STAGING THE PROMISES

STAGING THE PROMISES

Everyday Future-Making in a Serbian Industrial Town

Deana Jovanović

CORNELL UNIVERSITY PRESS   ITHACA AND LONDON

First published 2024 by Cornell University Press

Library of Congress Cataloging-in-Publication Data

Names: Jovanović, Deana, author.
Title: Staging the promises : everyday future-making in a Serbian
    industrial town / Deana Jovanović.
Description: Ithaca : Cornell University Press, 2024. | Includes bibliographical
    references and index.
Identifiers: LCCN 2024017416 (print) | LCCN 2024017417 (ebook) | ISBN
    9781501779091 (hardcover) | ISBN 9781501780134 (paperback) | ISBN
    9781501779107 (epub) | ISBN 9781501779114 (pdf)
Subjects: LCSH: Municipal government—Public relations—Serbia—Bor. |
    Post-communism—Economic aspects—Serbia—Bor. | Post-communism—
    Social aspects—Serbia—Bor. | Bor (Serbia)—Economic conditions—
    21st century. | Bor (Serbia)—Social conditions—21st century. | Bor
    (Serbia)—Politics and government—21st century.
Classification: LCC JS6933.A6 P756 2024 (print) | LCC JS6933.A6 (ebook) |
    DDC 320.9497109/05—dc23/eng/20240722
LC record available at https://lccn.loc.gov/2024017416
LC ebook record available at https://lccn.loc.gov/2024017417

For Beba

Contents

Acknowledgments

I am grateful to numerous people for supporting me and providing me with feedback, constructive criticism, inspiration, books, suggestions, information, and ideas throughout a decade-long journey. I spent my formative intellectual years at the University of Manchester where I learned a great deal from all the staff there, my supervisors, and my peers. This research has been developed with immense support from Stef Jansen. Stef, thank you for your guidance, for providing me with inspiration, reassurance, and understanding, for generously sharing your ideas about my work, and for the opportunity to learn from you. I am also grateful to Madeleine Reeves for motivating me and for the incredible feedback at crucial times, which allowed me to reach my intellectual maximum. Madeleine, thank you for all your support. I am also grateful to Frances Pine and Penelope Harvey for providing invaluable feedback. I also thank my anonymous reviewers for engaging thoroughly with this book manuscript, especially the reviewer who provided amazingly generous suggestions that helped me to polish my arguments in a sustained and creative way.

I would not have been able to start and complete this research without the Overseas Research Studentship Award (ORSA) from the University of Manchester, the University of Manchester Studentship, the Royal Anthropological Institute (RAI) Sutasoma Award, and the Fund for Young Talents of the Republic of Serbia. The Center for Advanced Studies of Southeastern Europe (CAS SEE, University of Rijeka) postdoctoral fellowship, the Leibniz Institute for East and Southeast European Studies (IOS) Visiting Fellowship, and the DAAD-Leibniz Fellowship at IOS were crucial in the stage of writing this book. The postdoctoral fellowship provided by *The Sociological Review* was the most important factor in making this book a reality, as it provided me with space and time to write, an incredibly scarce opportunity in academia today. Thank you, Michaela Benson, for all your support.

Part of chapter 2 of this book was adapted from my article entitled "The Politics of Simulation. Fake Repairs in a Serbian Industrial Town," published in 2018 in *Comparative Southeast European Studies*. A portion of chapter 3 contains adapted parts from my article entitled "Prosperous Pollutants: Bargaining with Risks and Forging Hopes in an Industrial Town in Serbia," published in 2018 in *Ethnos: Journal of Anthropology*. Part of chapter 4 is adapted from my article "The Thermodynamics of the Social Contract: Making Infrastructures

Visible in the Case of District Heating in Two Towns in Serbia and Croatia," published in 2019 as a book chapter in the volume *Post-Socialist Urban Infrastructures*. I thank all the anonymous reviewers as well as the editors of these journals and my book for providing comments that also shaped my work.

I am extremely grateful to the people of Bor in Serbia who shared their lives and knowledge with me and who offered me insights into their lives. *Hvala svima u Boru koji su podelili svoje znanje i vreme sa mnom, i koji su me pustili u njihove živote.* Unfortunately, to preserve their anonymity, I am not able to mention them here by name, but they certainly know who they are. I would like to express my gratitude to the workers of the Public Library Bor (*Narodna biblioteka Bor*), especially Dragan Stojmenović from the Local History Department (*Zavičajno odeljenje*), for helping me with this research. Your friendship and support over a decade have been inspiring. Thank you Vesna Tešović, Violeta Stojmenović, and Goran Milenković for intellectual inspiration and for making me feel at home. My gratitude goes to Marija Pešić, Miodrag Milošević, Dragan Ranđelović, Dragiša Trujkić, Vladimir Stanković, Jelena Miletić, Goran Jakovljević, Viktor Branković, Nebojša Ljubomirović, and Igor Velić. Thank you Marija for staying in my life.

I thank Thomas Hylland Eriksen, Ivan Rajković, Jeremy Morris, Ståle Knudsen, Elisabeth Schober, Jonathan Mair, Keir Martin, Karen Sykes, Maia Green, Jeanette Edwards, Tony Simpson, and the participants of the Social Anthropology postgraduate seminar at the University of Manchester for their engagement with my work. Thank you Berteke Waaldijk, Ildiko Erdei, Tanja Petrović, Dragan Stojković Klarens, Slobodan Naumović, Peđa Šarčević, Andre Thiemann, Pieter Troch, Alice Mah, Mateusz Laszczkowski, Ognjen Kojanić, Ger Duijzings, and Anouk de Koning. I thank Marina Simić and Brković Čarna for inspiration and induction into Manchester University. I finished this book in Utrecht where several people had crucial roles in supporting me and helping me through their incredible intellectual capacity. Rebecca Bryant, thank you for your suggestions that shaped the final contours of this book. David Henig, thank you for your friendship and intellectual engagement. Thanks are also owed to all my other colleagues at the Department of Cultural Anthropology of Utrecht University, especially Nikkie Wiegink, Hayal Akarsu, Marlene Schäfers, Aditi Saraf, Yvon van der Pijl, Kees Koonings, Martijn Oosterbaan, Tessa Diphoorn, Willy Sier, and Kootje Willemse-van Spanje.

I also thank Mark Featherstone and Ulf Brunnbauer for their timely advice and support, Attila Szeleni for making things work, and Brigitte Le Normand for the ultimate assistance, feedback, and friendship. I thank Imogen Hopker for a decade-long collaboration and Emma O'Driscoll for providing help in crucial times. Huge thanks are owed to the Čalovski family (Nada, Deki, and Vid), and the Manchester crew, Phaedra Douzina-Bakalaki, Theodoros Kyriakides, Angélica Cabezas Pino, Giuseppe Troccoli, Hester Clarke, Alice Stefanelli, and Adam Brisley. I thank my friends Kristina Stojanović Čehajić, Ineke Wijnsma, Tijana Ristić Kern, and Nataša Katić. I thank Viktor Marković for a decade-long support, as well as Zorica Nikolić Marković. Thank you, Vid. My grand-parents Maja and Deka and my aunt Mira would be proud to see this book as they also supported me. Although never acknowledging me in his songs, my dad Dragan Jovanović Krle provided me with all the rock'n'roll, and I thank him for that. I thank Bojan Tepavčević for always being there for me and for friendship. I am immensely grateful to my mother Jasminka Jovanović Beba for teaching me to think critically and for guiding and motivating me to make the future possible for myself, against all odds. Thanks to her, that future is now my present. Finally, I thank Miloš Veselinović, for wholeheartedly supporting me and with whom the anticipation of the future is a joyful blessing.

A Note on Pseudonyms, Language, and Translations

Throughout this book, I use pseudonyms to refer to people with whom I worked, and I have occasionally changed some of their biographical details in order to preserve their anonymity. All translations of my interlocutors' words and of citations from the literature published in Serbian or Serbo-Croatian language are mine.

I use letters with diacritical signs for the names of people and places throughout the book, using the Latin alphabet. I use Anglicized forms for place names that are in common usage (Belgrade instead of *Beograd*, Bosnia and Herzegovina instead of *Bosna i Hercegovina*). For people and relatively unknown places, I use the original spelling, including diacritics. The Serbian language is phonetic, which means that each letter of the alphabet represents one sound.

Basic rules for pronunciation are as follows:

The letter *c* is pronounced "ts" or "tz."
The letter *j* is pronounced "y" (*Jugoslavija* is Yugoslavia or Yugoslaviya).

Letters with diacritical marks:

ć is pronounced as a soft "ch," or "tj," like the "ci" in the Italian word *ciao*.
č is pronounced "tch" like the "ch" in *check* (harder than ć).
š is pronounced "sch" like the "sh" in *she*.
ž is pronounced "zh" like the "s" in *leisure*.
đ is pronounced "dj" like the "g" in the Italian name *Giorgio*.
dž is pronounced "dʒ" like the "j" in *joy*.

STAGING THE PROMISES

INTRODUCTION

In late summer 2012, I took a walk from the Fourth Kilometer toward the town center. Distance in the copper-processing town of Bor, in the far east of Serbia, is reckoned in kilometers from the inactive opencast mining pit. Close to where I was standing, I could see a newly built, sturdy iron construction with the sign "BOR—БOP," in both the Latin and the Cyrillic alphabet, which welcomed and bid farewell. Four faded and somewhat stained flags were attached to this construction: the flags of Serbia, of Bor municipality, of the European Union, and of the company called RTB Bor. RTB Bor, or Mining and Smelting Combine Bor (*Rudarsko topioničarski basen Bor*; hereafter "the company" or "RTB"), was (and still is) the only copper extraction and processing complex in Serbia. The complex produced mostly copper but also precious metals such as gold and silver. RTB had "fed the whole town" during socialism and was regarded as a Yugoslav mining, metallurgical, and chemical "giant."

On my way to visit a friend, I met Petar, a cultural worker in his mid-forties. We stopped by Dom kulture (the House of Culture), which was freshly painted in khaki color. A metal wire installation in the shape of a bird, which protruded above our heads, was spinning around its axis on the rooftop of the building (figure 1). Petar told me it represented a phoenix, a legendary bird, and had been placed there to symbolize the town's resurrection from the ashes. The company that installed it had never obtained the required permission for it, he explained, as Dom kulture was an antifascist state-protected monument dedicated to the fallen heroes of World War II. It was getting dark and the phoenix started shining bright red.

FIGURE 1. The statue of a spinning phoenix on the top of Dom kulture.

Milorad, a middle-aged man and president of one of the worker's unions, whom both Petar and I knew well, was just exiting the building after attending a meeting there. He lit a cigarette as he joined us in conversation and said to me in an amused tone, "They say that Sosa (the general manager of RTB) became inspired while visiting some American mining town which had a statue of a phoenix that marked its recovery. On his return to Bor, he decided to make a similar one."

Milorad and Petar laughed. "This giant eagle is his show" (*Ova orlušina je njegova predstava*), Milorad said. He did not use the word "show" by accident. The whole town was considered to be maintaining a plethora of stages onto which the promise of a mutual revival of the derelict town and the down-at-heel company was enacted. Staying in this town for longer enabled me to find out that many of the revived material sites, such as the repainted Dom kulture or the iron construction at the entrance of the town, made up the scenery widely referred to as "a scenography" (*scenografija*), "coulisses" (*kulise*), or "make-up" (*šminka*). Many people, like Milorad and Petar, considered them to be a more of a playact of a rebirth of the town. Some referred to these material representations as an "improvement" (*poboljšanje*) or as the town "washing its face" (*umivanje*). The phoenix was rarely referred to as such. Rather, it was more often called "the Merry-Go-Round at the Fair" (*vašarski hali-gali*), "the Chinese

Wire Installation" (*kineska žičana instalacija*),[1] or "the Large Bird" (*ptičurina*). Petar jokingly called it "the Penix."[2] The phoenix, in fact, was a symbol of ambivalence rather than a straightforward symbol of revival. Instead of being filled with hope and enthusiasm, many residents of this town encountered its promise both with hope that there might be some tangible outcome in the nearer future *and* with disbelief that the revival could be achieved in the long run. Such ambivalent encounters and multifaceted engagements with the staged promises of coveted futures and welfare lie at the heart of this book.

This book is about the transformative power of theatrically performed promises of coveted futures and what their staging could do for and to the individuals living in the town, whose raison d'être had been seriously brought into question by the global, post-socialist, and post-Yugoslav transformations. In the following chapters, I explore how individuals made their present and near futures possible for themselves amidst the gap between promises of revitalization made by the authorities and the uncertain conditions in the late-industrial environment. While I point out that the staging of promises played not an accompanying but rather a crucial role in the ways in which people reconfigured their present, I also argue that such practices simultaneously maintained hope and produced power. This book shows how staging of futural promises had an effect of withdrawing distant and long-term futures from the horizon of the very citizens who encountered them and among those who took part in them. The following chapters bring ethnographic examinations of the concept of the future together with questions about the production of power in order to better understand the mechanics of future-making practices and how the present is produced through them at the peripheries of global capitalism.

Staging as a metaphor and what my interlocutors felt as a "reality" enables me to theorize the social, temporal, and political transformations that have recently occurred in the global urban industrial peripheries at the aftermath of socialist modernity. Hence, the chapters provide insights into the broader experience of citizenship in the moment when the promises of reindustrialization, of state protection, and of social and economic revival were projected into the future, long after the promises of the abundant socialist state and of welfare had been withdrawn. Contemporary disturbing images of wars, widescale refugee crises, the COVID-19 pandemic, and rapid climate change, all produce a pervading feeling that the future is increasingly less tangible, difficult to imagine, and in crisis (Bryant and Knight 2019). Yet, in spite of widespread "future fatigue" (Gibson 2012), Bor is embedded within the global trend of populist political staging bursting with the promises of bright futures. For this reason, it is of the utmost importance to understand in detail how futures are today made possible within such paradoxical and contained conditions. The insights into the future-making practices and the political, economic, and temporal effects of staging of futural promises are not just topical but also vital and globally relevant in order to better understand the present within the landscape of global capitalism. The ethnography from this post-socialist, post-Yugoslav, late-industrial, and peripheral town provides a vantage point from which to look from the semiperiphery of Europe (Blagojević 2009) at the performative ways through which contemporary capitalist futures are remade. This is a story about how the present and the futures are performed into being.

Staging the Promises

I arrived in Bor in August 2012, around two years after the promises of revival started to circulate widely in the national media. I was intrigued by that fervent media frenzy, as everyone in Serbia, like I did, "knew" this town to be emblematic of post-socialist crisis, a polluted environment, precarious lives, and a devastated economy. The social, economic, and symbolic mutual revival of the company and the town (called *preporod* in Serbian, meaning rebirth, in the official representations) was surprising and sounded almost like an unbelievable "twist." Propelled by an increase in the copper price on the global market, the sudden revival was initiated by the Serbian government to enhance the future prospects of the down-at-heel company whose economy maintained the town.

I decided to carry out an ethnographic study of everyday future-making in this town, driven by my desire to broadly contribute to anthropology by exploring the dynamics in such an industrial and post-Yugoslav town. As I immersed myself in the communities in the town and carefully recorded fine-grained ethnographic details during what was widely experienced as a phoenix-like moment, I became occupied with questions, such as: How did engagements with the performances that enacted the promises of coveted futures and welfare shape the ways people imagined, contemplated, and acted upon their personal and collective futures? What did their engagements with such performances enable for them? What else did the promissory performances "do" for the audience and the performers themselves, apart from what they officially and supposedly represented? While spending time in the town where the company was still a nexus of anticipation, symptomatic of late-industrialism, and a locus of party-political power, another question that opened up was: How were power and authority produced through people's engagements with such performances? In the following chapters, I address these questions ethnographically.

I use the notions of staging and performing as well as the metaphor of the stage not just to describe the promises given by various actors in power through their utterances and to describe what they did (Austin 1962) but also to illustrate and examine the effects of the enactments of the promises. While I explore the promises, which I see as actions, as suggested by Simone Abram and Gisa Weszkalnys (2013), through which the actors projected collective futures, I look at the performances that were carried out by the company, the politicians, municipal actors, and individuals who aimed to assure the citizens that welfare and betterment would become possible in the future. The following chapters address the most prominent performative acts that served as promises of the futures that citizens were mostly concerned about and which they desired: successful industrial futures and the future of the company (chapter 1), revived urban futures (chapter 2), environmentally clean futures (chapter 3), abundant infrastructural futures (chapter 4), and opportunities to have post-industrial futures (chapters 5 and 6). Like any promise, they opened up spaces for expectations. The chapters illustrate how such performative acts were enacted on carefully crafted stages, such as the refurbished town or the site of the reconstruction of the polluting smelting factory, to name but a few. While those who engaged with the performances sometimes even became "both the audience and actor" (Reeves, Beyer, and Rasanayagam 2014, 4), often the very motives behind the performances were assessed by the citizens as artificial, fake, and/or insincere.

Drawing from insights into performances as elements of the political (Weber 1998; Yurchak 2006; Reeves, Beyer, and Rasanayagam 2014; Bryant 2021b), which may also take the form of simulation (Rajković 2018a) or bluffing (Newell 2012) and may entail humor (Kurtović 2019), irony, cynicism, or parody (Boyer and Yurchak 2010; Petrović 2018), the book examines what kinds of effects people's engagements with the staged promises had. The book shows how performances and engagements with them significantly transformed the present and how political, social, and even economic relationships were ordered through them (Abram and Weszkalnys 2013). The theatrical metaphor of a stage and the lenses of staging and performing serve here to achieve the main aim of this book, which is to document, illustrate, and examine the temporal, material, and political aspects and contingencies of future-making practices though which the present, power, and authority were produced. With such an aim, the book brings together the body of anthropological literature that inquires about temporalities and hope with the literature on post-socialist transformations and global industrial endeavors. The literature on production of power and authority is employed in relation to the latter to address how governance was maintained through engagements with the promissory performances. With this, I broadly show what experiences of living in the industrial and post-socialist environment entailed and what kinds of configurations of power governed the everyday life. The ethnographic explorations of these concepts help me to depict how the promissory performative practices were crucial for many to orient and rearrange their troubled present and to make some scales of futures (immediate, near, distant, or past futures) possible for them. Hence, the book contributes to anthropology in three ways.

First, the book joins the recent body of literature on post-socialism in the attempt to shift the dominant focus from studying the past (and nostalgia) to exploring futures (Laszczkowski 2016; Ringel 2018; Dzenovska 2018, 2020). While filling in such gaps, the book joins the broader body of literature that provides ethnographically more nuanced studies of the future and the quotidian (Wallman 2003; Appadurai 2013; Laszczkowski 2016; Ringel 2018; Bryant and Knight 2019). In this sense, the book focuses on the role of the future in shaping people's lives and the present (cf. Bryant and Knight 2019) and brings to the fore the performative elements of future-making, which are often overlooked.

Second, analyzing future-oriented practices in this Serbian town helps me to reframe how we think about post-Yugoslav experiences of everyday life. This area of study has become overdetermined by exploration of topics such as conflict, nationalism, violence, and the ways the national state appeared in everyday life (Denich 1994; Hayden 1996; Halpern and Kideckel 2000; Cushman 2004). This focus has had a significant impact on thinking about the post-Yugoslav space, leaving many other fields of social transformation largely unexplored. Such is the case of the disintegrated fundamental pillar of Yugoslav socialism—industry. By providing ethnographic data on the under-explored topic of future-making practices within this region and more specifically within such late-industrial settings, the book brings a fresh perspective to the ethnographic studies of post-Yugoslav industrial transformations, which started to emerge more systematically in the last decade.[3]

Finally, looking at the practices of engaging with the staged promises of coveted futures and welfare, assessed as not being entirely "the real thing," is extremely relevant in the light of what has been marked as the "post-truth" era. Promises of enhanced futures, materialized through theatrical performances, have played an important role within contemporary populist politics. Trustworthiness and authenticity of institutions and symbols have started to appear as fleeting qualities (Beek, Kilian, and Krings 2019, 425), also prompted by the process of globalization. Myriad claims of fraud and fakery have been documented (Bubandt 2009; Newell 2013) which point to "the social flaws and insecurities of a changing political, legal and moral landscape" (Beek, Kilian, and Krings 2019, 425) within an increasingly neoliberalized world. Performances of the promise of reindustrialization and of successful futures of Bor's down-at-heel copper-processing company, the symbolic and material revival of the derelict town, and the promises of environmentally clean futures were all embedded in the landscape of populist politics (cf. Kalb 2011; Hann 2019). However, the story of the revival of Bor cannot be reduced to merely a story about post-socialist transformations. Rather, Bor also tells us about the dynamics within the contemporary global moment, which Walter Armbrust (2017, 2019) marked as "the age of the trickster." This book recognizes that the promissory performances I witnessed in Bor, which were seen as "all show and no go" (*spolja gladac, iznutra jadac*)[4] and which promised that power would be reclaimed by performatively drawing on the crisis-driven present and better futures (Taş 2022), are crucial today in shifting social and political landscapes. Such shifting processes are especially visible in places like Bor, where political power is acquired by staging the promises to include the excluded, those who are "left behind," or those who are cast outside the circulation of global capital. The enactments of "the promise of something other to come" (Arditi 2015, 116) and promises of regeneration of futures that would give back (lost) agency to act upon the futures seem today very relevant. This is the case, for example, in the claims of the former US President Donald Trump that he would "Make America Great Again" and contribute to the industrial renaissance in Pennsylvania and West Virginia, or in the fascination with the promises of Brexit. As Gillian Evans (2020) noticed, the promises of the Brexit campaign that entailed the potential of post-industrial change were tightly connected to the experience of the failed promise of post-industrial society. This also included the experience of abandonment by "political managers" (Evans 2020, xiii) of the working class, who "were once the industrial and manufacturing powerhouse of the nation" (Evans 2020, xiii). The staging of the promises of revived, aspirational futures, often doubted and assessed by the audience as being not entirely the real thing, are very telling about the performative ways through which the social and the political landscapes are globally transformed. The projection of coveted futures and their staging in Bor are, hence, situated within such a global political performative moment. In this book, I look at how the material promissory performances resonated in a town that used to be an industrial, manufacturing, and symbolic carrier of the Yugoslav socialist system. The story of Bor goes well beyond the inspection of populist promises per se. Bor stands for all industrial towns and many other places around the globe, outcast from the circulation of global capital, where the performative promises of betterment and something else that is supposedly yet to come, enacted onto material ruins of past's futures, serve to acquire political power, profit, and production of new neoliberal policies that often widen social inequalities. This book shows one important and less visible element of their impact. Namely, as the promissory performances appeal to the (better) future, the temporal contracts between the performers and the citizens are being remade. Hence, the book ethnographically depicts how the futural performances alter citizens' futures and how such performances that appeal to the futures affect the present. Answering these questions provides a standpoint to inquire about the temporal, political, and material effects of promissory performances and the performative ways through which contemporary capitalist futures are remade within what David Harvey (2007) has identified as the unequal spatiotemporal configuration of global capitalism.

Making the Futures through Performing

In spring 2013, I agreed with Pavle, a twenty-eight-year-old newly employed worker at RTB, to have a chat over coffee at one of Bor's cafés on the main street. While talking about his future and his job, Pavle commented on the material transformations of the town that were visible.

Cynically, yet hopefully, he told me, "Yup, this story with Bor is quite interesting. Now it's *like* it's changing . . . but that is coming from RTB and its marketing. *Like* it's developing. . . . In fact, they are trying to change that image. It's changed for the better, in my eyes. They are trying to induce optimism, you know, like it is going to get better. Optimism for a better life. . . . Marketing is a real miracle." He laughed. "You simply start believing in some stories."

"You believe in it? You think life in Bor will get better?" I asked him.

Pavle replied, "You know how we are looking at it—it was really, really bad. This is absolutely great, so I don't think we will go back to it. At least I hope it will remain like this."

The logic of Pavle's utterance, "fake it till you make it," reveals an important performative aspect of future-making practices that is central to this book. Pavle (on whom I expand more in chapter 6) involved himself in performing "as if" the promises of betterment were happening. Becoming a self-fulfilling prophecy, "fake it till you make it" depicts some of the logic of practices through which the futures were produced in Bor. In the following chapters, I ethnographically grasp the performative practices which provide insights into "the relationship between the future and action, including the act of imagining the future" (Bryant and Knight 2019, 16). What I convey is that different kinds of engagements with the promissory performances shaped and *oriented* the present (Bryant and Knight 2019, 2) and that the very enactments made the present and some scales of futures (mostly nearer futures) a bit more of a reality (as they did for Pavle). The book reveals what kinds of engagements with such performances were necessary in this late-industrial town to orient the present and make some futures a possibility. What kept many people engaged with the broader project of the sometimes mistrusted revival was exactly the fact that the performances still enabled the individuals to maintain hope that life would become better in this town, as they did for Pavle.

The following chapters show that, in spite of the fact that the enactments of the promises were sometimes seen as "advertising tricks," as Pavle saw them, or as simulations and/or illusions, it was the very performative aspect that was crucial to their triumph. Anthropology has already demonstrated the transformational and powerful effects of performances. As almost all anthropological discussion implies, through the power of rituals as performative events, a community creates a sense of meaning, as they make it possible to imagine the political and social order and what the community could look like (Turner 1974; Graeber 2013a). Studies show that performances are socially and politically important and effective for state-making practices and the seeking of legitimacy (Weber 1998; Adams 2010; Ezrahi 2012; Reeves, Beyer, and Rasanayagam 2014; McConnell 2016; Bryant 2021b) while often being constitutive of the reproduction or subversion of hegemonic power. In this book, I argue that the process of imagining and performing by multiple agencies which entailed "redrawing the boundaries between facts and fictions, reality and theatricality in politics" (Ezrahi 2012, xi) was necessary in this town where the ruinations almost determined the futures and where the futures were very contained. In this town, it was not possible to build new buildings, due to lack of capital, or to quickly enhance copper production in order to make the industrial company prosperous again. Rather, staging the promises became an effective way of bringing the coveted futures closer in time.

This book draws from insights into the performative aspects of constructing political realities and places emphasis on the importance of metaphors of the stage to show how the performative dimensions of future-making practices in this post-socialist, industrial town had a crucial role in "the reproduction of social norms, positions, relations, and institutions" (Yurchak 2018, 25). Staging futural promises has a vital role in the production of political subjectivities and social inequalities. Studying how the present was produced through appealing to the future and how particular futures were (re)produced through people's engagements with the staged promises adds more nuance to studying the temporal dimensions of political performances that unfold within the landscapes of global capitalism.

The notion of staging in this book is closely related to the notion of performance, which draws on examinations of the concepts of representation and dramaturgy (Goffman 1969 [1956]; Turner 1974, 1986) that indicate how particular social situations and relations are performed. While drawing more broadly on literature that examines the politics of representations and recognition in social life, I build on Judith Butler's (1990) understanding of performativity to explore how the futural promises were enacted through continuous and repetitious enactments of the norms and established sets of meanings and how the present, the futures, and power were (re)produced through such continuous performances. Taking inspiration from J. L. Austin's theory of speech (1962), Alexei Yurchak (2006) analyzed "performative shifts" during late socialism in the USSR. According to him, the "performative" dimensions of ritualized speech acts were more important than "constative" dimensions (utterances that state facts and derive their power from the assigned authority of actors). He argued that between the 1950s and 1980s, it was the "performative dimension" that was central to how late socialism was organized, operated, and represented in Soviet life. The shift toward "performative utterances" was made possible by a simultaneous shift toward a standardized Soviet ideological discourse which no longer persuaded at the level of meaning. Hence, according to him, the performative reproduction of the form of rituals and speech acts took place in most contexts where authoritative discourse was reproduced or circulated, which enabled the emergence of diverse, multiple, and unpredictable meanings in everyday life, including those that did not correspond to the constative meanings of authoritative discourse. Drawing from Yurchak's (2006) approach to social and political consequences of such everyday performative practices, I look at the staging of promises as a constitutive part of the production of social relations, where, for example, true/fake distinctions or assessments that promises succeeded or failed were only one of many ways in which the distinction between "constative" and "performative" was sometimes made by individuals.[5] In the following chapters, I treat performances rather as ethnographic facts that provide insights into the process of producing social relations and individual and collective futures, which brings together concepts of agency and power into a dialogue (McConnell 2016, 34).

With this, the book throws different light onto the temporal dimensions of studies that focus on post-socialist, industrial, and post-Yugoslav transformations in three ways. First, it shows that experiences of socialism still continue to be a relevant temporal framework for understandings of contemporary capitalism (Rogers 2015; Morris 2016). I show how, on one hand, the authorities in power, including political and industrial elites, drew in their performances from an existing playbook of material remnants, images, memories, and narratives from socialism, which produced the feeling that *having* (capitalist) abundant futures was possible, which has been contested on a number of occasions. This town and the company were constantly on the verge of being "shut down."

The following chapters show how staging the promises was necessary to enable continuation of the town's existence and to renew political and social power. On the other hand, my interlocutors recognized slight improvements in the present by drawing on their experiences from the socialist past, which was also part of the staging playbook. In contrast to the body of literature on post-socialism that explores nostalgia as a widely investigated temporal orientation and a critique of the relationship between present and future (Berdahl, Bunzl, and Lampland 2000; Bach 2002; Boym 2002; Boyer 2006; Todorova and Gille 2012), I show how past futures (from late socialism) were used and made relevant in creating the possibility of capitalist futures in Bor. While I avoid taking "capitalism a priori, as an already determining structure, logic, and trajectory" (Empson 2018, 2), I attend more to "the diversity that exists within worlds that are cognized as capitalist" (Empson 2018, 2). This also means that I look at capitalist forms and relations "*as such*" (Gilbert et al. 2008, 11, my emphasis) and not just as their exceptional "Balkan" (Gilbert et al. 2008, 11), "post-socialist," or "East European" version.

Second, looking at the chronology of decline within studies of disruption of late-industrial development shaken by the global process of deindustrialization (Ferguson 1999; High 2003; Parry 2003; Mah 2012) and in the post-socialist context in Europe (Kandiyoti 2002; Kideckel 2008), this book offers a different insight into an announced revival after industrial decline and urban deterioration. There are still too few studies of post-socialist industries in anthropology that are not framed as straightforward stories of decline. In addition, I follow the anthropological work on late industrialism (Collier 2011; Walley 2013; Fennell 2015) and acknowledge the identified unease with having the post-industrial period neatly framed (Fox 2022). I draw from Kim Fortun (2012) to suggest that "late industrialism," which I use in this book to mark the present, takes into account industrial legacies deeply ingrained in the present in the ways that "the future becomes anteriorized" (Fortun 2012, 450), and as such, its contours are dictated by incorporation of the past into the present. The forthcoming chapters show how various temporal scales were evaluated by individuals, while the past (industrial) futures remained strikingly implicated in the ways in which individuals were engaged in the performances of coveted futures.

Finally, the book considers not only a particular time and chronology of global extractive capitalism but also a particular moment in which the post-socialist "decline" or "fall" has been located. So far, studies of Serbia have pointed to the experiences of "the great fall" (Simić 2010, 2014) and "suspended normality" (Jansen 2005) that are located after the 1990s, also a widely shared experience in the post-Yugoslav region. Post-socialist Bor, however, shows how those experiences of a "dramatic fall from grace" (Jansen 2009a, 826) were located long after Serbia entered the "democratic transition" after 2000. This is why the effects of some signs of a revival after the upheaval cast a different light on studies of Serbia. Before I elaborate in more depth on the theoretical framework, especially in relation to the notions of hope and power that support my arguments, let me briefly illustrate the context of my fieldwork.

The Town That Staged Its Rise from the Ashes

Bor looks fascinating when one approaches the town by car or bus. It is 250 kilometers from the capital and almost 90 kilometers from the main highway that heads toward the south from Belgrade. The city lights would start appearing under the heavy smoke from the smelter if one approached the town at night by bus or by car (figure 2).

I would always feel awe at the power of industrial endeavors and an awkward feeling of enjoyment of the red mine tailings and landscapes of toxicity (figure 3), which reminded me of Edward Burtynsky's photographs of landscapes altered by industry (Burtynsky 2007).

The town is located almost 100 kilometers from the Romanian and Bulgarian borders (see map 1). It counts as a medium-sized town, with a population of 34,160 in the urban area. Including the surrounding villages, the municipality had 48,615 inhabitants at the time of my research (Statistical Office of the Republic of Serbia 2014a).

I base the following chapters on the fieldwork I carried out in Bor between August 2012 and September 2013, and they also rely on the visits I made between this period and 2018. Upon my arrival in 2012, my plan was to follow public events and specific places related to the municipality and RTB's engagement with the local community. In the early autumn of 2012, I started volunteering in the *mesna zajednica*—the local community office—the smallest municipal unit where the town's governance is carried out on the microlevel. I was involved in the meetings, the organization of local events, and the everyday work of the office. I simultaneously spent a great deal of time with the individuals who worked in several cultural centers and with whom I established rapport.[6] I also built rapport with the union members by attending their meetings and with unemployed people by attending job fairs and retraining sessions. Through sharing an everyday life with the individuals from the local community office, cultural centers, and workers' unions, I met and spent time with the workers from RTB, who also gladly accepted me in their daily routines.

FIGURE 2. The view of the town at night. Photo credit: Taken by the author in 2013.

FIGURE 3. The view of Bor onto the Third Kilometer and the Second Kilometer. In the background are mine tailings where the town "starts." Photo credit: Igor Mitrović.

The workers later introduced me to their parents, relatives, partners, or close friends. As my access to RTB frequently required special permission, I mostly spent time with them while going out, having coffee, or having lunch with their families in their homes.

I also spent a great portion of my time in the recently renovated public spaces and had informal conversations with the individuals who used them. I attended public events organized by the municipality and/or RTB Bor. My experiences and daily routines of living in two rented apartments (on the Second and the Fourth Kilometer, which are unofficial names of the neighborhoods according to their relative distance from the inactive mine pit) provided insights into different neighborhoods. This greatly helped me to experience the provision of the urban infrastructure myself (chapter 4) and to have meaningful conversations about urban infrastructure, everyday life, and politics. As I wanted to explore the encounters with the promises performed, such a wide goal contributed to having open-ended networks of people that cut across gender, class, and age, which is reflected in the ethnography in this book. However, I tell the story here through a small number of people with whom I built rapport and who most illustratively depict the specific experiences of encounters with the staging of promises that I witnessed. The reader will also notice that some information that could have been included to, perhaps, more closely reveal the background of my interlocutors is sometimes omitted. This writing strategy was

MAP 1. Map of Serbia with Bor in the east. Created by Ivica Milojević.

necessary, as sometimes revealing more detailed information about them could have jeopardized their anonymity. Since the town is relatively small in size and the opportunities were still influenced by interpersonal relationships and power, I have had to be rather cautious about how much I disclose.

The reader will also notice that most of the individuals who appear in the first two chapters had some higher education or, at least, white-collar jobs. Mostly, they were the ones who spoke with more irony about RTB's performances. Although they were educated, with some of them belonging to the salariat, they were mostly invested in representations rather than practices related to RTB and the town's management. One of the things that divided them was that some would denounce the representations as fake while others would push them as "real," which was a common fault line in Bor. What connected them, however, was an investment in representations and how something would be seen. Those from the other side of the working spectrum, on the other hand, such as the villagers from the polluted land (chapter 3), those who were unemployed (chapter 5), or the very young (highly educated) workers of RTB (chapter 6), were more attuned to the material complexity of keeping things running and depending on them. Such contrasting examples also depict class and age differences.

Throughout my stay, many of my friends and acquaintances from Belgrade reacted in a very similar way when they heard that I would be living in Bor. They could not comprehend why anyone would willingly spend a whole year in such a place: to them, it was a town which had a reputation for being dull, depressing, and hit by poverty, unemployment, and outmigration. In fact, Bor used to be a prosperous Yugoslav town, a symbol of socialist industrial development and prosperity, a "giant," with its complex of mines, copper processing, and other factories. The citizens of this town, or Borani, as the people refer to themselves collectively, remember the period of hopelessness which occurred after the dissolution of Yugoslavia in the 1990s and long after Serbia entered its democratic and economic "transition" in 2000. Back then, nobody knew whether the town and the heavily indebted and technologically outdated company would survive. This period in Bor's history contributed to its widespread reputation among outsiders as an abandoned, peripheral, and heavily polluted town.

No one could imagine that I, as someone who had grown up in the bustling center of Belgrade, the Serbian capital, and had lived in various places around Europe (to work on my doctorate in Manchester and later to hold various academic positions across Europe), might come to live and share my everyday life with people from Bor. Many of my friends who had never visited the town before expressed their worries for my health and gave me a range of advice on how to take care of myself while I was there. This perception was the product of a hegemonic gaze from the privileged "center," but also was due to the fact that the town was heavily polluted and had not done very well in the past. The power relations could also be seen in how the Borani were amused by my stay in Bor. They made bets on how long I would last there, making jokes about how they would take pictures of the progress of my deterioration. Another of the jokes they made was how I would soon start drinking and smoking excessively (like many residents did) to ease my experiences in such a harsh environment, to become an average resident who was tough and endured various kinds of pollution well (see chapter 3). Although I held some conversations with some of my close interlocutors over a glass or two of Vinjak, a popular working-class brandy, drinking it only inspired me to make my fieldnotes even more abundant.

The individuals with whom I spent time were very much aware of the construction of Bor as an Other (the common struggle of all industrial towns). They argued that the negative image of their town was constantly recreated and reproduced through the media and movies. Even though they were proud that their town was so prominent in Serbian cinematography, they worried about the way in which it could perpetuate the image of a depressed town that they wanted to escape or misrepresentations that they wanted to contest. They were frustrated and irritated by the fact that *only* this negative image had been imposed on their town and maintained. The image of Otherness clearly motivated local politicians and RTB to actively dispel this negative image through the staging of (urban) futures. Taking into account the existence of the hegemonic, privileged gaze from the center (which included my own), the town's residents were aware of the stigma and many fiercely defended its credentials as modern. Surprisingly, being from Belgrade was not always regarded as a "posh" thing, a matter of privilege and class difference. I was surprised that many people did not like the capital and considered my hometown to represent a disadvantage. They sometimes saw it as a disgusting, bustling, stressful, oversized town full of frustration. Some even suggested that I should move to Bor, as for them it was a more convenient and self-contained town.

Borani were frequently happy to see a new face and helped me with books, shared their stories, or put me in contact with other people. Sometimes I was perceived as an intellectual and as a knowledgeable person. I did not much enjoy this kind of awe. I was also a "newcomer" or occasionally perceived as a stranger, which contributed to the fact that many people took the time to teach me what Bor was "really like," which made my access easier. The inequalities in terms of income were sometimes visible, as some of the individuals with whom I shared everyday life were impoverished, and my social capital clearly made my position different. They appreciated the fact that I was fairly well aware of, overt in discussing, and critical of these inequalities. While conducting ethnography "at home" (Jackson 1987), the exchanges between my interlocutors and me as a "local" enabled me to refer to "shared" experiences, such as economic crisis, NATO bombing, layoffs, precariousness, local and national political affairs, and so on. This became common ground on which we built meaningful conversations and relationships (Simić 2010).

The following chapters illustrate the social fabric of this town in the very last years of the company known as RTB Bor, when it was under the management appointed by the Serbian government. The company was managed by the same party-political representatives who were also the municipal councilors and representatives of the same political parties that were ruling the government on the national level. This book is therefore an ethnographic but also a historical testament to the last days of this former socialist "giant," whose former name remains ingrained in people's memories and bodies (and through pollution). In 2018, the majority of this state-managed company's shares (63 percent) were sold to the Chinese state-owned multinational company Zijin Mining Group Co., Limited, one of the leading copper and gold producers in China and globally. RTB Bor became registered as Serbia Zijin Bor Copper. The individuals who appear in this book could have not known these potential outcomes as they could not even have imagined or anticipated them. The following chapters look into their encounters with various staged promises of coveted futures and welfare, which were hope-instilling yet always on the verge of being potentially fleeting and inclined to disappoint. This book is a testament to such performances that tried to persuade but sometimes critically failed to deliver their promises. Tracking down these failures and understanding how they resonate among people is also my personal engagement as an appeal for political accountability.

Inquiring about the Temporal Scales of the Futures: Hope and Ambivalence

Involvement in and engagements with the theatrical promises in Bor were intrinsically related to the notion of hope. Hope, as defined by Stef Jansen (2009b) as a future-oriented disposition, was always part of people's futural orientations, as "a way of pressing into the future that attempts to pull certain potentialities into actuality" (Bryant and Knight 2019, 134). The futural orientation of hope has been vastly delineated, from Crapanzano's "imaginative horizons" (2004) and expectations that appear in different forms (planning, aspiration, despair, doubt, and waiting) to Bloch's philosophical perspective on hope based on a belief in the "not yet" (1986), to name just a few. This book goes beyond reaffirming hopefulness as a moral-political or disciplinary imperative.[7] Rather, I join the anthropological literature that explores the political economy of hope, and I treat hope as an empirical object of analysis that aims "to reveal the conditions of possibility for (particular forms of) hope" (Jansen 2016, 448). While exploring who hoped for something, what people hoped for, and what kind of hope existed (Jansen 2016, 449), I ethnographically describe "the production and negotiation of specific formations of hope and anticipation in particular settings and under specific socio-historical conditions" (Kleist and Jansen 2016, 373). With this aim, I inspect what types of scales of futures, by which I mean differing perceptions of distance to the future—immediate, near, distant, or past futures—appeared and how hope attached to them. For instance, in chapter 2, I show how hope of having a pretty, modern, and renovated town was related to the hopes the residents attached to (and which stemmed from) the past futures promised to them in late socialism. All the renovations, as part of the performances of revived urban futures, appeared as fake, as the newly made renovations did not fully match the expectations of the scale of the futures offered in the past. In this book, I inspect both the temporality of the performances and the temporality of various engagements with them.

Sometimes the encounters and engagements with the staged promises facilitated ambivalence. Ambivalence is examined in the first three chapters of this book, where I show how hope simultaneously "worked" with its conflicting orientation to futures. In particular, I examine how hope was coupled with doubt (chapters 1 and 2) and risk (chapter 3). When such *co-occurrence of conflicting orientations to futures* occurred, I refer to it as ambivalence.[8] Ambivalence always consisted of hope and its conflicting orientation, and both conflicting orientations attached to different types of scales of futures. For example, in chapter 3, I describe how hope of obtaining some more immediate compensation for pollution-related damage in the near future "worked" simultaneously with navigating and accepting risks to health that were projected into the distant, unknowable future.

When it appears, I treat ambivalence differently to how it has been used so far in scholarly work. Usually, ambivalence has been used as a descriptive tool to understand how social relations or institutions work and mainly to denote contradictory and ambiguous characteristics of the given focus.[9] Ambivalence is seen in this book as social and relational (Merton 1976; Smelser 1998; Palmberger 2019), rather than solely as an individual experience, and is differentiated from ambiguity.[10] Therefore, I look at how people *stood against* the ambiguities and lack of clarity that were part of everyday life. In other words, ambivalence is not synonymous with ambiguity. As a concept as it is used here, it denotes the ways in which people were oriented to futures in conflicting ways. Ambivalence was very frequent but not always present among my interlocutors.

When I looked ethnographically through the eyes of those who were experiencing ambivalence, I found something rather different from what has been recorded so far. More often than not, people did not work toward resolving, taming, or compartmentalizing conflicting orientations. Holding conflicting orientations toward the promised futures did, indeed, induce anxiety and frustration. Rather than experiencing such conflicting orientations as a threat or something that needed to be mitigated or successfully disciplined, as Zygmunt Bauman (1991) contended, the ambivalence provided some of my interlocutors with the capacity to engage with the futures in a meaningful way. In other words, such navigation of different scales of futures allowed individuals to make the near or immediate futures more possible. I discuss this especially in chapter 2. Thinking in ethnographic detail about different temporal scales of futures to which hope was attached shifts the scholarly focus from how uncertainty is employed as a concept (Samimian-Darash and Rabinow 2015). Hence, I move this focus to the question of how the navigation of different types of scales of futures in practice resulted in converting uncertainty into "at least some" possibility in the nearer futures. In contrast to a growing anthropological literature examining future-orientated practices steered by the orientations toward indeterminacy (Dostaler 2017; Alexander and Sanchez 2018), I rather emphasize the historically, politically, and socially conditioned practices through which the individuals translated uncertainty into some certainty. Identification of the precise constitutive elements of different types of scales of futures to which hope attached in the situations of a double bind (Bateson 1972) leads to a closer understanding of the workings of the broader landscape of capitalism that is itself predicated on uncertainty and on the process of imagining futures (Beckert 2016).

Staging the Political

There is a widespread understanding that politics is today more of an act, a parody, a simulation, and/or an illusion, that its intentions are often thought to be other than what they are supposed to be, and that it is merely a devalued and/or fake, manipulative performance. This is certainly a prevalent understanding in Serbia. In Bor, many of the performances that gave rise to promises of coveted futures and welfare, from promises of clean air to promises of providing possibilities for post-industrial futures, were often seen as manipulative performances enabling the politicians to win political votes. Even some academic discourses in Serbia were not excused from such interpretations, which entailed seeing politics as a mere performance of certain promises with particular temporal orientations. For instance, a prominent professor of economics, Miodrag Zec, who often publicly criticized the Serbian government, remarked that the "problem" with the Serbian "political market" was that there were "no authentic 'products'" (Đaković 2020, 38). According to him, "the political market is awash with fake products, because the state is considered a prey" (Đaković 2020, 38). This particular understanding refers to the notion of entrenched practices in which once the politicians got into power, they would never step down but would further use their positions only for their personal and party-political gains and not for the wider public good. A similar understanding of local politics as a fake performance was pointed out by sociologist Miroslav Ružica (2013). He argued that future-oriented practices such as "political promises, planning and strategies" lack a "long-term horizon of thinking" in Serbia. By this, Ružica meant that the interests of the next generations were not envisioned and taken into account by such future-oriented practices. He concluded that, in Serbia, "from the short-term thinking one cannot live, but thanks to it (unfortunately) it is being governed" (Ružica 2013). Ružica's contention is important here, as it resonates with the ways in which many of my interlocutors engaged with the promissory performances and how through their engagements with the promissory performances precluded the possibilities of even imagining the distant futures.

In this book, I draw from anthropological insights into the performances of the political and engage with the theory of the state and power to point to such temporal (futural) aspects of governance. As I show, it is through staging the promises of coveted futures and welfare and through people's engagements with them that power and authority were also performed into being (Weber 1998; Wedeen 1999; Adams 2010; Bryant 2021b). By following Fiona McConnell, who examined everyday state practices through the process of "rehearsing" the unrecognized Tibetan state and found that "claims to legitimacy are staked on a notion of desired futures" (McConnell 2016, 187), I argue that through people's engagements with the staged promises, certain authorities of power strengthened their capacity to govern everyday life. Through showing how promissory performances particularly used hope and "the future" as governmental tools, I illustrate how a particular kind of governance was also hoped for and desired by the residents themselves.

The following chapters show that neither for the state, the municipality, or the copper-processing company nor for quotidian practices was the hold on the near and immediate future lost. This is, in fact, in contrast to what Jane Guyer (2007) indicated in her analysis of the temporal perspectives in the public rhetoric of macroeconomics. Namely, Guyer (2007) showed how the focus on the immediate future (supply and demand time) has the aim of achieving stability over the long-term futures, which results in evacuating the medium-term or the near future of significance or potential for action. Her concept of enforced presentism shows that people are pressured to live only in the immediate present, where the (better) future seems to be lost to the realm of fantasy together with the ability to plan ahead (fantasy futurism). Her distinction between enforced presentism and fantasy futurism is certainly relevant but was not always in correspondence with the ways in which many of the individuals who appear in the following chapters made their near futures slightly more possible. Similar to Simone Abram's (2014) critique of Guyer and to what Felix Ringel (2018) also indicated in his analysis of a shrinking post-industrial town in Germany, I found that the near future had not been evacuated of intention, activity, or its potential. In fact, distant futures were evacuated from both the state's, the municipality's, and the company's projections of the futures and from the quotidian future-making practices.

The ethnographic descriptions in this book show that obtaining some tangible opportunities for the immediate or near future required knowledge about how and with whom to engage, which kinds of forms of connectivity to mobilize, and what kinds of appeals needed to be made. The book shows the plurality of "faces of power" that were not necessarily always "faces of the state." Such "faces of power" strongly brought out a desire sometimes for regulative frameworks of "the state" and sometimes for the company to regulate the everyday life (Jansen 2015). Sometimes it was the power of individuals who desired the authorities in power to regulate the everyday life. Because of the specific sociopolitical setting of Bor in which it was historically dependent on industrial endeavors which were contingent on state support, the residents often appealed to the role of "the state" as critical in their hope for their betterment in the future. The book argues that it was through future-oriented performances that "the state" and the company appeared as "hope-generating machines" (to paraphrase Nuijten 2003). My approach to understanding the state, the "everyday company," and their overlap relies on interrelated bodies of literature on the "state effect" (Mitchell 1999; Hansen and Stepputat 2001; Migdal 2001; Ferguson and Gupta 2002; Aretxaga 2003; Das and Poole 2004) and the "corporate effect" (Shever 2012; Golub 2014; Rogers 2015). My aim here is not to develop an ontology of "the state" so much as to understand how, when, and where different "faces of power" were configured to become desired regulatory frameworks of everyday life. This book brings the performative aspect of future-making practices to the fore for the exploration of how these different forms of power were produced.

The following chapters also show the material contingency of future-making practices in terms of not only how promissory performances were materialized but also how they took place through the material stages. The materiality that appeared was neither as "prior to politics" (Anand 2017, 13) nor merely as an effect of social organization and "the effect of the politics" (Anand 2017, 13). The materials which constituted the social, political, and economic fabric of this town had a capacity to exercise agency in a Latourian sense of things as mediators (Latour 1993), as active elements capable of altering the course and effects of the agency of others, and which might, to an extent, provoke humans to undertake particular actions. It was through human articulation of materials and their involvement in affective interactions that subjectivities, identities, and the sense of belonging were formed (Laszczkowski 2015). I look at how material conditions for the articulation of the futures were remade and how materials were involved in affecting relations. I also inspect how the relations affected the materials through the performative articulations of the futural promises. Having introduced the framework from which the arguments in this book are drawn, I will finally introduce the structure of this book and the following chapters in more depth.

The Stages, the Performers, and the Audience

The first part of this book, entitled "Make Believe," inquires about performances of pretense through which the futures were remade. Chapter 1 provides a deeper historical and political context of Bor. The chapter familiarizes the reader with the context of the performances carried out by the politicians and the company managers who performed the promises of revival of the company and of copper production. In this chapter, I show how the promise of the bright future of the company was conveyed through what was seen as a fabrication of the company's success. Chapter 2 explores how the town's urban texture became a stage that served the town's and the company's officials by mimicking the mutual revival and performing the promise of the revived urban futures. The chapter specifically delves into the ambivalence of embracing the partial renovations as being "at least something."

The second part of the book, "Hope of Sustaining Everyday Life," pays attention to the requirements for living urban everyday lives (decently), such as having clean air to breathe (chapter 3) and keeping houses warm during the winter (chapter 4). Chapter 3 inquires about the promises of nonpolluted futures that were engendered through the implementation of new copper-smelting technologies, which were there to replace the obsolete polluting ones. I show how the imbrication of risk with hope, as ambivalence, produced particular subject positions vis-à-vis the company performances. Chapter 4 shows how the derelict district heating system was a material stage that served for the performance of political power by providing the promise of welfare and care through the abundant, yet instable, infrastructural provision. The chapter offers new insights into so-far underexplored post-Yugoslav afterlives of urban infrastructures.

The third part, "Hope for Post-Industrial Futures," illustrates two contrasting examples of how certain groups engaged with the possibilities of making post-industrial futures. Chapter 5 focuses on older unemployed women who needed to conceive their alternative, post-industrial futures away from the company. Here I show how the practices of pretending helped to make the future goals more of a reality while they engaged in improving their handcrafting skills as a particular investment in their futures. Chapter 6 portrays how the youth, onto whom successful futures of the company were mapped, engaged themselves in obtaining what they saw as "artificially high salaries." The two chapters inspect contrasting temporalities of individuals' actions that emerged vis-a-vis specific staged futural promises, namely waiting (chapter 5) and urgency (chapter 6).

Overall, the chapters highlight the everyday navigation of the futures within the global production of "instability between appearance and the genuine" (Newell 2013, 138). The ethnographic insights from this peripheral late-industrial town where the futures were remade through engagements with the promissory performances help us to interpret and understand better our present within an increasingly unpredictable, deindustrialized, and crisis-ridden world.

Part I

MAKE BELIEVE

FABRICATING

The Revival of Industrial Futures

Ever since I started living in Bor, I really enjoyed having inspiring conversations with Petar, a cultural worker, who became my friend. I collaborated with him on several cultural projects, and he helped me with the literature and connected me with other residents of the town. Petar was married with a daughter. In April 2018, I visited the town for just a couple of days. When I met him, we sat on a bench with small solar panels over our heads. This mushroom-like bench, called the Strawberry Tree, was installed in October 2012 in the square in front of Dom kulture (the House of Culture). The bench was supposed to serve as a solar charger for mobile devices and was advertised as a successful endeavor of some young entrepreneurs from Serbia who had collaborated with the state mobile network provider. At the time of our meeting, the bench did not work and the cables for charging phones were gone. Petar reminded me that it had been faulty ever since the first day it was installed, and it stayed faulty, perhaps, because the residents did not need such an innovation or because many times the projects were done only for the sake of doing them, since they brought more immediate results to those who accomplished them, by performatively testifying efforts to improve the urban living conditions, but they never envisaged their long-term usage. The public sites were destroyed many times, and the projects rarely envisioned their maintenance and repair. Sitting in the shadow of the Tree's broken promise of innovation and sustainability reminded Petar and me of many projects in Bor that had promised sustainable or alternative futures (other than the industrial ones) but had failed to deliver their promises. The very mention of the failed promises led us to discuss the ever-present question of the future of the town and the company. At that moment, Petar said something that encapsulated an interesting aspect concerning imagining copper. There is no better way to start illustrating the specific historical, political, and social context of Bor than by briefly illustrating the shared ethos of how copper was imagined to offer possibilities for the town's collective and individual futures.

"Everything here is centered on copper which does not exist. Like nationalism, constructed from something which does not exist . . . it is invented in the period of crisis," Petar said to me, smiling. He knew that this would entertain me. His statement was clearly a reference to Benedict Anderson's (1991) notion of imagined community and alluded to his somewhat skeptical stance toward the prospects of having copper in the future. For Petar, the promised revival and its potential failure, "crisis," was carefully brought into being through performances carried out by the company for the sake of party-politicking and to produce a sense that there *was* a future. The idea of privatizing RTB was lingering in the air, but it was not certain. His statement also pointed to a particular kind of production that entailed a performative aspect of industrial production: producing "something" out of "nothing." In fact, the campaign that promoted the company's revival conveyed the message that it produced a record amount of copper, which was a matter of widespread doubt and dispute among the residents. The question of whether the company had a future at all was also a matter of contestations.

Interestingly, Petar's ironic assertion of the performative aspect of industrial production has been captured in the past by the famous Yugoslav comedy-sketch television show called *Top lista nadrealista* (*The Surrealists' Top Chart*). The show, which aired on TV Sarajevo in the 1980s, had one particular sketch that focused on poor industrial production and referred to the Yugoslav economic crisis. The sketch illustrated the act of faking the industrial success of a still functional state while on the brink of collapse. In the sketch, one could see the head director of a company, who gave a statement to a journalist that his factory produced "nothing" by importing two kinds of materials from abroad: "*nema ničega*" (there is nothing) and "*đe je, ba, ono nestalo?*" (where the hell is it gone?). Such a sense of an insufficient capacity to produce, the importance of the faking of industrial (hence state) success by the factory's head directors (usually party-political authorities), and the widespread practices of stealing by the local directors (and sometimes even the workers) seem to be a continuous leitmotif in the narratives of the potential futures of Bor. The *longue durée* of such representations speaks about the continuum with late socialism, where the performances of successful industrial production served to strengthen the state power or even maintain the illusion of a still functioning state in the midst of the crisis.

Yet there was a difference between such performances in these two different periods. During socialism, there were some promises of the futures that were realized and made material and whose realization existed until today. For instance, the very presence of district heating that covered the whole town (see chapter 4) and the vast majority of building blocks in which the residents still lived were the outcomes of socialist future-oriented urban planning projects.[1] The whole company became an industrial "giant" during that time too. However, many projects that failed to deliver their future-oriented goals, failed investments, and myriad unfinished projects built after the abundant period of socialism still stood in the town. They were also important for the cognition of the (im)possibilities and especially of the potential failures of the realization of the promised futures. At the time of my fieldwork, a sense of failure and abandonment haunted Bor, as much as the promise of the revival that was frequently attached to the future promises from late socialism. This temporal dynamic significantly influenced the notion that many future-oriented promissory projects could be always on the verge of being disappointing, yet possible.

The very doubt in the (in)existence of copper was subject to frequent interpretations by its residents, especially when I was there in 2012 and 2013. Copper, a material that had the potential to grant stable and promising futures, to use Anderson's (1991) metaphor of imagined community, was a "thing" that the majority of the people could not see or feel in person but could experience through the by-products of its processing, such as through the incredible amount of sulfur dioxide in the air from smelting (see chapter 3). Nobody could know for certain how much copper there was. There was even a dispute among many engineers who worked at RTB or at the RTB Copper Research Institute (engaged in researching of copper deposits) with whom I had conversations. The existence of copper was almost like Schrödinger's cat: it was at the same time an abundant and a deficient matter—it existed and it did not.

Schrödinger's Cat: The Paradox of Insufficiency

Anyone in Bor would certainly explain to any stranger, such as me, that copper had enabled national and local prospects in the past. According to this widely shared understanding, copper was seen as a material which enabled past futures by building "the whole of Yugoslavia," as my interlocutors would phrase it, through its system of redistribution of income. This narrative was constantly repeated on social media and by the individuals with whom I spent time, who told me (and each other) stories about how Bor's copper built many

Yugoslav sites. Those were, among others, the main Yugoslav railroads, parts of the Serbian capital Belgrade, and essential cultural institutions. They were allegedly built from the profit RTB made that was redistributed through the self-managed system of economic redistribution. Copper was also seen as a deficient matter, which people often viewed as stolen by the politicians who were transferring the profit (and gold) for their own private accounts, which cast the town to the periphery, especially during the 1990s. In spite of the reminiscences of the potential futures that copper could have granted in the past, and in spite of the conditions that distributed its potential elsewhere, the potential of copper still managed to produce a collective sense of intimate belonging to the "copper town."

Milica, who was a fifty-five-year-old accountant at RTB Bor and the mother of one of my interlocutors from the local community office where I volunteered, would often emphasize to me that she was still hopeful, in spite of some doubts. For her, the potential of copper, which could provide (better) futures, was a reason why she praised the government's decision to provide support to the highly indebted post-socialist company to keep it alive. Such support consisted of myriad incentives—from providing subsidies to protecting the company from debtors, overwriting debts, being a guarantor for massive loans, and so on. However, as much as these acts served the political parties in power by helping them to win the next election, such decisions were also supported by global capitalist economic configurations inherent in mining endeavors and the very fact that the copper price increased on the global market at that point. Her daughter (aged thirty-five) added that there were still some "irrational" decisions. It was said that there was a poor concentration of copper in the ore and that 2,500 workers out of approximately 5,000 to 5,200 were working as surplus at RTB.[2] Milica reacted affectively: "It's a positive thing!" She explained to us that, through such acts of keeping the surplus workers, what she called "social peace" was maintained. This was a widely shared notion which meant, in this context, that the higher number of employed workers was "artificially" maintained, in spite of the economic rationale, as a populist measure to maintain the power of the political elite. Milica added: "It's a good thing . . . because such politics do not allow the workers to end up 'in the streets.'" Such praise for such protectionist politics was something that could often be found in Bor. It also entailed praise for the support given by the government to the indebted company, which otherwise might not have been able to compete on the global market.

Even though Petar, the cultural worker, was more skeptical about the existence of the copper, which he, of course, could not know for certain, his life, just like the lives of the majority of the town's residents, was also intimately connected with this material and the company. His father had worked at RTB, as did his close friends and relatives. He even thought that no privatization of RTB would bring some good. He, Milica, and many others sometimes expressed doubts that there would be enough copper to make up for the debts incurred historically by the company. They thought that the company's capacity to produce without making a loss required additional investments that were lacking. Such investments were necessary due to the very "nature" of the production. The Schrödinger's cat phenomenon that I mentioned earlier—the perception that copper was at the same time an abundant and a deficient matter, both existing and not existing—resonates with the concept of "doubtful hope," which Gisa Weszkalnys (2016) delineated as an intrinsic element of capitalist dynamics of resource potential and of its temporal imagination (cf. Ferry and Limbert 2008; Limbert 2010; Weszkalnys 2016; Empson 2018). "Doubtful hope" consisted of hope and doubt and relied, as Weszkalnys (2016) argued, on the potential of oil. The "doubtful hope" in São Tomé and Príncipe comprised visions of material betterment and personal and collective transformation, as well as anticipations of failure, friction, and discontent (Weszkalnys 2016). The specific entanglement between such inherent global dynamics resonated in Bor and it elicited ambivalence with regard to the prospects that copper might grant in the future. While on the one hand, there was doubt about the sufficiency of copper to realize abundant and prosperous near futures, on the other hand there was still hope, which drew from the promises of the past futures, of having abundant amounts of copper that could be granted in (undefined) futures. Such ambivalence was constitutive of why Bor was at the same time seen paradoxically as *both* a marginal (post-socialist) site and central to projects of modernization, like it was during socialism.

From 2010, a vast number of politicians who visited the industrial premises in Bor promised revived and successful industrial futures that would be relevant on both local and national scales. The performers changed just as the governments and the ruling parties were changing, one replacing the other. The deputy prime minister and minister of interior affairs, Ivica Dačić (who later served as first deputy prime minister of Serbia in the government that sold RTB to the Chinese company) said in 2010 that Bor was "Serbia's pillar and initiator of the development of the whole state, just like it once was" (B92 2010a). He added that "Serbia has learned lessons from the past, so in the future it will not easily give what is its national and state resource, like RTB" (B92 2010a). The minister of the economy, Mlađan Dinkić, who initiated the revival of Bor, claimed that "with a new smelter and sulfuric acid plant, RTB will be one of the largest copper producers in Eastern Europe" (B92 2010b). Together with him, the director of the World Bank for Southeast Europe, Jane Armitage, in her visit to RTB and Bor, stated that there would be an enhancement of employment through various training courses and development of the Incubator Center (B92 2010b). The promise that Bor would flourish tomorrow was enhanced by foreign officials and ambassadors who occasionally came to Bor and created the media frenzy I already mentioned. For instance, back then the current UN resident coordinator, William Infante, who was frequently present in Bor at the time of my visit (and with whom I exchanged a couple of words on several events we both attended) visited Bor the day before Miners' Day (August 6) in 2013. He noted that "a renaissance of Serbian mining" (B92 2013) was on the horizon. During a visit to RTB with a nine-member delegation from many Western embassies, he added that that the revival (also called "progress") would certainly bring an influx of money and new jobs (B92 2013).

Unlike such predictions that widely circulated, which indicated that Bor would experience remarkable social and economic development in the future, there was a sentiment of not quite believing such positive forecasts. For instance, in the alternative media (those outlets that did not support the politics of the ruling political parties), one could read how the company was a remnant of the socialist period, oversized and indebted (Radenković 2015). Some news reports claimed that the extractive potentials were rather unknown or at least ambiguous. In fact, the company itself appeared as a highly conflicting entity. It was significant and valuable, the backbone of local, regional, and national development in the futures, an asset, and an obligation of the state, *and* simultaneously a Serbian "economic black hole" which pulled Bor and the state into the abyss. In spite of these conflicting potential futures that the company might bring, no one in Bor could imagine their own existence and the existence of their town without the prospects that copper could guarantee.

The popular disbelief in the promise of prosperous industrial futures was usually dismissed by the company's very active public relations (PR) department. In their public appearances on social media, on national and local broadcasts, and in the newspapers, the company's representatives, usually either the general manager or the company's PR representative, claimed that such negative projections of the futures were an attempt to politically discredit the new managers or the government. The company claimed that the widespread doubts represented a malicious and negative outlook on Bor that did not allow this peripheral town to fight against the negative image of a rundown town that haunted it. In spite of such PR representations, in public there was confusion as well: how could the money be labeled as "profit" and *"pozitivno poslovanje"* (positive business), which was frequently heard on the news, if the company was highly over-indebted? There was also confusion about how it was possible to maintain suddenly increased good salaries (above the national average). A related question was what would happen to the company, its employees, and the whole town if (and when) the copper price eventually dropped. The questions that appeared were myriad: Was it a state-owned or only a state-managed company? Was the investment in the new smelting technologies a backdoor to privatization in the future? The numbers were also ambiguous: How much copper did RTB actually produce and have in its reserves? Could the company produce enough copper from its own resources? Did it need to import copper ore concentration? Nobody knew this for certain as the numbers were a party-political matter too. They usually served to perform an image of the company in the "superlative" to create proof of the government's and the company's successful governance. The numbers were vague, nonverifiable, or even sometimes claimed to be fabricated. A search for the "real" facts that may have been concealed or manipulated would be impossible and here rather unnecessary. It would be a futile endeavor to determine the "real" numbers which could potentially tell us how the company was *actually* doing business. What was certain, however, was that all these ambiguities were a constitutive part of how the whole company as an entity came into being performatively. As such, it became the stage for the protagonists who continually promised bright and successful industrial and company futures.

However, I cannot help but notice that, at least when I was in Bor prior to RTB's privatization, instead of finding the "paradox of plenty" or the "resource curse," there was a certain sense of a "paradox of insufficiency," so to speak. As the Schrödinger cat's phenomenon in relation to the potential of copper indicates, there was a particular sense that there *could* be a possibility of copper insufficiency that haunted the estimation of Bor's resources. Of course, when people doubted the sufficiency of copper, they only guessed, as they could not know it for certain. However, together with that doubt, a strong sense of the possibility of *having* prospective futures was still there: there could be more copper, but it was uncertain. In spite of the notion of copper's insufficiency and its potentiality in undefined futures, there was a collective desire for greater economic development, for potential (what Bor could have achieved in the past and might achieve in the future), and for greater development of the town through the completely rundown company. Before I illustrate the various actors on the "front stage" of the company's performances and the very specificity of the resource curse, first I would like to make the reader familiar with a brief history of Bor and Serbia, the background against which the following chapters are set.

Rewind: From Mining Colony to Yugoslav Giant

The year that Borani count as the beginning of copper extraction is 1903, when the mine was opened by the Czech engineer Franjo Šistek and the Serbian capitalist and industrialist Đorđe Vajfert, who sold the concession to a French capitalist company (from 1908 until 1941) in the capitalist Kingdom of Yugoslavia. The town emerged as an ad hoc mining settlement, and the entire development of Bor village was subordinated to the needs of the capitalist mine. Several workers' colonies were built very close to the mining pit for the accommodation of the workers, along with a number of houses and apartments for the upper-class management of the mines and for the technical and administrative personnel. At that point, the town had an overground sewage system, a limited electricity network, and a very limited heating system. Relying on corruption among the local population and the corrupted state, the French administration was dominant in the mine and influenced everyday life.

The main institutions in the town were built and founded during the interwar period (administrative buildings of mines, hospitals, schools, post office) (Jovanović 1987). Bor was developing as a town, but at the same time, it maintained the characteristics of a mining colony. The ambiguous status of the settlement was also reflected in its name: it was neither Bor village nor a proper town but was known as Bor Mine, the name used in the press, official documents, and everyday speech for a long period (Jovanović 2001, 36). The movements of urban–rural migration were intense and constant. In this period, the number of inhabitants increased from 1,000 to around 5,500 before World War II. During the war, the mining complex was turned into a work camp. The local labor force and other ethnic groups were recruited for forced labor in the mine, among them Hungarian "Work Jews," Soviet prisoners of war, and Italian military internees. The profit and gold went to the German government (Rutar 2005). Bor Mine suffered heavy damage during the withdrawal of the Nazi forces.

From the 1950s, the town started developing linearly and expanded toward the south, owing to the super-productive (*udarnički*) enthusiasm for building a new Socialist Federal Republic of Yugoslavia (SFRY) from the wreckage of World War II (see map 2). The shape of the town became linear as it "ran away" (as my interlocutors would say) from the mining pit. The smelting factory was built in the middle of the old town and, paradoxically, stood for a long time next to the green market in the town's old city center. The urban conglomeration developed with expanded industrialization, adding one Kilometer (as parts of the town were called by reckoning the distance from the mining pit) after another towards the south. The old part of the town built during the period of the French colony started crumbling, and collapsed into what was an inactive open mine pit on the Zeroth Kilometer (figure 4).[3] The remaining part was populated by old dilapidated houses inhabited by impoverished citizens.

When Josip Broz Tito split from Stalin in 1948, Yugoslavia introduced third-way self-managed socialism, which was characterized by a unique mixture of socialist and market-economic principles. It had a liberal socialist system of

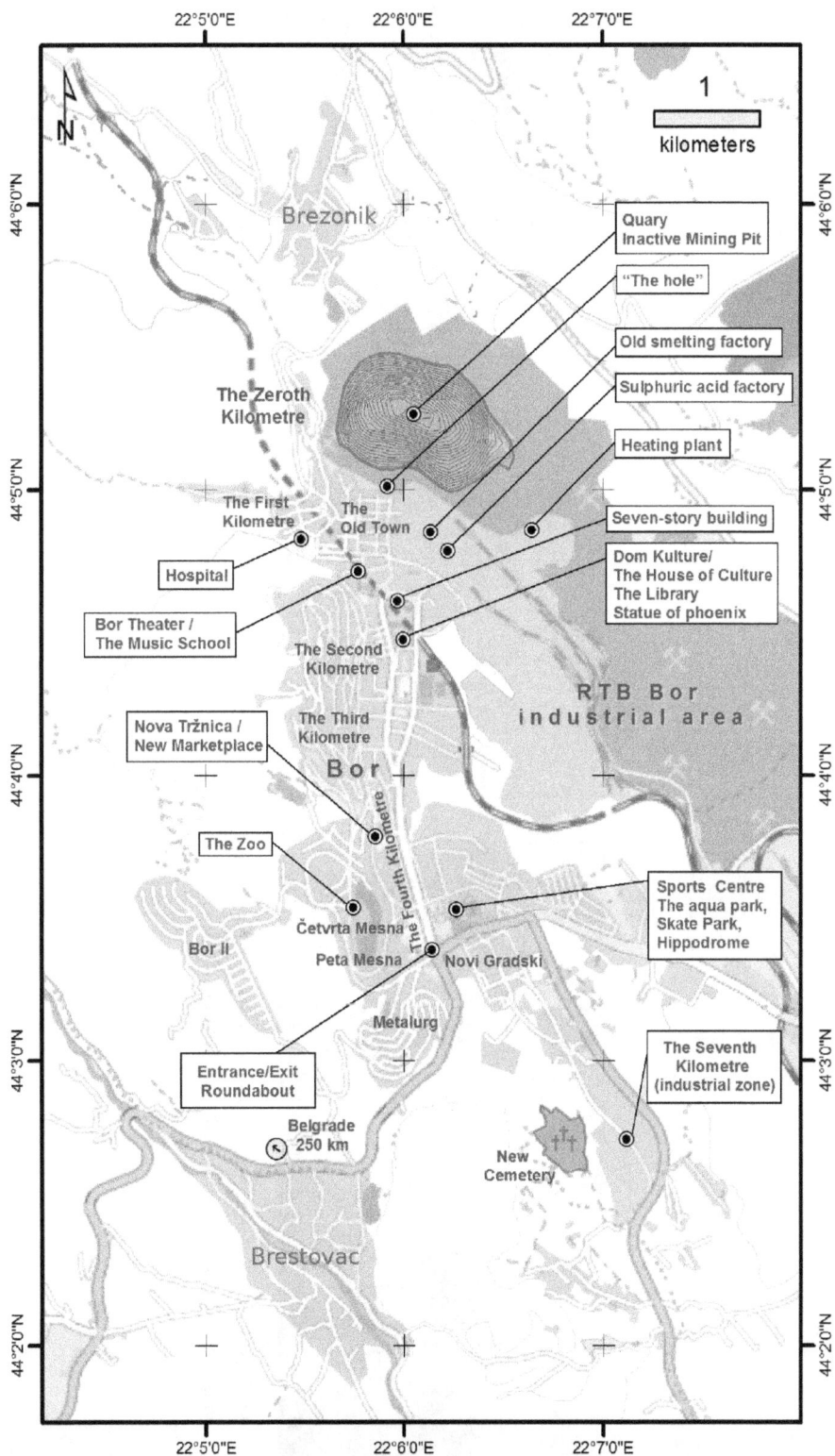

MAP 2. Map of Bor, representing the town in 2012. Created by Ivica Milojević.

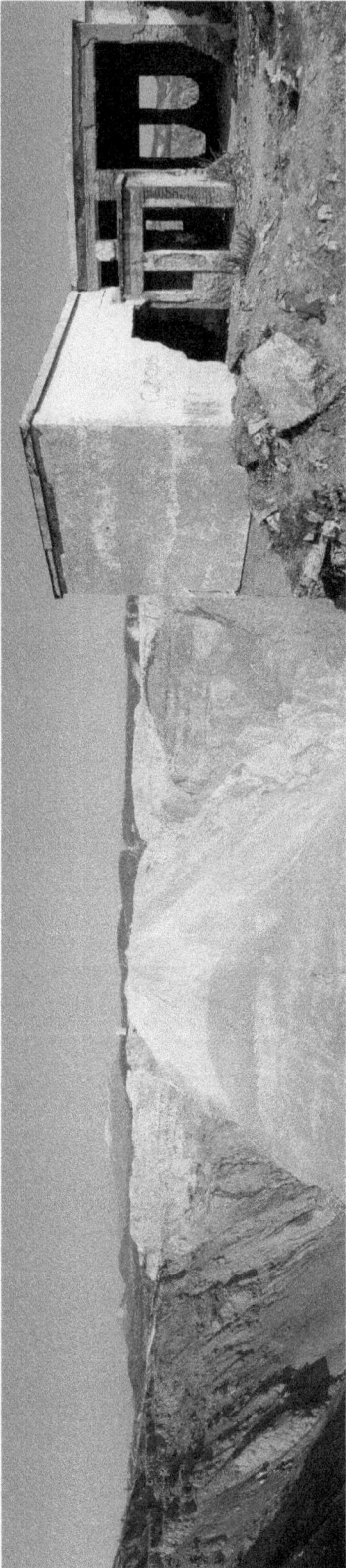

FIGURE 4. The Zeroth Kilometer. The view on the inactive open-cast mining pit, called "the hole" where the town begins. Photo credit: Taken by the author in August 2013.

government, and the borders were open to goods, people, and ideas from around the world. This was an exceptional socialist principle that combined a limited market and relative freedoms, such as the freedom to travel abroad, with high living standards. This form of socialism was different from the socialism in all other Eastern Bloc countries, where it was characterized by central planning and centralized management of their economies. Therefore, Bor was neither a "closed town" (Kotkin 1995; Collier 2011) nor a proper "company town" (Solecki 1996; Green 2012), as the shops, facilities, and housing were not owned or provided solely by the company. Rather, they were built through the workers' self-management (RTB workers made up the majority, although not all, of the workers) and other funds on the state level.

Workers' self-management was based on the idea of transferring management and decision-making over to the workers (through "workers' councils") in the enterprises and other spheres of life. The idea was to separate the state from industry, although this was never completed in practice (Simmie and Dekleva 1991). Self-management was conducted in several ways. A redistribution of the workers' contributions (*samodoprinosi*) was carried out by taking a percentage of workers' salaries to contribute to the infrastructural development of the country. The workers were included in the decision-making on the matter of the distribution of funds through the workers' councils and *mesne zajednice* (local community offices). In practice, self-management had its limits. For instance, the workers did not have any influence over the price of copper or its distribution. Altogether, the most important decisions of the company were made by the head directors and the company managers, who were always high-ranking members of the Communist Party.

RTB Bor, like other Yugoslav companies, exported to both Western and Eastern markets and even to the Global South. This was possible due to its geopolitical neutrality and its leading role in the Non-Aligned Movement.[4] In the socialist period, the economy went through very different phases, and the export of copper was controlled by the state and limited until the 1970s (Cvetanović 2005). In this period, it was essential to increase copper production to meet the restoration needs of the country. The ideology of Titoism, like other socialist ideologies, meticulously constructed images of workers and the working class as symbols of progress and prosperity (Petrović 2010, 145). Miners occupied a particular symbolic position among the workforce in former Yugoslavia, since mining represented a competitive socialist form of work par excellence (Matošević 2015).

A strong economic, demographic, and spatial expansion of the town occurred in the period from 1961 to 1981, which also matched a time period when the market price of copper was higher. Economic development was characterized by an increase in production at RTB. There was also a transition to surface exploitation along with horizontal expansion in/toward neighboring towns and villages. New factories were opened for making the final copper products. The Copper Mining and Smelting Complex, established in 1961, became one of the ten biggest companies in SFRY. It was envisaged as a self-sustaining copper-processing complex that consisted of the very places where raw mineral materials could be extracted and which could finalize the products as well. Apart from exploitation and processing of copper ore and the production of cathode copper, gold, and silver, the company also produced (and it still does) sulfuric acid, copper II sulphate pentahydrate, selenium, platinum, and palladium.

From the 1960s until 1975, the copper price was favorable, but from 1975 onward, it began to drop (Cvetanović 2005, 151). By the beginning of the 1990s, RTB Bor had become a huge metallurgical industrial conglomerate which excavated copper but also performed secondary copper-processing and housed other industrial facilities (semifinished and finished copper products). It consisted of nineteen industrial companies across Yugoslavia. At that time, when copper production also reached its peak, RTB employed around 24,450 people across Yugoslavia, which included the daughter factories spread out through the country (Jovanović and Miodrag 2005, 489). It is estimated that in the town of Bor, which had roughly 40,000 citizens at that time, from 11,900 (Jovanović and Miodrag 2005, 489) to 14,000 workers were employed by RTB.

The period between the 1960s and 1970s is well known as the flourishing "Golden Age of Bor," during which the town gained its urbanized infrastructure. Many institutions like Dom kulture, the Medical Center, and the Sports Center were established in this period, and many comfortable apartments and buildings, holiday resorts in Croatia for RTB workers, and institutions for cultural and social life were built. An infrastructural network started developing, such as railroads, electricity, district heating (which I address in chapter 4), and so on. RTB was also taking out foreign loans to enhance production and invest in urban development. The workers' salaries were among the highest in the country at that moment. A lot of people in Bor talked about the period as a time of abundance, consumerism, and connectedness. A fast business train even took Borani to Belgrade along the railroad which was removed during the 1990s.

Ruptures: 1990s Decline and Post-2000s Crisis

The citizens of Bor experienced radical ruptures in their lives several times after the 1990s. The collapse of SFRY started in the late 1980s and culminated with the secessions of Slovenia and Croatia (1991), Bosnia and Herzegovina, and Macedonia (1992). The Yugoslav successor state, the union of Serbia and Montenegro, abandoned the name Yugoslavia in 2001, and Montenegro declared its independence in 2006. The Serbian province of Kosovo declared its independence in February 2008. The 1990s were marked by economic crisis, the rise of nationalism, and Serbia's involvement in the wars in Slovenia, Croatia, Bosnia and Herzegovina, and, later, Kosovo. Citizens of Serbia were subject to a strict visa regime (up until 2009, its residents needed a visa to travel to the European Union, and it was difficult to obtain) and, in 1992, the United Nations imposed economic sanctions that had a negative impact on the economy.

During the government of Slobodan Milošević in the 1990s, RTB maintained its production under difficult circumstances. At that point, RTB had a surplus of workers and was not able to produce without losses. RTB Bor was heavily subsidized by the Serbian government. There were almost no layoffs because Milošević's politics relied on the politics of "buying social peace," which referred to populist acts of the government that ran counter to economic rationality (like maintaining low food prices or avoiding privatization of factories) in order to pacify the population and prevent revolt among them. Due to the difficulty of importing industrial oil, factory parts, and other necessities for production, the technology became worn out and outdated. In 1999, Serbia faced North Atlantic Treaty Organization (NATO) air strikes during the Kosovo war, which included several air strikes on some industrial areas in Bor, which contributed to further devastation of its industry.

Even though the 1990s were remembered as a very difficult decade, an even more difficult period was about to come after the fall of Milošević's government in 2000, when the state entered the so-called democratic transition.[5] The new democratic government had the task of introducing a state of law and democracy, regulating the local market, normalizing foreign relations, and conducting hasty privatization of malfunctioning companies in order to remove the burden on the state budget. At this point, RTB's technology was severely outdated, the global copper price was extremely low, and salaries at the company were below average. RTB was still heavily dependent on state subsidies for all wages and the colossal debt (stemming from socialist times). The government introduced the distribution of severance pay programs to deal with the surplus of workers. They were distributed in two "waves" in 2002 and 2006, when around 5,900 workers left RTB (RTS 2009), followed by an additional wave at the beginning of 2009, during which only a couple of hundred workers left. Some parts of RTB were sold or bankrupted, especially those in the industrial zone in the Seventh Kilometer (the town's final Kilometer). The factories were sold as property to insolvent companies whose intention was not to revitalize industrial production but to sell the property and its machines, lay off the workers, and perhaps resell the factories in the future. Chapters 4 and 5 provide the contours of everyday engagements of the people laid off from several factories in Bor in this period and illustrate the consequences of this period.

RTB Bor has been in the process of restructuring since 2003 and retained this status throughout my fieldwork. The process of restructuration meant a complete reorganization of the formerly socially owned company with a goal to secure its market position and operations for the future. In Serbia, restructuration of socially owned and state-owned companies was usually an attempt to keep them "alive" under government subsidies, loans, and bylaw protection from their creditors.[6] The introduction of restructuring was first and foremost a political decision to maintain company viability, especially those that were assessed as economically "strategic" for the state, which meant that they had great financial potential. In this period, there were only a few potential clients that could buy the company, which declined drastically. Selling the company was also not the most popular political move, as the government feared it would probably be sold as a weak company and then further resold and, due to such a transaction, the political parties would lose their voters.

Around 2014, Serbia was spending a quarter more than it produced, with imports exceeding exports (Savić 2014), and RTB relied on imports of copper. Since 2010, loans had been taken out many times to enable the company to survive or for building some other projects (like the reconstructed smelter discussed in chapter 3). This particular economic status, especially since 2010, protected the company from its creditors. The company's debts were temporarily blocked. The government would usually claim that the solutions for this company would be taken from the state's budget, but since the state did not have any major revenues, it would, most probably, be paid for by all taxpayers in Serbia. The company, however, tried to reassure the citizens that the debt would be returned from the company's own copper production, which would especially benefit from the high price of copper, presented as if it would never drop in the future.

The Revival: Until It Is Not Anymore

In 2009, the price of copper returned to the level of the 1980s and then grew progressively to reach $9,631.75 per metric ton on the London Metal Exchange (Mining.com 2021). The effects of the continuing rise have been felt across the globe. There are a variety of factors behind this rise, of which the biggest by far was China's economic boom. At the end of 2011, China increased its imports of copper due to high usage in its industry, which resulted in a record deficit of this metal on the global market in the next two years. At the same time, China limited copper exports, which prevented other countries from accessing copper, strongly impacting the global market and contributing to new geopolitical tensions (European Commission 2016).

In spite of a favorable copper price, in 2013, RTB Bor could hardly produce more than a third of the copper it had produced in the 1990s. According to data from the Customs Administration of the Ministry of Finance of the Republic of Serbia, RTB Bor alone contributed 0.8 percent of the country's gross domestic product (GDP) in 2018 (Bjelotomić 2018), whereas it had previously contributed 18 percent of the GDP of Yugoslavia (Cvetanović 2005). According to some Serbian raw metal entrepreneurs who were at one time interested in buying the mining complex, in 2016, RTB was able to produce 60,000 metric tons of copper every year, which had a value of 300–500 million US dollars (this sum is without counting gold and silver) (Marković 2016). Bor's gold was sold exclusively to the National Bank of Serbia, as mandated by law, which enabled the state to maintain and enhance its gold reserves to protect the state economy. Copper and silver were sold on the London Metal Exchange and depended only on demand on the global market.

It was estimated that RTB's debt in 2016 was approximately 1.3 billion euros (Lakićević 2018), but the numbers vary. The debt structure included foreign companies to whom RTB Bor owed a significant amount of copper and cash based on loans from the socialist period until today. RTB also had debts to the Development Fund of Serbia, the Tax Administration of Serbia, and companies supplying raw materials, intermediate goods, and spare parts. The biggest part of the debt (more than 70 percent) was owed to the Serbian government and was, again, part of its foreign borrowing and transferred funds from taxpayers. For instance, the company owed the state (its main provider) for electricity, the state provided subsidies and loans, and the company did not pay appropriate taxes to the state (so the state basically owed itself). The debts dated back to the 1960s, including years from the socialist period when the old smelting factory was built, the flats were built using the loans, and the town was developing. With the financial measures such as keeping it alive to save it from bankruptcy, by delaying the repayment of the debts and preparing the company for restructuring, the government and the company were "buying time" until the company started becoming slightly more profitable.

The favorable price of copper was not the crucial impetus for the decision to provide freedom to RTB to avoid repayment debts. However, both the rise in the copper price and the state's protection contributed to raising RTB salaries to extremely high levels compared to the national average. In March 2012, the national average salary was 40,562 Serbian dinars (at that time, approximately

483 US dollars/366 euros) per month (Večernje novosti 2012). The average RTB salary was around 60,000 Serbian dinars (approximately 714 US dollars/540 euros) per month at that time, but it was quite uncertain whether the company was paying the workers' social security contributions (toward health care or pensions) (B92 2012). For higher managerial positions, salaries rose to 1056 US dollars (800 euros) and above, which was regarded as an incredibly high salary. This amount would allow a better quality of life, which could even include, apart from the everyday spending, affording a modest holiday at the neighboring Montenegrin or Greek coast, the most common summer vacation sites for Serbian citizens, or buying an average price laptop and/or a smartphone. The debt cycle of RTB was not broken—it was just put on hold. Due to the extremely good salaries, the company started to figure again, after so many years, as the most desirable employer in the town. The following chapters follow particular temporal, material, and political contingencies of future-making practices set against such a particular moment in the history of this town.

Stronger Than Fate

During the first months of my fieldwork, I toyed with the idea of obtaining access to the newspaper *Kolektiv*, which became a part of the RTB Bor PR office. *Kolektiv* was the oldest factory newspaper in the former Yugoslavia and used to be conceived as a tool for informing the workers of the self-managed company.[7] I was interested in exploring the transformation of this newspaper from the "backstage" (Goffman 1969) of RTB's performances. I decided to give it a try and asked to join this office as a journalist or photographer (or any other role they were willing to assign me to). The PR office, which had a role in creating the image of the company's performances, was in charge of granting permission for such access. My request was straightforwardly rejected by the PR officer, to whom I had to propose my idea first. In spite of this rejection, the PR officer, a woman in her mid-forties (I assume), with short black hair and a lot of confidence in her posture and talk, explained in our telephone call that she would, instead, gladly have a cup of coffee with me and would reply to all my inquiries. According to her, my presence in the newspaper (PR) office was out of the question because, she explained, they did not want "to be observed." I was not surprised by this decision, as this is one of many issues that ethnographers encounter while conducting ethnographies in business organizations (van Marrewijk 2014).[8] In general, access to the shop floors and industrial landscapes that belonged to this company, for which one needed to apply for permission from the RTB headquarters, was also not easily granted to outsiders.

In its active involvement in maintaining the image of the company's successfulness, the PR office maintained control of critical writing about the company. The PR officer of the company was sometimes involved in scripting of the company's performances both in the town and in the (social) media. The PR office had good collaboration with the local and national news agencies and journalists and, thus, tried to react to any other kinds of representations that were not aligned with the company's vision of itself and the town. The PR officer explained to me, while we were having coffee in the garden of one of the popular cafés on the Fourth Kilometer, that the company's goal was to perform the "glittering" image exactly as illustrated in its redesigned newspaper, now printed on glossy colored paper in the style of a magazine (figures 5 and 6).

According to the PR officer, the emphasis of the company "was on optimism and not on hopelessness and despair," on renovated façades and the zoo or children's playgrounds rather than on "dilapidation and dirty corners," and on the newly opened miners' underground café rather than on "dirty factories and shop floors with page-three girls on the wall." She added that the preferred emphasis was on the renovated hotel on Bor Lake (managed by RTB) and not "the mining tailings or pyrite fields that had a 'whiff' of the apocalypse," landscapes which the local filmmakers and photographers often utilized for their own artistic representations. She revealed that she was also affectively engaged in her role as a PR officer to "defend" the town's credentials as revived and modern. She herself had grown up in this rundown town, and all the negative images bothered her. According to her, such representations were false. The PR officer recounted her life trajectory to me along with stories about her early days as a journalist at the local TV station. When she became more prominent in her coverage of the local news, according to her account, the company recognized her work and persistence and offered her the opportunity to work in the PR office, which she gladly took. The PR activities which she carried out sometimes entailed acts subsumed under corporate social responsibility (CSR) discourse, which also played an immense role in the performances of the promises of successful futures of the company and the town.

It was not always clear in the media whether the representation of the town was conducted by the company's PR department or by the municipality or the tourist offices. However, in the end, it was always the company which was behind such news, sometimes even pretending that the representation in the news was not its official PR statement but only an image painted by some random journalists interested in the sudden revival. The following abstract of the reportage in the national media from 2015 best captures the ethos of the company's performances. The abstract appeared in a news article entitled "Like a Phoenix. This Serbian Town Was a Synonym for Ruination, and Now It Is One

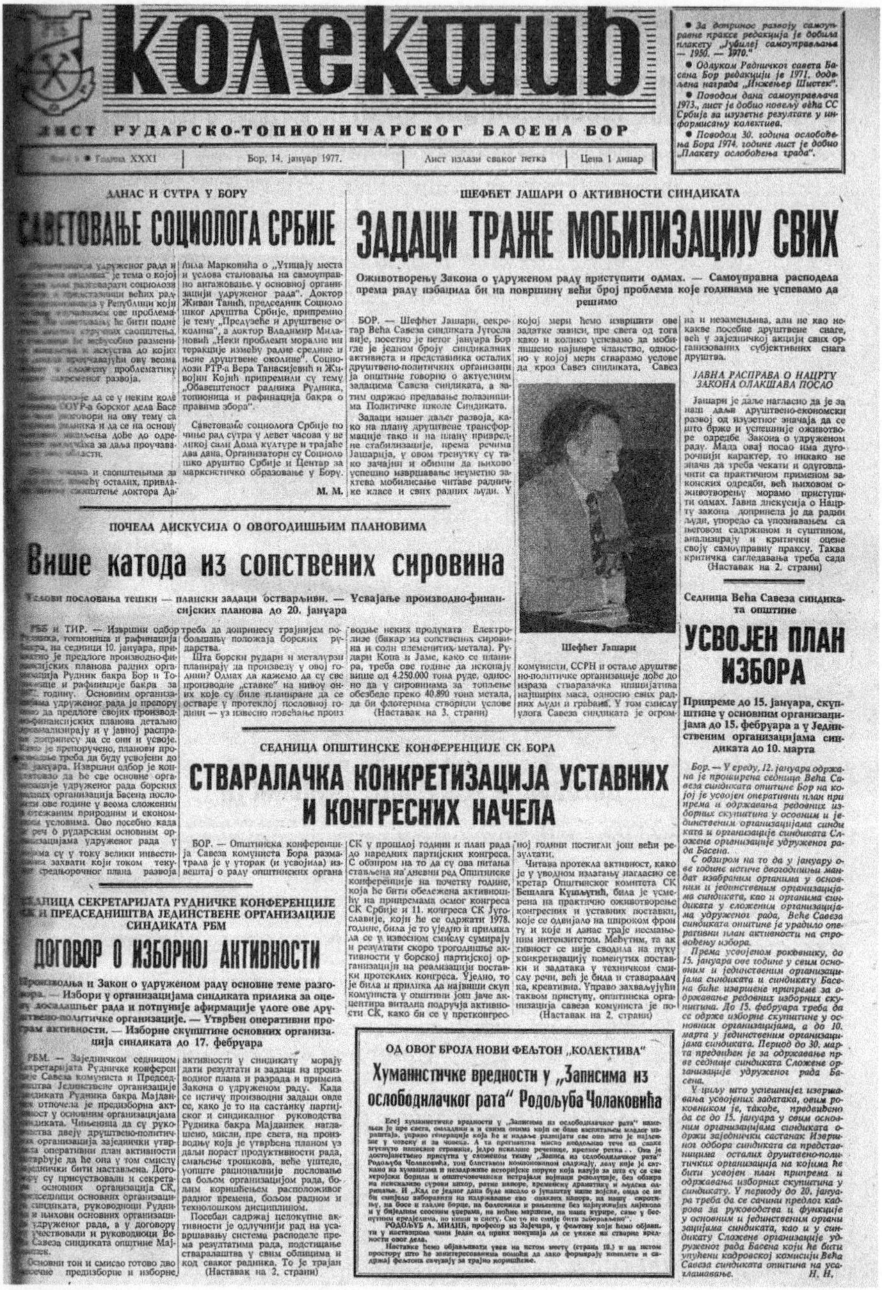

колектив

ЛИСТ РУДАРСКО-ТОПИОНИЧАРСКОГ БАСЕНА БОР

Година XXXI | Бор, 14. јануар 1977. | Лист излази сваког петка | Цена 1 динар

- За допринос развоју самоуправне праксе редакција је добила плакету „Јубилеј самоуправљања — 1950. — 1970."
- Одлуком Радничког савета Басена Бор редакција је 1971. додељена награда „Инжењер Шистек".
- Поводом дана самоуправљача 1973., лист је добио повељу већа СС Србије за изузетне резултате у информисању колектива.
- Поводом 30. година ослобођења Бора 1974. године лист је добио „Плакету ослобођења града".

ДАНАС И СУТРА У БОРУ

САВЕТОВАЊЕ СОЦИОЛОГА СРБИЈЕ

ШЕФЌЕТ ЈАШАРИ О АКТИВНОСТИ СИНДИКАТА

ЗАДАЦИ ТРАЖЕ МОБИЛИЗАЦИЈУ СВИХ

Оживотворењу Закона о удруженом раду приступити одмах. — Самоуправна расподела према раду избацила би на површину већи број проблема које годинама не успевамо да решимо

Шефќет Јашари

ЈАВНА РАСПРАВА О НАЦРТУ ЗАКОНА ОЛАКШАВА ПОСАО

ПОЧЕЛА ДИСКУСИЈА О ОВОГОДИШЊИМ ПЛАНОВИМА

Више катода из сопствених сировина

Услови пословања тешки — плански задаци остварљиви. — Усвајање производно-финансијских планова до 20. јануара

Седница Већа Савеза синдиката општине

УСВОЈЕН ПЛАН ИЗБОРА

Припреме до 15. јануара, скупштине у основним организацијама до 15. фебруара а у Јединственим организацијама синдиката до 10. марта

СЕДНИЦА ОПШТИНСКЕ КОНФЕРЕНЦИЈЕ СК БОРА

СТВАРАЛАЧКА КОНКРЕТИЗАЦИЈА УСТАВНИХ И КОНГРЕСНИХ НАЧЕЛА

СЕДНИЦА СЕКРЕТАРИЈАТА РУДНИЧКЕ КОНФЕРЕНЦИЈЕ СК И ПРЕДСЕДНИШТВА ЈЕДИНСТВЕНЕ ОРГАНИЗАЦИЈЕ СИНДИКАТА РБМ

ДОГОВОР О ИЗБОРНОЈ АКТИВНОСТИ

Производња и Закон о удруженом раду основне теме разговора. — Избори у организацијама синдиката прилика за оцену досадашњег рада и потпуније афирмације улоге ове друштвено-политичке организације. — Утврђен оперативни програм активности. — Изборне скупштине основних организација синдиката до 17. фебруара

ОД ОВОГ БРОЈА НОВИ ФЕЉТОН „КОЛЕКТИВА"

Хуманистичке вредности у „Записима из ослободилачког рата" Родољуба Чолаковића

FIGURE 5. The cover page of the old *Kolektiv* newspaper from January 14, 1977 (XXXI).

КОЛЕКТИВ

ЛИСТ РУДАРСКО - ТОПИОНИЧАРСКОГ БАСЕНА БОР

www.rtb.rs
www.kolektiv.co.rs

KOLEKTIV
ONLINE

Број 2227 · Година LXVI · Лист излази месечно · Понедељак, 22. октобар 2012. · Примерак 15 динара

БАСЕНСКИ ГЕОЛОЗИ ОТКРИЛИ НОВО ЛЕЖИШТЕ РУДЕ

Страна 7

БАКАР И ЗЛАТО НА КРИВЕЉСКОМ КАМЕНУ

МЕТАЛУРЗИ У СЕПТЕМБРУ

Страна 9

ОПЕТ ВИШЕ ОД 4.000 ТОНА АНОДА

Министар рударства упутио снажну подршку менаџменту РТБ-а Бор

„БАСЕН ДОБРО РАДИ, КРИТИКУЈУ ЗЛОНАМЕРНИ"

Амбасадор Канаде у Србији Роман Вашчук у радној посети РТБ-у

НОВА ТОПИОНИЦА НОВО РОЂЕЊЕ „БОРА"

Јубиларни додатак

65

година Колектива

FIGURE 6. The cover page of the rebranded *Kolektiv* on glossy colored paper from October 22, 2012.

of the Most Beautiful" (Popović 2015): "Previously gray-covered with clouds of smoke, and synonymous for hopelessness, and today a town full of life. It experienced its rebirth after a complete fiasco. Now it has a higher average salary than most Serbian towns, rich nightlife, frequent theater visits, a skateboard park, and a karting route, which most cities in Serbia (with the exception of Belgrade and Novi Sad) cannot boast of. Welcome to Bor!"

According to the company, the renovations of myriad sites in Bor, which preceded my arrival in the town, had the purpose of building a "much better social ambience in Bor municipality" (Stanojević 2011). Many of the newly refurbished spaces were also given space on the official municipal calendars for 2013, on postcards, and in the new official tourist brochures, which represented Bor as a "modern town." A few Serbian actors, movie directors, singers, and some bands occasionally came to Bor for work and also took on the role of the performers at various locations in the town. When they were in town, they took tours of the company's industrial sites or visited newly built sites, such as the zoo. Their visits were always publicized by the local and national TV. These public figures usually gave statements on how they were amazed or even "shocked" by the development of the town, which had transformed so much to the point of unrecognizability. Some of these individuals were also members of or sympathizers with the same political party which the RTB managers represented and/or who had business deals with that political party, which managed a substantial number of cultural institutions in Serbia. As I already illustrated, the performers of the promise of revival were also foreign delegations, representatives of foreign companies, and representatives of foreign embassies of the countries where their companies had an economic stake in the business with RTB. On their visits to certain locations, either industrial ones or revived urban sites, they usually made public statements to the present journalists in which they all gave assurances that the future of the town and of the company would be successful and that that future could be even felt in the present as well. For these visiting delegations, a particular stage would be set by the company. At the time of their visit, the whole town would turn into a temporarily smoke-free town. As the smelting plant was positioned in the very city center, usually worked twenty-four-seven, and rarely stopped working except in cases of repairs and maintenance of the plant, the smoke was often present. The smelter was (in)famous for its production of a great amount of "smoke" (*dim*), which, depending on weather conditions and the wind, would fall onto the town. Since the winds were unpredictable and no one could estimate whether there would be smoke in the streets and onto which part of the town it would eventually "fall," when the delegations arrived, the smelter would be ordered to temporarily stop its work. In this way, the important visitors would get an opportunity to enjoy smoke-free tours through the town or the company's premises and to breathe without any difficulty.

A crucial role in the performances was played by an unavoidable performer: the general manager of RTB, a man in his mid-sixties then, who was a well-known and powerful local politician in the town. This charismatic actor, usually referred to by his nickname, Sosa,[9] was already mentioned by Milorad in the introduction of this book as the person who placed the phoenix installation on the top of the building. Sosa was a frequently mentioned figure. People would just simply refer to him as "he" (without even introducing his name) or even through familial nicknames such as the Daddy Sosa (*tata* Sosa) or uncle Blagoje (*čika* Blagoje). The general manager spoke about the refurbishment of the town as though Bor would become "just like Barcelona, Amsterdam, Prague . . . meaning fresh new hope, light, eyes wide open, looking ahead to the future . . . as the Americans say: 'dreaming with the eyes wide open.'" People frequently described him, as some individuals in this book do, too, as a knowledgeable and elegantly dressed (like a gentlemen), eccentric, decadent, haughty, and imperious person. He was also the "sheriff," "the micro-oligarch," "the master of everybody's lives," or "the master of the Universe," as some referred to him, denoting the extent of his power and the autocracy he represented. Sosa had been the general manager since 2008 (until the privatization) but was well known to the residents as the director of one of the RTB companies during socialism and as the director of the Copper Mines Bor company during Milošević's regime in the 1990s. He was the epitome of the continuum with socialism.

Particularly amusing anecdotes circulated in which everyone in the town told each other stories about how Sosa would sometimes take on the role of an actual entertainer. The pictures of him performing circulated on social media as well. Namely, usually at the company's celebrations or even at high school prom nights organized in the restaurant (e.g., the RTB refurbished restaurant in the vicinity), Sosa would sometimes be their VIP guest. At these celebrations, Sosa would at some point insist on taking the microphone and would sing with the band a popular folk song with the following lyrics:

> Nobody's got nothing on us,
> we're stronger than fate,
> those who don't like us,
> may only resort to hate.

> (Mirić 1989)

> *Ne može nam niko ništa,*
> *jači smo od sudbine,*
> *mogu samo da nas mrze*
> *oni što nas ne vole.*[10]

These promissory and hope-instilling lyrics were known by almost everyone in Serbia, belonging to a corpus of general knowledge. Allegedly, Sosa insisted on performing the song whenever he could grab the chance. He was surely a performer stronger than fate as he did not leave anything to fortuitousness in his political career: he managed to stay in power as a general manager of the company by constantly changing his membership of political parties according to whichever was currently in power both locally and on the state level. These conversions enabled Sosa, as he said in the media, to "always play for the best team"—an expression by which he compared himself to the renowned footballer Ronaldo, who would also do a similar thing in his job (Medija Centar Bor 2013). Since the managers of the company were appointed by the Serbian government and, therefore, by the political parties in charge, the conversions from one political party to another enabled him to stay continually in power both as the general manager and as the president of every local party branch that was in power in the municipality. On top of his other engagements, Sosa was a local councilor in the municipal assembly, and his party comrade was the town's manager, whose decisions Sosa controlled. Sosa's position represented the common situation in Serbia where the ruling local parties always overlapped with the ruling governmental parties, and the politics always trickled down from governmental to local level. For this reason, the municipality and politicians in power were often understood as not having genuine and autonomous political power. The municipal power, equated with the state power, was actually located in the management of the company, which was, through its management and power, actually running the municipality. The power was centralized in the director and his clique. Sosa was referred to as *vlast* (power, usually referring to the governance or the ruling elite in power/those who govern), and he was associated with "The State," and had the power to structurally influence and regulate everyday life. The municipal bodies and politicians were the embodiment of the state, but the corporate managers, especially the general manager, had even more authority and power.

Many of my interlocutors were telling me how Sosa could also control the business in the whole town and employment in the public enterprises as much as in the private sector. One of the workers at the union meetings told me how they had seen Sosa measuring the sizes of the bars' summer gardens so that the owners could be warned if they were taking more space than was legally allowed. The worker thought that, perhaps, this could be the way in which bribes were taken as well. This situation of power reflects findings that Serbia's economic and industrial elite (at the same time a political elite) constituted itself as a rent-seeking rather than a profit-seeking group (Lazić and Pešić 2012). This was particularly true as all the public enterprises in Bor, as in many parts of Serbia, were controlled by the political parties, as the managers and directors were elected as politicians by the party membership, and employment in these enterprises was mostly a political game and a matter of informal connections and *veze*. Many RTB workers, my neighbors, and my friends told me that Sosa had the power to "bring people to work" almost anywhere in the town but could also fire them from anywhere, too.

On one occasion, I also became a part of the performances of the promissory revival, as my own presence as a researcher became, for a brief moment, a public political issue. On June 5, 2013, some turmoil occurred in the local government as the ruling party (at that point, Sosa's party) lost its majority in the local town council. The ruling party on the state level was supposed to form a new local government in Bor. On waking up, I turned on a live online broadcast from the local council, which I followed regularly. Still in my pajamas, I stirred my coffee while listening to Sosa's usual long talk about his own great political and economic achievements. This time he was congratulating the new local government of the town. Underlining the success of his political party involved in the revival in the past couple of years, he continued:

> As well as by the citizens, this [the revival] has been confirmed by a girl named Deana Jovanović, from Belgrade, who is staying in Bor for some time, and—you won't believe it—she is going to defend her PhD at the University of Manchester on the topic of what was done so well in Bor that the town and then the company were so quickly and so nicely transformed! Anyway, we can invite her to our next meeting to introduce herself, to talk to us, to record her.

I dropped my spoon on the floor. Sosa had just publicly invited me to become a performer myself in the widely broadcasted local council meeting, to become a very witness of the revival. I had never met Sosa in my life and was surprised he knew my name and my research. Feeling shaken up, I sat down to think about this unusual event. I remembered that a couple of months earlier I had submitted a letter to RTB headquarters through the *pisarnica*, an administrative office where all requests and letters to the company and its management were officially handed in. In the letter I asked to conduct an interview with Sosa and briefly explained the aims of my research. Several months had passed since then, and no one had responded to my request. When I coincidentally met his political party comrade in the street, with whom I had collaborated earlier when I attended training sessions for the unemployed, I mentioned to her the letter I had submitted. I asked her if she could draw the attention of anyone (anyone in charge) to it, simply so I might receive a response. Usually, one had to pull strings to get anything in the town, so my nudge was appropriate.

I could only guess that she had, perhaps, told Sosa that morning about my request and maybe about my research. Even today, I am still not sure what sequence of events led him to mention my presence in Bor, but it is not important anymore.

As the local council meetings were broadcast live on the local TV, radio, and Internet and publicized on Facebook, and, to my surprise, were widely followed, this led to a number of reactions among people I knew, from serious advice and concerns to jokes, mockery, and cynicism. A young RTB worker, Jovan (see chapter 6), advised me in a serious tone to immediately make use of the opportunity if I was reconsidering living in Bor in the future, saying that it would be a perfect moment to go and ask Sosa for a job (as many people in Bor had obtained jobs in this way). He contended that I would immediately get that job, which would enable Sosa to stage his success. Petar joked that I had become "Sosa's guy" and that I should start preparing my speech soon. Some individuals from the nongovernmental sector with whom I collaborated on one project saw through this event and commented that that the "egomaniac" was only using my research for his own political campaign. One of the unemployed individuals with whom I was close asked me timidly whether I could mention their financial problems to Sosa if he ever accepted my invitation to an interview and to recommend them to Sosa for some kind of job. I must admit that it would have been an amusing ethnographic experience if I had given my own speech at the local council and then followed up the reactions and subsequent events. Not surprisingly, not only did I not receive any invitation from the local parliament, but also Sosa never responded to my interview request.

The Resource Curse Otherwise

It is necessary to mention that the revival of RTB occurred in a paradoxical moment when in other sectors, such as employment, health care, social services, and civil society sectors, the ideology of neoliberalism justified austerity-driven public-sector retrenchment in Serbia. In his study of the moral ideology that justified such neoliberal policies as redress for an immoral redistribution of societal resources, Marek Mikuš (2016) pointed to particular persistent structural conditions in Serbia, such as a scarcity of jobs, cutting public-sector employment and salaries, privatization of the remaining public enterprises, strengthening of the private sector and market competition, increasing labor market flexibility, and internationalization of the market. Thus, according to Mikuš, this popular discourse has been established about the excessive and corrupt public sector. While this discourse could have been found within many state and public institutions in Bor, such as in the municipality and within public enterprises, it did not apply to RTB. In fact, RTB was a social welfare entity but also a protected site as a strategic company, a niche where the redistributive role of the state was visible. The company pursued this role by emulating the Western style of governance by using, for example, CSR and PR discourses which resulted in their performances, which also, among many other things, promised steady job provisions with high salaries, regulation of the local market, and improvement of the environmental conditions.

I always wondered why it was that such an intimately embedded company needed this corporative PR and CSR discourse to be implemented within the local community. Why was investing in building a brand-new elderly care home or a children's playground sometimes called a CSR act by the company, since RTB, as a state-managed company, was already legally obliged to allocate a certain amount to the municipality's annual budget as a normal part of how decentralized governance worked in Serbia? In practice, it was influenced by formal and informal political and personal connections, which resulted in the prioritization, for example, of the zoo's budget in the annual municipality budget over the budget of the library and the mining museum.[11] This was one of the reasons why on many occasions it was not clear whether the investments of the company were a donation, a CSR act, or a gift to the municipality and whether the company's endeavors in the town (like renovations of the façades discussed in chapter 2) were a regular investment in the municipality or an investment by a political party that had its own interests in the company. The responsibilities were also blurred. Issues such as street lighting and new candelabras in the main street, which served as pedestrian areas on summer evenings, were also in practice the responsibility of RTB. Any works conducted on these matters were also navigated by Sosa, even though they were officially run by the public utility services.

The intimacy with the company was so ingrained that there were no clearly delineated *combatants* who needed to be turned into *collaborators*. This was usually the main motivation for the CSR and PR activities of extractive companies (cf. Rajak 2011; Appel 2012; Hönke 2014). RTB was not an external enemy due to its historical embeddedness. On the contrary, there was an ethos that everything surrounding the company was "ours": RTB, "the smoke" (which was what the air pollution was called), the smelting factory, the mine, and the urban and mining landscapes were people's allies and enemies, all embedded in a peculiar "cultural intimacy" (Herzfeld 1997). Some, like Petar, for example, would be, perhaps, frustrated, irritated, sarcastic, bitter, and angry about pollution or how the whole town worked through clientelistic relationships. However, Petar's relationship with the company was not antagonistic. This dependency on the company and collaboration between the company and its residents was already there, and therefore, it was not supposed to be created by the company. There was an almost folkloric phrase that could be heard from the residents when they tried to explain the logic of what it took for the town to have stable and long-term futures: "When RTB is doing well, the town is doing well too" (*Kad je RTBu dobro, dobro je i gradu*). People were not critical toward such dependency. They would explain the math in the following way: if RTB employs 5,000 people, one should multiply this number by three (members of the family that he or she supports), which would make 15,000 or 20,000 people that RTB supports, which was nearly half of the population of the whole municipality. It was a known fact that the functionality of the service industry and private entrepreneurship in the town depended upon the living standards of the citizens. Those who worked in the secondary industry that cooperated with RTB depended directly on RTB having good production figures.

In practice, the "money-go-round" and the increase in salaries of RTB employees (as part of the performance) did enable the hairdresser I visited to serve more customers than he had in the past. As this town experienced a significant drop in real estate during the 2000s, the prices became slightly higher but remained cheap in comparison to other towns in Serbia. The owners of private shops made slightly more sales. In practice, the improvement was only experienced to a limited degree and the official unemployment rate in the town increased slightly. For example, in 2012, it was almost 2 percent higher than in 2007. However, the statistically high average salaries masked the rising pay gap and poverty in the town. In fact, in practice, the "money-go-round" even had negative consequences. The prices in supermarkets and shops in Bor increased by 10–20 percent due to the higher RTB salaries, making groceries and other necessities more expensive than in Belgrade and other big cities like Novi Sad in the north of the country (Mitrović 2013).

This limited economic and urban reconfiguration in Bor was the reason why the revival did not make this town a "boomtown,"[12] as it was represented to be through its performances. In Bor, the labor market was only somewhat changed (and not immensely), and the flats had rarely been rented anyway since the 1990s; hence there was no shortage of housing, which is usually a characteristic of a boomtown. In addition, the living costs went up only moderately. As outmigration had been so high in the past, the population dropped by approximately 11,375 inhabitants since the census in 1991 (Statistical Office of the Republic of Serbia 2014b). Therefore, the increase in population, also one of the traits of boomtowns, could not even be felt. For this reason, there was also no pressure on services and infrastructure.[13] Some ethnic diversity and transience were ever present in this town. Hence, Bor was a boomtown that only performed as such.

Performing as a successful company through CSR and PR actions can reveal the local specificities of the resource curse or the paradox of plenty. The literature that pays attention to CSR discourses implemented by the extractive companies provides significant insights into the interplay of social relations and economic and power struggles. This literature mostly focuses on how transnational companies exploit the mineral wealth of "weak" or "fragile" states and on "the unaccountable, inequitable and at times corrupt, mismanagement of resource revenues by political elites" (Gilberthorpe and Rajak 2017, 186). In such settings, CSR programs and tales of "doing good" were usually a strategy by which mining corporations would gain control of local situations to the detriment of environmental and social conditions (Kirsch 2014). While these studies help us to understand RTB's CSR and PR strategies in terms of leading the company's (moral) campaign to move local communities toward capitalist futures (Welker 2014), the social, political, and economic dynamics make Bor a different example. In fact, Bor even provides a contrasting example to a great number of studies that focus on the private companies which disperse the power of the states, bypassing them through local enclaving (Ferguson 2005), or the ones which exploit the local workers and natural wealth in the transnational context (Solecki 1996; Halvaksz 2008; Li 2011, 2015; Gardner 2012; Cross 2014). The celebrated profit made by the company was not going elsewhere to help the extractive company justify its operations, at least not in the period of 2012 and 2013. The "profit," or surplus value, as part of the performances, was projected into the future in spite of the fact that there could be no profit as such in the near future, since there was a colossal debt that had to be repaid. Only owing to the state's protection on the market, provided by the process of post-socialist restructuration (especially since obtaining strong governmental support in 2010), was the company not legally obliged to repay any debt. The catch was that such an economic (protective) configuration made it legitimate to represent the income as profit, which could be further invested in, for example, unusually high salaries.

Many individuals thought that fiscal fabrications (and general fabrications of numbers that relate to production) made it impossible to distinguish "real" from "fake" numbers, statistics, and/or achievements and even success from failure. RTB often celebrated *poslovni dobitak* (operating profit), which was meant to be presented as a surplus value. The company performed its success by providing in the media some numbers from business operations before deduction of interest and taxes or any debt. Therefore, claiming *pozitivno poslovanje* (positive business) or *pozitivan finansijski rezultat* (positive financial results) was done only to give an impression that there was profit. The calculations never took into account the overall structure of debts and other obligations and expenses. The "positive financial result," however, was used by RTB to perform the notion of "the most profitable company," which made substantial exports.

In fact, CSR and PR activities were in place to justify the enormous loans invested in the company (guaranteed by the state) and to assure the residents that there *would be* a prosperous and stable future of the company and of industry, and that some of those promises about the future could already be felt in the present. CSR and PR activities, therefore, turned the widespread doubt into some capital that could be potentially sold in the future. Instead of the goal of achieving market domination, the performances of a successful company served to create a corporate effect for the future, something that was badly needed by the company after being previously known as a failed one. Such staging of promises had an effect of instilling hope and convincing people that a successful government and politicians existed (in order to generate electoral votes) who were capable of fulfilling the promises of the revival. Performing the successful future of the "black hole," as Bor was popularly called, and of the Serbian economy served in the present to maintain and justify the state as the main intervening body on the market. It also served to justify the domination of the clientelistic party-political relationships through which the state institutions worked. Through such performances, the revamped industrial "loss maker" enabled the state to retain a strong redistributive role (Lazić and Pešić 2012, 96).

The End of Staging: The Phoenix on the Modern Silk Road

In light of what I have described so far, how can we then understand such evidently specific economic and political configurations of capitalism that the company represented? Sociologists Mladen Lazić and Jelena Pešić (2012) characterize Serbia as a state where "state-centered capitalism" dominated. According to them, such capitalism had a long trajectory, which fed the expectations of the citizens that the state should be the main welfare agent (Ružica 2010). While this notion could resonate with the ways in which RTB functioned, I believe that there is a more suitable analytical approach that captures better the capitalist configurations that the company represented. In her study of Chinese resource-based companies in Zambia, Ching Kwan Lee (2017) used Victor Nee and Sonja Opper's (2012) notion of "politicized capitalism," which they developed in their approach to the Chinese economy to explain capitalism marked by the state's direct intervention in transactions at the company level. According to Lee, politicized capitalism is characterized by state support in external transactions or by state ownership of firms in strategic sectors, where a politicized governance structure is installed by appointing party officials as senior managers and by setting up party committees inside firms (Lee 2017, 6). This description, I believe, best describes the sociopolitical and economic context of RTB in Serbia (until the 2018 privatization of the industrial complex).

Of course, the differences between China and Serbia are vast. Serbia does not have a state-controlled market (at least not in theory) and, for instance, foreign companies operate freely on the market. Perhaps as a result of its extractive potential, which carried futural potency for the state and party-political actors, and because it was economically strategic, RTB was a suitable site for the functioning of politicized capitalism. Fabricating numbers, performing the economic and industrial success of the company, and staging the promise of its successful futures was the constitutive part of how politicized capitalism functioned and was made possible. The particular configuration was specifically enabled by a specific post-socialist economic measure—restructuring of the company, as a targeted state decision, which enabled the government to regulate and protect this particular company on the market. Hence, this industrial site, a legacy of socialism on "life support," served as a stage for performances to expand governmental and party-political projects. In addition to this, we could see how political capital in Serbia was not only the pool of party political members and party sympathizers reproduced through employment in the public sector (Rajković 2018b). Political capital was also gained through the management of this former socialist, rundown (and in-need of foreign investment) industrial giant. The site of the "failed company," the famous "loss maker," was a site for the residents to engage with the staged promises and take part in the performances. As the following chapters will show, through their everyday future-making practices in the town, where this company played a pivotal role, individuals often appealed to the state and sometimes to the company in their hope for betterment of their lives and their town.

While they were happening, the performances of the "strong company" primarily served to secure political power in the near future and to secure the power of certain individuals representing particular political parties. Such power was secured by providing reasons to hope. The electoral results eventually paved the way for only one party—the Serbian Progressive Party (*Srpska napredna stranka*), a populist party described by many as centrist, center-right, and/or right-wing—to seal the historical deal for the company's final sale. In particular, Serbian president Aleksandar Vučić, who was the leader of the Serbian Progressive Party, made a direct deal with the Chinese president. Upon his return from China in August 2018 (less than a month before it was announced that RTB had been sold), the Serbian president stated that he had "begged" president Xi Jinping to take RTB while "literally kneeling in from of him" (N1 2018b).

Coincidence or not, the sudden decision to sell the company coincided with the International Monetary Fund's (IMF's) plea to the Serbian government in 2016 to finally deal with loss-making institutions. Immediately after this plea, the performances of Bor rising from the ashes like the phoenix were suddenly gone. The media started to portray RTB as a loss-making factory again. There were no longer any statements from the politicians who were forecasting bright futures for the company.

In 2018, the company was eventually sold in what has been criticized as a "fake bid," according to economic journalist Miša Brkić. According to him, the other two companies that applied to buy the company played only "an unimportant role of a ficus tree (weeping fig)," and the sale of RTB to China was prepared in advance and put through (N1 2018a). Only one year before it bought RTB, Zijin Mining Group Co., Limited, was ranked the twenty-second mining company in the world and was the second-largest copper producer in China and one of the largest gold producers in the world (Janković 2018). Besides owning mines for other metals in Myanmar, Peru, and Russia, since 2005, the company had produced or explored gold through joint ventures or subsidiaries in five other countries: Tajikistan, Mongolia, Kyrgyzstan, Australia, and the Democratic Republic of Congo (Daly 2017). In 2018, Zijin acquired 63 percent ownership of RTB, for which it paid 350 million US dollars, and pledged to invest a further 1.26 billion US dollars in the next six years (*Serbia Energy Mining News* 2019). This company promised that it would conserve 5,000 jobs for the local workers for a limited amount of time and preserve the high salaries, which RTB had increased greatly as part of its performance. Zijin's other main goals were also to provide new jobs, increase income for the entire region of eastern Serbia, and repay all of RTB Bor's debts (*Serbia Energy Mining News* 2019).

In contrast to what had been promised by the government during the period of the revival, especially when I was living in Bor for a continuous period (in 2012 and 2013), it was Serbia that eventually became Zijin's strategic partner and not the other way around. Such development, contrary to what was promised, brings to mind Ching Kwan Lee's (2017) question of whether and how Chinese state capital is a different kind of capital, which she posed in her analysis of the presence of Chinese state capital in Zambia. In contrast to the perception of global private capital, which is focused on the pursuit of profit maximization, Lee argues that Chinese state capital in Zambia embodied "both the logic of capital and the logic of the state" (Lee 2017, 28) and that it was "driven by an encompassing set of imperatives, which include profit making, extending China's political and diplomatic influence, and gaining source access to strategic minerals" (Lee 2017, 28). This characteristic of Chinese expansion in that period was exactly what brought China to Bor as well. Through the sale of RTB, a formerly post-socialist, down-at-heel company, Bor found its place in the landscape of the global crisis of copper overaccumulation that was expedited by increased extractive endeavors by China. Further research will illuminate whether, and if so, how, Chinese state capital would contend (or not) with Serbian political, economic, and social pressures.

What we can learn from Bor is how the prospects of this company were conditioned and made a reality not *only* by the global configurations of extraction-based capitalism in a world dominated by finance capitalism. Rather, its futural prospects were also secured by the local post-socialist economic and political configurations and performances of the company's successful futures. The global economic condition was an *occasion* to make the frameworks of the state increasingly even more relevant (which was also desired by the people themselves) for the economic and social transformations of this town. The Schröding-er's cat that was present among the Borani, at least when I was in the town, where copper was at the same time an abundant and a deficient matter, one which existed and was subject to doubt, was constitutive to multiple temporal layers of the performance of the potential of what copper *could make possible* in this town. In fact, staging the promises of the revival of the company (re)made the possibility of *having* resource-based futures. In other words, performing as though the rundown company was successful and projecting the promises of reindustrialization of this former Yugoslav giant made it possible to arrange the particular party-political configurations, which then gave power to enable the company to reconfigure its position on the geostrategic map. The performances of the industrial successful futures, hence, paved the way for the Chinese capital to enter the European market for raw metal. It is through such historical, economic, and political entanglements that Borani's relationship with the state and the company was remade in this town. By buying RTB, the Chinese company was drawn into the circle of the performances, but only to secure its power and pave the modern-day Silk Road with gold (Daly 2017). With this move, China positioned its political and economic influence at the very borders of the European Union, not only making use of resources and the workforce in Bor but also bringing workers from China, of whom some worked in precarious conditions and some with limited freedom of movement and without a possibility to unionize (Dragojlo 2021). Such new social, political, and economic configurations slowly caused RTB and the state to lose their sovereignty over the protective welfare mechanisms, especially over matters of the environment and workers' rights. The Chinese company often undercut the Serbian rule of law. Yet the novel capitalist and geopolitical configurations made through the performances allowed the town and the company to "stay alive" in the present until the arrival of some new, yet still not predicable, crisis.

Forward: For Whom Was Staging Done?

While there was a lot of "going along with" the fabrication of the company's success among the citizens, I cannot say the same about the newly arrived Chinese company. The Chinese company made its decision to buy RTB on the basis of geopolitical and economic interests based on estimates of precious metal resources, especially gold (and copper). This move was in line with the Chinese national strategy of the Belt and Road Initiative, a global infrastructure development strategy implemented by the Chinese government in 2013, which served to make China's reserves of copper sources more secure. In 2019, China became the world's largest consumer of refined copper, taking a 51 percent share of global copper consumption (Statista 2019). In addition, China has become a major investor in Serbia, with Chinese companies constructing infrastructure across the country. In Serbia's struggles to geopolitically position itself between the power of the European Union, China, Saudi Arabia, and Russia (and make economic and political deals with all of them), China started to figure as a friend of Serbia.

The performances carried out by the RTB management, various politicians, foreign delegations, and other protagonists in 2012 and 2013 never emphasized the major potential of copper or gold deposits. In fact, speculation on these deposits came into the spotlight after I left the town in late 2013, when it was confirmed that the amounts of precious metals in the surrounding areas were significant. Before Zijin, the US copper exploration company Freeport-McMoRan, together with the Canadian company Nevsun Resources (through a company called Rakita Exploration), held exploration, concession, and mining rights. They had been present in this area since 2010. Only in 2012 was an important extraction site named Čukaru Peki found. The first preliminary report in 2014 provided some indications that this site could be an extraordinary one. In 2016, the company Reservoir Minerals finally published a study according to which this location, located within the central zone of the Timok Magmatic Complex, was officially pronounced to be a potentially extremely abundant deposit of copper and gold. This was the same year in which IMF requested the Serbian government to sell the company and when the performance of the revival started to disappear from the horizon.

The mining complex in this area was split into two parts, the Upper and Lower Zones. It was estimated in 2021 that the Upper Zone amounted to 1.28 million tons of copper metal, with an average grade of 3 percent, and 81 tons of gold metal, with an average grade of 1.91 grams per ton. In the Lower Zone, there were reserves of 14.30 million tons of copper metal, averaging 0.86 percent, and 299 tons of gold metal, averaging 0.18 gram per ton (*Zijin Mining* 2021).

The reserves of copper and gold that the company claimed to have were extraordinary.[14] Immediately after making a deal with the Serbian government in 2018, Zijin acquired exploration rights over the copper and gold deposits in the area by buying these two companies. With this move, Zijin became the only owner of both companies that had exploration and mining rights in both zones for a significant amount of money (Reuters 2019). What kinds of contracts the two companies had previously had with the Serbian government was never made public. Zijin has already invested 474 million US dollars in the new underground mine (*Mining Technology* 2021). The opening of the mine of Čukaru Peki in October 2021 was followed by calculated estimates that this site would become the second-largest copper producer in Europe after Poland (*Mining Technology* 2021). However, the profit made by Zijin most likely will not go to the Serbian state at all, since the company might be using ways to avoid allocation of profit to Serbia.

In the public discourse, it was not clear why and how Serbia lost its foothold over such incredible copper and gold reservoirs. Soon after the Chinese acquisition of golden and copper assets, RTB started to look like it was only a side target that *had* to go together with what the Chinese company turned out to be mainly interested in—the main target—gold and copper deposits that were more economically profitable than the current infrastructure of RTB. I believe that the Chinese company did not opt for the fabrication of the company's success and its promises but for the potential that existed in the vicinity of Bor, a site which was never used in RTB's performances of the revival. Six years before this immense and sudden economic transformation, such performances only targeted the residents' hopes (while leaving out the Chinese prospects), which perhaps managed to induce the feeling that there *was* some prospect for RTB after all and that the new potential buyer would be a suitable and deserving one.

A great number of people whom I met back in 2012 and 2013 contended that they would not like to live in the town if RTB was owned by a global industrial company. Petar, Milica, Milorad, and many others hoped that the company would remain the state's responsibility in the indefinite future. In fact, there had previously been several big uprisings of the whole town of Bor, especially in 2004, when the workers blocked the highway, asking for the state to provide more support and subventions. The same thing happened in 2007, when the company was supposed to be sold to a Romanian company, which was never accomplished. Thus, it was rather surprising to me to find out that there was no major public articulation of any opposition to the announced sale of the company among its residents. We can only guess that the performances may have managed to convince the residents that the privatization of the company might not be a bad choice, since no globally weak company would buy a "corpse."

Perhaps around six years of continual performances, and people's engagements with them, made the very surprising transformation more acceptable.
Owing to the immense emotional connection with RTB, which was historically made, staging the promises of the industrial success might have enabled
the transition to the new social, economic, and (geo)political order to be more
easily accepted by the residents. Staging the promises, which instilled hope,
in that sense might have not only made the transformations less painful, but
welcomed the unexpected arrival of the new futures, which brought onto the
horizon new expectations in Bor.

2

MIMICKING

Inadequate Refurbishments as
"at Least Something"

I woke up on the morning of August 18, 2012, to hear the local TV station reporting that the most important information, promotional content, and pictures from the copper-producing town could be seen on the LCD screen (figure 1) at the renovated Plateau close to the old town center. The report added that the new screen was attached to the front wall of Dom kulture. The screen, it was said on the news, had been secured by the management of Mining and Smelting Combine Bor (RTB) with the help of its business partners and provided to the Regional Television of Bor to fit the image of a new, modern Bor, which was, according to the TV station, gradually becoming a synonym for progress, development, and urban life. That evening, I decided to walk down to the town. It was 8:30 p.m. and very warm, and the screen was active from 7 p.m. to 10:30 p.m., as had been announced on the news. It was crowded in the nearby park, where the company had recently placed new exercise equipment and a playground for children. A couple of older people, parents with their children, and several couples were sitting on the benches around the Plateau. A group of younger men (in their twenties) were taking pictures and seemed to be friends with the security staff of the building. The screen was on, but with no sound, and people were only sporadically looking at it.

The screen showed the town's landscapes in the form of a promotional video. My impression was that one had to know the town pretty well in order to know which locations it represented, as there was no information about them. On the video was a logo, "For a prettier Bor," which I had heard before. It was the name of a joint campaign between RTB Bor and the municipality to enhance

"Bor's potential." On the screen, one could see the landscapes of the lake near Bor. Then, the process of renovating the old hotel, owned by the company and located by Bor Lake, was followed by scenes from the ceremony of the hotel's reopening and how the hotel looked today. A close-up of the general manager of RTB patting a lion cub in the zoo came next, along with scenes showing the zoo's opening ceremony and how it had been built from scratch. Then scenes of the construction of a new roundabout were shown, together with close-ups of the politicians attending its opening and the audience standing around the roundabout applauding. Sights of a pond-like geyser could be seen too, again showing the process of its construction. One could also see renovated fountains and a couple of frames of refurbished parks and children playing there. Then came the scene that struck me the most: the scenery from the Plateau in front of Dom kulture, where I was standing at that point. The screen was showing what I could actually see around me: the fountain in front of me, the building of Dom kulture, and some people sitting around the square. A lady in her forties, smoking and walking her dog, probably noticed that I was amused by these scenes as they reminded me of a form of Baudrillard's simulacrum, a "picture in a picture," which I felt was there to convince us all of something. Smiling, the woman commented, "It's all Potemkin villages," and left.

The representations of the revived town that I encountered that summer evening, which were supposed to denote the revival of the company as well, were an attempt to make the renovations seem even more "real." This was exactly because of frequent assessments that the renovations were fakes or imitations. Yet, at the same time, besides often being labeled as fake, after I had been there for a couple of months, I found out that frequently the Potemkin villages succeeded in providing a feeling of being "good enough" for many. Let me illustrate this briefly by going back to Milorad from the book's introduction.

Milorad, the activist from the workers' union, who worked at RTB and with whom I followed the events organized by the union, always liked to draw my attention to the recent transformation of the town in our conversations. Milorad tended to pinpoint the things that were happening in the town, so I could understand them properly. He mentioned one "achievement" that particularly annoyed him: an "aqua park" behind the sports center (figure 7). The aqua park in Bor was a "sort of" aqua park. Built to enhance the space behind the center, a wide and empty field before the intervention, the aqua park resembled a small, shallow, artificial pond with a thin geyser in the middle. For Milorad, the aqua park was "fake," a proper fraud: "You cannot swim in it, but that is what an aqua park should serve for. What kind of aqua park is it? Aqua park? It is more of a swamp [baruština]."

The name "aqua park" was given by the local media. I also heard from one of my older interlocutors, who worked at RTB, that he and his colleagues called it "Sosa's puddle" (Sosina bara), referring to the way in which all the endeavors

FIGURE 7. The aqua park. Photo credit: Taken by the author in June 2013.

done in the town were ascribed to him. Despite such criticisms, Milorad agreed that this investment enhanced the space. According to him, it had been an ugly wasteland and did not work properly but "at least" it "looked like something" (*barem sad liči na nešto*) (Jovanović 2018a, 28). Milorad's opinion was shared by many. The aqua park belonged to the list of "things done in the town" that were criticized but also praised for being a "sort of something." How can we understand such simultaneous embracement and criticism of seemingly "out-of-order" reparations when "good enough" becomes "at least something"? In this chapter, I explore this question in order to understand such ambivalence facilitated by engagements with the wider project that materialized the promises of the revived urban futures.

Laying the Urban Coulisses

The vast renovations of the town were conducted by the officials of the company and town to make Bor look like a livable and enjoyable town again.[1] They were carried out especially through refurbishing the material sites from socialism. For example, the monuments of heroes from the socialist (and also pre-socialist) past were displayed more visibly now. A bronze sculpture of a miner which had been made during socialism to celebrate heroes of work and which used to be situated in front of the headquarters of the company was now placed at the very entrance of the town in the middle of the roundabout. The bronze miner had a rock-drilling machine on his right shoulder and a mining lantern in his left hand. It was illuminated and rotated on a pedestal on the roundabout twenty-four seven.

In addition to moving the monuments, some tarnished gray façades of the buildings built during the socialist Golden Age were refurbished. The industrial soundscape was enhanced, too: after eleven years of silence, the mining siren could also be heard again. In the past (until 2018), it could have been heard three times a day—at 7 a.m., 3 p.m., and 11 p.m.—to announce three work shifts (as the complex worked nonstop). The siren used to be turned off during the NATO bombing in 1999 to allow citizens to hear the air-raid siren properly. My neighbor, who was in his late fifties and worked in the municipal administration, told me that every time he heard the siren, he would instantly feel emotional. It reminded him of the good, secure, and abundant life during the 1970s and 1980s. However, unlike him, my friends were rather more sarcastic and turned my attention to a comical situation that this revival of the siren had provoked. They asked me to open my window at the time the mining siren started and to listen carefully. When I did this in my flat in Peta Mesna (see map 2), to my surprise, I could also hear wolves howling. The wolves were new residents of the revived Bor, placed in the newly built zoo. During the night, their howling triggered by the siren could be heard for the next ten minutes. This was something which was definitely new in Bor.

In spite of the different ways in which the residents understood these performative changes, the attempt of the town and the company to create a continuum with the socialist and even pre-socialist past was an attempt to shift the reputation of the company and town away from the derelict one. The renovations had a theatrical character: besides always being conducted in visible and representative places, their representation and opening were often ceremonially organized. For example, in the past, some of the newly built roundabouts had been ceremonially opened and visited by the media and sometimes even by the residents. The very acts of renovating and their constant representations in the media and on the TV screen in front of Dom kulture had the goal of performing an image of a strong and capable company and of a revived town that was *already happening*, promising the town's revived urban futures. Many people with whom I spent time, regardless of their age, occupation, or gender or whether they worked for the company, claimed that the town's appearance could not be compared with what it had looked like only two or three years earlier. Some renovations were necessary, as many façades were tremendously dirty from pollution, buildings had started to fall apart, and sidewalks were cracked due to decades of neglect, lack of state and municipal funding, and increased unemployment. The criticisms of the repairs usually targeted the legal, administrative, institutional, material, or even esthetic domain. Criticisms of how RTB avoided legal procedures or how all renovations and construction works were done without public procurements were extremely common. Many complaints emerged: inappropriate locations were selected for new leisure sites without respecting the town's urban spatial plan, as in the case of the newly built zoo, which did not even have a construction permit and was built in the middle of the residential area. The new "things" were sometimes regarded as not only amusing, inappropriate, or kitsch but also superfluous. The sturdy traffic light made of iron in the Second Kilometer was sometimes represented among the residents as a symbol of money laundering by the local officials (RTB and municipality). The fact that the company avoided the laws and state institutions and that its representatives could do whatever they wanted with the renovations always sparked heated discussions.

During my first months in Bor, I spent time with Lidija, a woman in her mid-thirties, who had just had a baby and ran one of the very few active civil society organizations in the town (cf. Jovanović 2018a, 32–33). Lidija was very much engaged in projects that offered incentives for young people and ensured better futures were secured for them. I was interested in getting an insight into several educational courses for young entrepreneurs and was considering attending one. These courses, unfortunately, never happened due to a lack of the external funding on which Lidija's projects relied. While smoking and sipping Turkish coffee in her office, Lidija told me how the town had changed. She saw only positive sides to Bor's refurbishment and said that Bor had changed and "turned out so much for the better." This was because, according to her, a very capable man (the company's general manager) had become the head of the company—a man who actually knew what needed to be done. She explained that Sosa had been politically "taken off and put back" (by the government and political parties) many times and also used to be one of the directors during Milošević's time. She talked about him in terms of him "coming to power" (došao na vlast). According to her, Bor had started to look much prettier thanks to him: "they put a bit of make-up on the town" (malo su našminkali grad). Then she explained, "When you saw Bor from the distance, only various shades from gray to black could be seen. Today, those are multicolored buildings" (figure 8). I smiled a bit and she reacted: "Perhaps it might look funny to you, but the town is now much prettier . . . it is much more pleasant now when you pass through the town. And the objects from the Mining Museum have been scattered throughout the boulevard (figure 9). Now when one walks down the street, one can see the whole history of Bor."

FIGURE 8. Multicolored buildings, called the Comb (*česalj*) in the old center. Photo credit: Taken by the author in 2013.

FIGURE 9. The mining dumper relocated on the Boulevard. Photo credit: Taken by the author in 2013.

Lidija continued to speak in one breath, as she usually did: "The town used to be all dilapidated and decayed, but it is not like that anymore. And the people who work for RTB are much more content: they have monthly salaries of 700 euros, and it wasn't like that before. And you can feel the liveliness again, lots of people in the streets . . . the smiles are back on people's faces."

She explained that the mine had started to work again, that the price of copper was very high and "favorable," and that the state had invested in the development of industry in Bor. "New workplaces are being opened. The zoo is hiring. The hotel [on the nearby lake] has not been working for ten years and now it is working again." After a while, she showed me an email she had received that morning from the local tourist office, which offered a two-day tour of Bor. She commented that such an offer was great because it showed that the town was "becoming a new tourist attraction" that would include the development of mining tourism in the future.

The newly underground mining café that was included in Lidija's email was represented as the only café in Europe embedded in a still active pit. This tourist offer at the time of our conversation gave Lidija hope for betterment of the town and emulated the trends employed in many other sites of extractive mining ventures on a global scale. Such endeavors are usually known as a quick solution to diversify the economic offer. These offers are normally seen as an opportunity for developing win-win solutions, especially in places that struggle to make alternative futures (other than industrial ones) a reality and places that struggle to stay in (or get back to) the flow of global capital.[2] However, the mining café turned out to be a short-term project. This café was opened sensationally in 2012, and the ceremony was attended by one of the most popular singers in the Balkans, Zdravko Čolić. Six years after my conversation with Lidija, the newly opened café was closed when the Chinese company took over the business. Before that, the café worked with only a limited scope, as a lot of administration and upfront preparations were necessary to organize the tours. During its short-term span of operation, this tourist performance served a purpose other than what it initially seemed to be: for performing successful (party-political) management.

Even though the *šminka* (make-up) that Lidija mentioned might have denoted cosmetic and hence only superficial or temporary changes (of which the underground café would be an example today), Lidija still used the idea of "make-up" while at the same time underlining its potential temporary effect and using it to denote a positive and optimistic evaluation of Bor's recent material transformation. In addition to Lidija there were people like Milorad, who was more critical and who emphasized that even though the awfully dirty buildings had been repainted at last, they revealed the extremely substandard work carried out during the renovations. Other residents were also more skeptical about the renovations than Lidija, pointing out the illegitimately implemented (irregular) improvements by the corrupt RTB (political) leadership and arguing that material renovations were not "authentically" (or "genuinely") for the common good (Jovanović 2018a, 33).

Katarina, a law student in her thirties with whom I worked in the local community office, and her boyfriend Kosta, a software engineering student who lived in Bor at that time but studied in Belgrade, were both affectively involved in criticizing the things done in the town (cf. Jovanović 2018a, 33–34). One day I met them in a café. I was holding the new February edition of RTB's newspaper *Kolektiv*, which I had just bought at the kiosk (where it was usually sold for a symbolic price of less than half a euro). I placed it on the table while taking off my coat. Kosta took the newspaper in his hands. He seemed very amused by the new issue as it was full of news about the renovated Bor and the cultural life that had started to develop due to RTB's investments. He said in a cynical tone: "I wish I could live in that Bor. . . . I need to go there, at least once, just to experience in one day all that freshness, cleanliness, positive vibrations, to see painted buildings, refurbished streets, the zoo, hippodrome, fountains, roundabouts, and, most of all, smiling people full of hope, faith, and optimism, full of life. . . . Yeah, right."

Kosta did not think that the material refurbishments contributed to an enhancement of the social life in Bor. According to him, the refurbishments were false as they did not resonate with reality and they had a different purpose. Katarina, nervously lighting her cigarette, agreed with him, claiming that nothing was actually new in Bor in the way that RTB presented it. Such representation annoyed her. She explained that what "they" were doing were things that were supposed to be "normal": "Do you paint your walls in your home, Deana, when they get dirty?" she asked me. Painting buildings was supposed to be seen as "normal," and Katarina was upset because the politicians were capitalizing on such a "normal" thing that had to be done while making theatrical representations of it, trying to make it look sensational only for the sake of winning electoral votes and acquiring power in the town. Even though Kosta said that it was "about time" the awfully dirty buildings were painted, both of them indicated the substandard work carried out during the renovation and construction.

Things That Were Not Quite What They Were

For most people (perhaps except Lidija), the cosmetic, temporary, partial, fake, or superficial aspect of the repairs in the town revealed a mismatch between the "proper" ways in which people thought "things" should have been done, or what they thought they should have looked like, and the actual material outcomes, which failed to meet certain standards (cf. Jovanović 2018a, 35–36). Such discrepancies and normative ideas intrigued me, as they induced a feeling that things were "not quite what they were." Sometimes, such apprehension not only called into question the authenticity of the intentions behind the promissory material interventions but also, for some people, indicated particular desires of obtaining "at least something," no matter how partial, substandard, or superficial the transformations were considered to be.

Not Quite Refurbished

The façades were refurbished, but not fully. The painted façades of the buildings built during the Golden Age in the old town center were located close to the smelting plant chimney. The problem with them was not so much the choice of colors (turquoise, light green, orange, yellow) but rather how the façades were refurbished in a superficial manner. I heard from Kosta that "they" had done it very quickly, in a rush, and that they had had to do it in such a manner because some politicians from the government had been coming to Bor, two years previously, on Miner's Day (August 6). I was sitting with Kosta and his parents in their nicely decorated apartment in the *Sedmospratnica* (Seven-story building), whose façade had been repainted in yellow and green tones (figure 10). Kosta's

FIGURE 10. *Sedmospratnica* (Seven-story building). Photo credit: Taken by Kosta and Katarina in September 2013.

parents were quite talkative, and I spent a lot of time at their flat. His mother, a blonde women in her sixties who was a clerk in a state institution, would occasionally invite Katarina, Kosta, and me for coffee or a snack at their flat. During one of my visits, Kosta spoke about the refurbishment: "It was all tarnished and the façades were black from the smoke. But when you paint, you first need to put on a base for painting, right? First the undercoat, then the color." He claimed that only one layer of color had been put on, which clearly revealed that things had been done hastily to satisfy only short-term esthetic and ostensible renovation. "And since the undercoat paint was not put on, the paint has already started to crumble," Kosta added.

The refurbishments were not comprehensive. One problem, for example, was that the rain gutters on the *Sedmospratnica* were old and ruined and had not been changed since the building was built. "How can you renovate the building and leave those things out?" Kosta's father, an engineer who had worked for RTB for over twenty-five years, joined our conversation. Kosta and his father both started telling me that there were parts where the rainwater was not diverted from the wall and was destroying the new paint. Kosta and his parents were dissatisfied that only the façades had been refurbished while the shabby interior of their building had been ignored. They told me that everything around them was done in a similar manner. Then they asked me to look through their kitchen window, which looked onto the square, where a big modernist building, the old Belgrade Shopping Mall (*robna kuća Beograd*) was situated (figure 11). They asked me if I could see how the new red color (it used to be only gray) from the upper part of the newly repainted façade of the shopping mall was cracked and falling off, only a couple of years after it had been refurbished. We all laughed. It seemed as though they were amused by the situation and were trying to entertain me with what seemed to be a ridiculous situation.

The refurbishments were selective. Some residents of Bor also reacted to the other parts of the town that had not received the same attention as the buildings that lay along the main route through the town. The secretary of the local community office where I volunteered told me that he was writing many letters to the municipal headquarters to start renovations off the main route as well. In fact, many buildings along the main street, where I also lived for the first months of my stay, were painted in a pale rose color. I was asked by my landlord, a retired engineer who had worked in the Enamel wire factory, which was formerly owned by RTB before it was privatized, whether I had noticed that only the visible parts of my building had been painted and that the back part of the building had not even been "touched." When I asked him to explain the possible reasons for such partial interventions, he explained that most of the

FIGURE 11. The view onto the old shopping mall "Belgrade" and the peeling red façade. Photo credit: Taken by the author in 2013.

renovations had probably been done for the benefit of visitors, mainly for the general manager's partners, who came to Bor occasionally. My landlord used to go to middle school with the general manager and, although he also saw the renovations as self-serving, he praised the transformations made by someone who he described as a very cunning man.

The Theater Which Was Not One

Bor had a theater, but not quite a real one. As Anica was preparing for a rehearsal of her children's theater group, led by her at the Cultural Centre, where I spent one day a week, she told me in a cynical tone that Sosa had placed a huge sign with metal letters spelling out "The Theater of Bor" above the entrance to the Music School (figure 12). Anica, a forty-year-old who lived with her mother and devoted her whole life to the theater group, contended that Sosa had put up the big Cyrillic sign "overnight" a year before. She did not refer to this particular institution as a theater but explained in detail that the institution was actually "a music school": "It's not a theater. I mean, we have a music hall, a very good music hall with almost 350 seats, and it belongs to the Music School. The Center for Culture (a municipal institution funded by the municipality) sometimes brings theater companies from Serbia. But a local theater does not

FIGURE 12. Bor Theater (The Music School). Photo credit: Taken by Kosta and Katarina in November 2013.

exist," she said. While standing in front of the very sign, she added that this "move" to camouflage the music school as a theater was the general manager's idea to outcompete the neighboring, rival, and bigger city of Zaječar, which had a "real theater." By "real theater," she meant that it had its own acting company and its own repertoire. However, even though the theater did not seem to be very genuine, Anica, like many others, appreciated the fact that she did not have to wait for a new theater institution or a building to be founded and built from scratch. This did not spoil her joy in catching the performances of some well-known theater companies from Belgrade that had recently started to perform again in Bor under the sponsorship of RTB (as a part of the revival).

On occasions, the famous Belgradian theater group Atelje 212 performed some of their acts from their current repertoire. Their plays sold out quickly, as they performed well-known, good-quality plays that usually only Belgradians had the privilege of seeing and the theater had a limited capacity. Anica told me with amusement the story of how Sosa even appeared once during the applause after the play to take a bow with the actors, taking credit for the play too. After this amusing detail, she immediately referred back to the well-repeated narrative of RTB's involvement through contributing with cash to the construction of myriad things, reminding me that the Belgradian theater in the very city center was built from exactly the profit that had been redistributed during socialism (the narrative about the central place of RTB in modernity that

I explained in chapter 1). She also recalled that during the 1970s and 1980s, Bor used to be the first town to receive copies of internationally acclaimed films only one day after they premiered at the renowned international film festival (FEST) in Belgrade. The story of Bor's past futures and the centrality of this place within the discourse of modernity were often repeated and not just by Anica. The theater, in fact, approximated such memories of the past futures in late socialism. Even though she thought that the experience of this period might never return to such an extent, the theater still represented something important for her.

"At Least Something"

The criticisms which targeted things "done in the town" implied that they were not done appropriately according to a particular order, that they did not look as they should, and that the intentions of the renovations were not quite genuine. The interventions were seen as superficial and the transformation as selective, instrumental, and having been achieved in a shady and disordered way. The existence of the new things was not denied, but rather their (material) qualities were questioned. The questioning of the "genuineness" of the progress embedded in material performances served as a way for these individuals to express and criticize the existing social relationships as "out of order."

Even though the examples of "things that were not quite what they were" implied that the change was not a "proper" one but rather a calculated strategy to provide only the appearance of transformation and potential progress, they included some positive evaluations. Except for the comments made by Lidija from the civil society organization, all the examples of the things that were "not quite what they were" (the aqua park, the seven-floor building, and the theater) referred to the refurbishing as *šminka* (make-up) in the negative sense: insufficient and shallow, explicitly staged for a quick, short-term effect. While showing limited signs as potential steps in a larger, truer process of revival, the renovations were not criticized through a straightforward rejection but as *insufficient*— many Borani wanted more, more genuine, and more extensive renovations. They were seen more as a short-term scenography which still managed to produce some tangible effects. The criticisms indicated that the material transformations were marked by their temporary effects, not being what they were supposed to be.

Although the "things" were not achieved in the "right order," Kosta and my other interlocutors demanded more paint and more thorough interventions, asked for more investments, and wanted things to be even more visible. Even Katarina, who was very critical, thought that the zoo was not visible enough if its purpose was to show the "new face" of Bor. The questioning of the "genuineness" of the renovations constituted a simultaneous disbelief that more comprehensive transformations could be achieved in the distant future. Even when they doubted the genuineness of the intentions behind the performances, the renovations were still acknowledged as a (poor) substitute, an *ersatz* for the "real," like the theater that was not one (cf. Jovanović 2018a, 37). The theater was an indicator of modernity (of the past) and, as such, it was more "real" for Anica. For her, it was still better to have a theater that was not an actual theater (as a substitute, an *ersatz*) than to have none. For all of my interlocutors, the present was judged for its ability to produce a future. In other words, as the improvements in the present were not perceived as having a productive force necessary for making the long-term proclaimed better future, they seemed fake. At the same time, a clear sense of the future (and also a feeling that one was "going forward") was necessary for them and for their practices in the present. As short-term solutions, the material performances, with their pro tempore, immediate effects, managed to offer a sense of an immediate fulfillment for some, a satisfactory compromise to be felt in the present. For the audience who embraced and criticized them at the same time, the fake performances entailed hope for approximation of the past futures embedded in what seemed to be more a "real" thing. Because of this, the "fakes" sometimes became "at least something" or "good enough," "similar enough," a sort of something "as opposed to being 'absolutely something,'" "the objectification of the ideal" (Crăciun 2012, 860, cf. 2013). Those who embraced "at least something" extended the past's futures,[3] the kinds of future imagined and promised during Bor's Golden Age in socialism.

The simultaneous disbelief that the transformations would be more permanent and that they would last and have effects in the distant futures, together with hope that attached to the past's futures, constituted the ambivalence of "at least something." Those future outcomes were surely better than having nothing in the future. Such an embracement points to what Ståle Knudsen (2018) argued in his critique of corporate social responsibility (CSR) studies, which usually tend, he argued, to consider the agency of CSR activities as being merely "top-down" processes. Bor precisely shows how CSR activities of painting and renovating, even when they were not represented as CSR but looked like it, were ambivalently claimed "from below."

In order to better understand the role of the past experiences in formulating the ambivalence, one also needs to understand the role of half-dilapidated buildings, which stood together with the half-refurbished buildings in the urban landscape. Knowing more about them will help to fully grasp the practices of mimicking the revival that pervaded the everyday life in Bor.

What Else Was "Real"?

After the end of Milošević's regime in 2000, there were rumors that the whole company might close down along with all its subsidiaries. It was hard for Borani to imagine what would happen if the company were privatized. One of the possible scenarios could be that the privatization of this rundown, state-managed company would ultimately lead to the bankruptcy and downfall of the whole town. This was because there were many other factories across Serbia being sold, usually as property. At that moment, there was no money in the town's budget, RTB was less privileged by the state than during Milošević's time, and the town was decaying. The various palettes of gray mentioned by Lidija ruled the town's landscape. The period after the rupture in 2000 was an almost unspeakable experience. My interlocutors could not easily translate this experience into words. They only used expressions and words such as "you cannot imagine," "grayness," "darkness," "depression," "people walking like zombies," and "deserted streets." The real-estate prices dropped dramatically, so one could buy a flat for "ridiculous money." The devastation of the company realized its material form in the urban landscape as well. The description of the town in decay was a material reflection of hopelessness.

In the context of post-socialist transformations of Bor and socialist modernist industrial projects, which once brought the promise of prosperity to the community (and some experience of prosperity), the notion of "abjection" was back then relevant in understanding everyday life. The economic stagnation and sudden destabilization of the modernization narrative implied not merely an economic crisis but also a crisis of meaning (Ferguson 1999, 14). The promise that prosperity of the community was accessible to all was lost. Moreover, the unpredictability and the prediction of a possible collapse of economic and social life that might happen "tomorrow" not only to the individuals but also to the collective mattered as well. The life of the town and of the people was brought into question—it was a matter of not only individual continuity but also a collective future. A social death was lingering in the air.

During one of the walking tours I made with Petar, I asked him to show me certain places of significance in the town. He decided to take me to the half-dilapidated building called *Nova Tržnica* (New Marketplace; see map 2) in the area known as Četvrta mesna, located next to the old post office. It was a long, oblong, modernist concrete building block built from white bricks during the period of socialism.[4] It used to have an elegantly designed interior. Petar and I walked around the building and then stopped. He explained that it used to be a place where a fine pastry shop, a high-class restaurant, and a huge modern supermarket were located during late socialism. He used to go bowling there when he was young. This center was owned by Centroistok, a chain of supermarkets that had gone bankrupt due to, as the locals interpreted it, an "unsuccessful" privatization and suspicious circumstances related to the privatization scam, in which the state bodies were also allegedly involved. Due to dubious responsibilities and unresolved ownership, the building stood half-dilapidated, broken, and abandoned for a couple of years, which prevented the renovation of the building. At the time of our visit in October 2012, the first floor of this building, where the restaurant had been, was decayed and decrepit, with broken windows and a ruined interior. I looked through a broken and dirty window and saw parts of broken furniture, upturned and broken chairs, tables, and half-wrecked white modernist chandeliers. Lost and fractured sociality and the promise of a good life in the past were framed within Petar's story about this building that had been functional only a few years ago, before it had gone bankrupt. Petar was not the only one to bring my attention to this building—Katarina as well as Lidija also did. The stories about pleasant celebrations of weddings, New Year's eves, and army send-offs that had taken place in this modern building, as well as buying supplies in the supermarket, were central in his narrative as we were observing the "horror." At the time of our visit, this half-dilapidated place, with a polluted entrance on the first floor that stank of urine, was not a "fake" thing or a thing that was "not quite what it was." Rather, for Petar it was very real and genuine. What was "real" were the very memories of *having* the futures in the past and a sense of abandonment.

The ground floor of the building was still functional—it provided a space for the local community office, a grocery shop, and a fast food stand, all operating in poor and unhygienic infrastructural conditions. At the time of our visit, the youth went to *bleji* (waste time) during the night next to the entrance of the restaurant on the first floor, where they sat in the dark on concrete blocks marked with the graffiti *Deca Dima* (Children of Smoke) by the supporters of the sports club Red Star. As a result of takeovers, bankruptcies, and unsolved issues over ownership, there were many half-dilapidated or abandoned buildings in Bor that were very relevant for everyday experiences of the promise of revival. Nova Tržnica was just one example of a place which became dilapidated as a consequence of such privatization. Barely working factories in the Seventh Kilometer (separated from RTB and privatized), workers' canteens that were not operating anymore, and the Stara Tržnica (Old Marketplace) green market located in the town's city center were just a few examples. All of them were in either a semifunctional or nonfunctional state. The example of Nova Tržnica tells us about the experiences of continuity, futurity, and (potential) social order and how individuals, like Petar, cognized their social relations and relationship with the town through encounters with these half-dilapidated socialist material remnants through which they imagined potential futures and alternative possible future relations. This decay represents a material prop against which the ambivalence facilitated by the Potemkin villages should be interpreted as well.

Victor Buchli argues that "the actual death of buildings, their physical collapse, and destruction are vitally important occasions for collective thought and action" (Buchli 2013, 167). Hence, collapses, according to him, then become "opportunities for a postmortem, as death refigures social relations, creating new ones and new temporalities" (Buchli 2013, 167). Nova Tržnica had not collapsed, but it did represent a material place that was a painful reminder of the promise of a good life and modernity in the past. *"Ko je dopustio da ovo propadne?"* (Who let this go down the drain?) was a question about this building that I very frequently heard from people, including Katarina. The half-dilapidated space of Nova Tržnica was a materialization of suspicious privatization processes on whose outcomes many lives depended and of ambiguous ownerships and responsibilities.

Being ambiguous and liminal, still awaiting its destiny at that time, this site recalled and warned that the choices could still be made for the Centroistok, since the privatization had not yet taken place (fully). It materialized corrupt relationships within the state (and the corrupted state) and enabled people to express their desire to continue to be cared for by the company ("Sosa should fix this," a common reasoning heard by my interlocutors) or the municipality and by avoiding privatizations that would lead to massive layoffs and retraction of state responsibility. Following Caroline Humphrey's (2007) insightful analysis of the privatization of public city space in Ulan-Ude, the capital city of the Republic of Buryatia, Russia, after the 1990s, "whereby the values and meanings of objects embedded in earlier relations are externalized and suddenly made visible in a new light" (Humphrey 2007, 177), what Nova Tržnica pointed to was the possible social relations that *could* occur. The horror was materialized in the destiny of this building. Nova Tržnica stood for and spoke about "abjection" (Ferguson 1999) and about the future that was once promised. This sturdy building, left to exist in a half-dilapidated state, offered a "sneak peek" into some potential future and alternative possible future relations. The way it appeared at the time of my visit in 2012 and 2013, it told a story about how life in Bor *could* potentially turn out. It signified two kinds of futures. One was the future that *could have been* for all. It embodied not only the negative and horrific potential of a social death but also the traces of a future that one could once aspire to in the past: the ordinary things of modern life (restaurants, bowling, supermarkets, etc.) experienced during socialism.

It was precisely because of the latter appealing dimension that its horrifying ruination was so powerfully affective.

We should think about the affective narratives around this building in terms of "yearning for change for a way out of present circumstances" (Pelkmans 2013, 21). The building remained an ultimate and genuine example of how economic, social, and political relations might go wrong in the potential future or how Bor's futures could be jeopardized. It was a material reminder that haunted Bor's townscape and people's cognition. Moreover, its fate reminded many individuals of their own destinies and those of their parents who had lost their jobs as a consequence of privatization, just as in Katarina's case. Nova Tržnica was a threatening promise of a haunting social order that could potentially arrive if the company did not do well. It was an alternative future that could have been—all too near, too possible, just around the corner.

For some, this sentiment contributed strongly to a yearning for state support, which was often seen as corrupted and contributed to praising the state's protection that RTB Bor enjoyed as a company. The management of RTB and the politicians used these sentiments for the electoral campaigns and imaginations of the horrifying potential futures that people vividly remembered. However, what we can clearly see here is that there were two different kinds of temporalities at play. On the one hand, there were expectations of the "good life" like the one experienced during socialism, where the promised future played an important role in orienting the present. The socialist "golden" period and the past's future were remembered as a period that enabled material prosperity, social security, chances for employment, and equal access to the company's benefits. On the other hand, there were the horrifying *potential* futures that people vividly recalled from the 2000s, which included the possibility of closure of the whole industrial complex. When evaluating these two material potentialities, "at least something" in Bor became fairly appealing.

Perhaps now we can better understand Lidija, at least, from the local civil society organization, who was, like other residents of Bor, faced with a decayed town of "different shades from gray to black" and how the "new things" (which were not that new at all), even when they were "things that were not what they were," still managed to represent a minimal degree of satisfaction. "Grayness," as an emic metaphor for the early 2000s,[5] can then be contrasted with the images that Lidija presented to me, which she considered to be representative of the revived Bor: smiling people in the streets and liveliness that could now be felt again. That was why it was so significant for the people to obtain at least the *ersatz* objects that would allow them to obtain the objects of their hope (a prettier town) more quickly and that could maintain hope for life in a town that was not dilapidated. The feeling of abjection and grayness recalls the sense of post-socialist emptiness, which Dace Dzenovska documented in places that were also shattered by deindustrialization (Dzenovska 2018, 2020). Dzenovska's (2018) insights into (im)mobility in an emptying village in Latvia bring to the fore how orientations to futures have a particular political dimension. In particular, she shows how those who decided not to leave the emptying village and who were working to maintain life in it drew "on futures past to resist the new futures inherent in contemporary forms of neoliberal capitalism" (Dzenovska 2018, 26). When faced with the present promise of the revival, after the experience of emptiness during the 1900s and 2000s, my interlocutors did not resist such new futures. As a consequence of the experiences of the past futures (from late socialism) as abundant, the material renovations of the town made it possible to more easily reimagine what had been promised to them: better lives, a good living standard, stability, and a modern town. With their experience of the near past when people were "walking like zombies" and of abundancy during late socialism (different past futures), the performances of the revived urban futures made a difference in the case of Bor. They managed to spark hope.

Producing the State at the Earliest Possible Time

So far I have shown how Petar, Katarina, Kosta, and Anica uttered a "shared concern" (Jansen 2015) that the material renovations revealed the gap between appearances (surface) and reality (depth). These individuals were constantly "ordering" things around them and "saw through" the intentions that lay behind the renovations of their town. By valorizing them and by talking about the "order" of things, they employed normative ideals concerning how the things should have been done or what they should have looked like (Jovanović 2018a, 39–40). The embedding of normative ideas in the material "order" is not something new, of course. A great number of ethnographies have shown how citizens in post-Soviet cities, for instance, including officials, bureaucrats, and urban planners, often raised normative ideas (imbued with moral values) concerning urban material appearances that pertained to Western and/or European ideals (Fehérváry 2002, 2013; Alexander 2007a, 2007b; Buchli 2007; Collier 2011; Laszczkowski 2011). Interestingly, the frequent insistence on ordering was measured by several assessments through different space-time ordering. First, it was ordered in relation to people's aspirations to an idea of a European/Western state (Greenberg 2011, 2014). Second, it was also measured in relation to the normative standards stemming from the socialist past, which entailed memories of a much more ordered state. And finally, the renovations were also evaluated in relation to past modernist aspirations, expectations that Bor had never fully lived up to.

Katarina, Petar, Kosta, Milorad, and Anica insisted that "those in power" should respect what they considered to be the basic rules, whether in the domain of the general rules of masonry and esthetics or in the domain of urban plans and other state and local laws and legislation. In other words, they insisted that they were supposed to be respected by those who were actually the regulators themselves: sometimes the municipality, sometimes various politicians; Sosa and his clique also appeared as the desired regulatory powers. The legitimate actors in the renovation—the company and the politicians—were usually regarded as promoting impaired, immoral political and social relationships and infringement of the laws, which contributed to "the decline of standards," as Anica would say. For Kosta and Milorad, the encounter with the repaired objects labeled as fake, irregular, inauthentic, and substandard almost awakened anxiety over how they perceived their own (and social) integrity, credibility, competence, and moral judgment. Through their encounters with the material reparations, they all constituted themselves as moral and competent citizens, sometimes perceiving themselves as even more competent than the people in charge of the town. By ascribing a "fake" status to the repaired objects, they positioned themselves as being on higher moral ground than the "system" in charge—the company and "the state"—which they held responsible and accused of never sanctioning but instead tolerating, and even enabling, RTB's infringements of myriad laws and rules. By emphasizing such (dis)orderliness, they constituted themselves as moral and state subjects who desired a regulatory and regulated state (Jansen 2015) and company.

In order to unpack further the implications of ambivalence that the renovations facilitated, it will be useful here to introduce Janko, a man who worked at RTB headquarters, and how he saw the temporality of the promissory performances. Janko was experienced in advertising on social media. We met in 2012 through a mutual friend with whom Janko was also active on the online platforms (mostly blog forums, which were important for generating political and social critique at that time) that he used for criticizing the government. It was a surprise for me to find out that Janko had accepted an offer from RTB to work for the public relations office, as this meant that he could no longer be critical about the government. Janko and I had spent time together discussing the politics in the town and of the company. As we established close relations, Janko invited me to visit him at his office at RTB. This was an unusual experience for me, as access to the company premises was very limited. As I entered the building headquarters, a receptionist asked me in a formal tone if I had an appointment. She politely requested my name and identification. After I had waited in the lobby for a while, she approved my visit and told me to walk to Janko's office, where he was waiting and smoking. As soon as I entered the room, he offered me an espresso. A polite waiter in a catering uniform brought it to us quickly, almost immediately after Janko had ordered it by phone. As usual, we started talking about RTB and politics. Janko said that his political views had changed since he started to work for the company. He saw a lot of good things happening. We started talking about a public affair that was happening at that point which involved the reconstruction of the old smelter. The process of the reconstruction was paused at that moment due to the lack of some official state documents. Janko commented on the accusations by the local media that RTB had not followed many regulations in terms of how the smelting plant should have been built. Many legal approvals from the state offices were missing, including the allegedly missing construction permit. "While you wait for the system and everything else to change, your life goes by."

"That is interesting," I said, and I asked him if that temporal "logic" could also apply to the recent renovations in the town.

"Yes, definitely," Janko said, "Today the 'business' in any sector is in a very gray area. . . . Everything always involves nepotism, money laundering, and party-politicking." He added that "such a 'system' needed to change and get ordered." By the "system," Janko meant those in power, by which he meant the state administration, politicians, and the management of the company, which all contributed to its "out-of-orderness." Even if it was possible for this (political) system to become "ordered," Janko told me that it would take a long time. According to him, "real" progress would have the chance to happen in Bor only if there were an orderly state and an orderly company that could (and should) enable it.

In fact, those in power, which included "the company," were commonly regarded as incapable of managing the social relations, the town, and society. This notion resembles widely documented dispositions in ethnographies of post-socialism in Serbia and Bosnia and Herzegovina (Greenberg 2011; Spasić and Birešev 2012; Jansen 2015; Rajković 2017; Simić 2017). For instance, Marina Simić (2014, 2017) found that her interlocutors from the city of Novi Sad in Serbia saw that there was an expectation that the state was supposed to manage society as a structural form of social interactions that had certain values, rules, and regulations. The notion they shared was that without the state's control, society would fall apart. While understanding that the state was incapable of managing society, similar to what has also been found in post-socialist Russia (Ssorin-Chaikov 2003), Simić found an apprehension among the urbanites of Novi Sad that in order to *have* a society, there had to be "a state" that would, with procedures and rules, produce the citizens (Simić 2017). My interlocutors shared a similar disposition that the society, usually referred to as "the town," would become an orderly one *only* with the help of the functional "state" and an orderly "company." In other words, the state's institutions were seen as necessary frameworks to create conditions for the existence of the "orderly" company and as something that would (sometimes in tandem and sometimes not) produce frameworks for the existence of the "orderly" town. However, when the rules of the state were not respected by the company (when, for instance, the phoenix was placed on the top of Dom kulture prior to getting institutional approval), it was seen as an infringement of the legal frameworks of the state. Hence, the individuals were left to their own devices to produce some effects of their actions that could bring about the desired outcomes more quickly. Having "at least something" produced more immediate, albeit partial, fulfillment for some.

The ways in which the state and the company appeared through people's encounters with the Potemkin villages can be understood better through the great body of literature that pays attention to the shifting relationship between corporations and states. The literature that theorizes neoliberal corporations in places of extractive industries especially shows how disparate and conflicting agents, parties, and events contribute to the ways in which corporations appear as unified and powerful entities. For instance, Elana Shever (2012) and Marina Welker (2014) argue that corporations appear as singular powerful entities despite their inconsistencies, just like the "state-as-idea" (Abrams 1988) or the elusive "state effect" (Mitchell 1999) do (cf. Golub 2014; Rogers 2015). By focusing on the ways in which corporate personhood and the disarticulated "bodies" of corporate organization appear with their shifting boundaries and responsibilities, this body of literature mostly looks at what kinds of effectiveness and impacts the "corporate effect" may have on the society, on its political implications, or on how people negotiate it. In the example of the inadequate, insufficient, and partial reparations in Bor, we can see something peculiar. RTB as an entity did not appear as separate from the society or from the state. Rather, the frameworks of the company and of the state were seen as the structural conditions for the existence of the orderly town (as the society and a set of relations). In other words, "the town" did not appear as a coherent entity that was structurally separated from the company and the state. Rather, both the company and the state were seen as necessary manifestations of power that were needed to enable social relationships and to create "the town" and the society. Such inseparability, of course, should be seen as a product of a particular historical development of this company in relation to the state during socialism, which I explained in chapter 1. This finding also reflects the current broader landscape of political power in which Bor was located and shows the ways in which the authorities in power were maintained and produced through staging the promises.

The individuals I introduced in this chapter were not eager to delay what they saw as short-term, quicker solutions, even when they mocked them. The Potemkin villages as fakes had their immediate effects, and this was the reason why "at least something" seemed appealing. They allowed the individuals to experience something "during their lifetime," to paraphrase Janko, as his explanation speaks for many. The pro tempore renovations, which were embraced and served to perform the promise of the revived urban futures, produced a feeling of the existence of certain manifestations of power that had the potential to, at least partially, produce (alas, disorderly) society. For Janko, the "disorderliness" appeared inevitable, since achieving a "normal" social order and society, that would be produced though the frameworks of the state, would take a lot of time. It also seemed impossible that the orderly company would emerge any time soon either. The logic of "at least something," an ambivalence which consisted of conflicting orientations to futures, managed to produce the frameworks of the company and the state at the earliest possible time. With such temporality, at least some "state effects" and some corporate effects were produced as well.

Embracing the blurred lines between the real and the fake calls for attention, as pointed out by Alexei Yurchak (2018) in relation to new interest in the fake today. Yurchak depicted this by using the example of the contestation of representations of facts that has come to dominate much of the political and media discourse in the contemporary politics of the United States and Russia. He argued that the main effect of blurring the boundaries between real and fake effects is not necessarily that the audiences are fooled into believing every imaginary story and fact. Rather, they learn that "facts" may be read not for how true or false they are but for how effective or ineffective, "patriotic or unpatriotic," or "pro-Russian or pro-Western" they are (in his example) (Yurchak 2018, 96). Erasing the boundaries between "facts" and fakes, he argued, had an effect of redirecting "different representations of the world from how true and untrue they are to how effective they are and what interests they allegedly serve" (Yurchak 2018, 98). Borani's practices of embracing "at least something" reflects this global performative shift that Yurchak (2018) identified. The material reparations as "at least something" were evaluated exactly on the level of their performative dimension of how successfully or effectively they represented and extended the past's futures. The performative shift to the *effectiveness* of the representations of the past's futures was assessed not only in terms of what interests the renovations allegedly served (in this case corrupted stated power, personal gains, and acquiring party political power). The material renovations were also assessed in terms of the ways in which the present's futures were made possible through them. In other words, embracing the partial material renovations is a story about the assessments of how effectively and how *quickly* the fake reparations, as material performances, could produce some partial approximations of the past's futures.

The Promise of Urban Revival: Ambivalence

In this chapter and in the previous chapter, ambivalence was facilitated by performances of the promise of revived industrial and urban futures that allowed us to better understand the temporal scales to which hope attached. When we think about ambivalence, we might, perhaps, think of it as something which may constrict the capacity to engage with the future. The notion of such constriction by ambivalence could be noticed in how Zygmunt Bauman (1991) in his classic book *Modernity and Ambivalence* analyzed the transition from the modern to the postmodern condition. Bauman argued that the counterpart of the global modern project is not its disorder but ambivalence. In his view, ambivalence is seen more as the possibility of assigning an object or an event to more than one category, which produces a feeling of acute discomfort when we are unable to read a situation properly in order to choose between alternative actions. Bauman contended that modernity is tremendously marked by such a specific struggle *against* ambivalence. This struggle produced attempts to undo it, to categorize everything neatly, and to tame ambivalence, which are doomed to fail: "We experience ambivalence as discomfort and a threat. Ambivalence confounds calculation of events and confuses the relevance of memorized action patterns . . .[;] the outcome is the feeling of indecision, undecidability, and hence loss of control. The consequences of action become unpredictable, while randomness, allegedly done away with by the structuring effort, seems to make an unsolicited come-back" (Bauman 1991, 2).

Of course, we can debate whether ambivalence from such a macro-sociological view is a trait of the world (Bauman 1991). However, I found that ambivalence was experienced differently. Faced with the experiences of a "fall from grace" (Jansen 2009a, 826) as consequences of deindustrialization (associated with mass layoffs and economic decline), which are also constitutive of the global modern project Bauman indicated, citizens often embraced ambivalence rather than attempting to tame it. As I have shown so far and also in the next chapter, instead of experiencing conflicting orientations to futures as a danger that needed to be struggled against, ambivalence was a way through which individuals assessed different temporal aspects of the futures, to which conflicting dispositions attached. By embracing the navigation of different scales of futures, they obtained the capacity to engage in future-making practices. In spite of the fact that they felt a reduced ability to negotiate their own agency and to understand themselves as social actors participating in the public sphere, as could be found across a range of towns in Serbia (cf. Petrović 2016), "at least something" enabled some of these individuals to exercise some agency, as the objects of their hope (e.g., insufficiently renovated objects) could have been obtained in a nearer future. Lidija from the civil society organization, for instance, believed that the performative revival contributed to the development of her projects and gave her a feeling that something could be going forward, although it was far from perfect.

The material repairs that were "almost the same but not quite" had an effect of mimicking the revival of the town. The quality of being "fake" ascribed to the material repairs, which carried moral, social, emotional, and affective attachments, was a quality ascribed to the final outcomes produced by those in power. Many hoped that the make-believe would eventually (and partially) succeed as they had felt abjected and excluded in the previous two decades from the economic and social conditions that they themselves regarded as "modern." This was especially a feeling induced in relation to Belgrade, the capital of Serbia, where most of the "opportunities" were located. Hence, the mimicking, which relied on partial resemblances that were "not quite the same" and "not quite different," was an attempt at social and economic (collective) membership that would enable access to modernity and progress (past promises). They simultaneously learned from the "difference" in relation to being classified as the Other when they were regarded by many as "outsiders" or peripheral, abandoned, and hopeless. However, unlike mimicking in the post-colonial context (Bhabba 1994; Ferguson 2002), which has a power to subvert the hegemonic discourse, mimicking of the revival of the town did not represent a threat to hegemonic power. There was no subversive "slippage" (Bhabha 1994), as the performances did not challenge the norms or any disciplined powers. When the audience encountered these performances, they appealed to the company and the state as being *insufficiently* involved in regulating the everyday life. Hence, their encounters and ambivalence facilitated by such encounters did not subvert the hegemonic regimes, even though some of them may have acted "as if" they respected the disciplinary aspects (Wedeen 1999). In fact, mimicking animated the involvement of the company, the politicians, and the state, making them all hegemonic administrative, financial, and political authorities which became necessary frameworks for the regulation of everyday life. A desire to request and to continue to receive care from the company and from those in power also reveals the hope that make-believe acts would succeed.

The focus on ambivalence here also enables an escape from the model of "domination versus resistance." The studies of hegemony and domination under colonial rule showed that this was based, inter alia, on ambivalence (Taussig 1993; Bhabba 1994; Ortner 1997; Wedeen 1999). The examples from this chapter indicate how ambivalence, as a conflicting orientation to futures, was not just an outcome of "top-down" styles of statecraft which (re)produced power and inequalities. Rather, it was *also* part of the "noninvasion" of the "state" (desire for the state to regulate) (Jansen 2015). In its presence and its fractional and random absence and presence, "the state" and the company became the regulative frameworks that (ought to) generate social order and even moral selves. It is in this context of the material "fakes" being "dispersed material traces of the state" (Laszczkowski and Reeves 2015, 3) that extended the past's future were "not quite" but "similar enough" and in the context of settling for less ("at least something") that the company's appearance in this town should be understood. Through such dynamics, the material spaces for hopes of progress and of prosperity and modernity were framed by the dialogue with the past's futures, precisely as performed on the screen that summer evening in front of Dom kulture.

The embracement of "at least something" which maintained hope is not only bounded to the examples that I provide in this book. In fact, ambivalence in which people orient themselves to futures in a conflicting way is a widely relevant experience in the contemporary contestations and navigations of capitalist futures. We can think of numerous practices driven by the logic of orienting oneself to futures in a conflicting manner via settling for less as a minimum requirement due to a lack of options and less likely or less viable ones. This could be, for example, when people invest themselves in appreciating the "bullshit jobs" (Graeber 2013b), which often promise coveted futures. The ethnographic inspections of different scales of futures to which hope and its conflicting orientation to futures attach open up a space to better understand the temporal, material, and political contingencies of future-making practices within the "contradictions of contemporary global capitalism" (Eriksen 2018, xxii).

The crucial role of staging the promises through the semirevived ruins, as in the case of freshly painted but still crumbling façade, allow us to think about the revivals that never get their objects completely revived and which, perhaps, are never intended to be fully revitalized. While the promises of better futures and welfare may look like simulations, play-acting, and illusions, the unfinished surfaces become the field that demands further interventions. While the play-acting still leaves doubt and room for both contingency and possibilities, such sites remain actionable for various performances of their future revival. The encounters with the half-revived ruins, which are "at least something" but still not good enough, help us to think about their central role in reframing the temporal frameworks in which we embed our everyday life and act accordingly. For the residents of Bor, the performativity was part of their cultural repertoire, as the performance as a form of social action was known also during socialism. The staged promises were then realized many times and their material outcomes lasted for some time, until today. The blurred lines between falsity and reality were, however, in Bor necessary to maintain hope for frail improvements of their derelict town, which was less possible to gain in the present. The partial signs of such improvements as "at least something" provided a long-desired feeling that hoping itself was finally possible in this town.

HOPE OF SUSTAINING EVERYDAY LIFE

BARGAINING

All I Need Is the Air That I Breathe

"The sky will be clean just as it was in 1903 when the smelting of copper started!," the general manager of the company promised in 2012 at one of the press conferences held at Mining and Smelting Combine Bor (RTB). Bor, the most polluted town in Serbia, was about to experience clean air, promised by "the biggest ecological project in the Balkans" (RTS 2013). This project promised the reconstruction of the old smelting factory and the construction of a new sulfuric acid factory, since the old ones polluted the town significantly. The reconstruction of the old smelting factory was followed by a media frenzy on a local and national scale. It was promised that clean flash smelting technologies would be implemented in the old smelter. They were supposed to eliminate nearly 98 percent of all the harmful particles, primarily sulfur dioxide, produced by copper smelting. After three and a half years of its reconstruction, the smelter, often misrepresented as "the new smelter," was finally ceremonially opened. Aleksandar Vučić, who at the time held the position of prime minister, theatrically opened the smelter at the end of December 2014. In his speech broadcast on the local and all national news, in front of the smelter, he called the project "our little wonder" and "the pride of Serbia" (*Telegraf* 2014). He stated that "by building the smelting factory, Serbia has demonstrated that it can industrialize the country" (*Telegraf* 2014). The notion of "the future" appeared in his speech many times, followed by myriad promises: the promise of securing the future of the citizens of Bor, of becoming wealthier in the coming years due to the smelter, of better lives, and that the whole of Serbia would benefit from the reconstructed smelter. He emphasized that people could always criticize and never be satisfied with anything, so he ensured that those who took part in the reconstruction would be remembered as the people who enabled the future of the town, the region, and the whole country (*Telegraf* 2014). The prime minister ended his dramatic speech with the mining greeting "*Srećno*" (Good luck!) and "*Živela Srbija*" (Long live Serbia!).

Following the smelter's opening, the next two years were remembered as unusually unpolluting. The news reported that the amount of toxins in the air was within the normal limits. Alas, the relief was only temporary. As soon as the new Chinese management took over the company in 2018, the reconstructed smelter turned out to have less capacity than would suit the new owners. The company assessed that the sulfuric acid that RTB also produced (which turned sulfur dioxide into sulfuric acid) was not as profitable as copper. Therefore, only the production of copper was prioritized. The sulfuric acid factory, which was supposed to collect sulfur dioxide from the smelter, could not even process the newly increased amount of it. As a result, at some point a vast amount of pollution was again simply expelled through the smelter's chimney onto the town (Vlaović 2019). It also turned out that the reconstructed smelter may even have been built improperly and hastily. There were rumors that its opening might have been rushed before it had been completely checked by experts and made ready to work. The new Chinese management blamed the previous management for equipping the old smelting factory with "an obsolete technology," designed to smelt 80,000 tons of copper cathodes, which was too limited for its desired goal of 180,000 tons (Stevanović 2021).

In spite of some limited local protests back then, the state mechanisms to limit the increased pollution turned out to be powerless. Even though the sales contract was not available to the public (at least until some years after the sale), it was made public in the media that the ecological clause had been omitted from it. There were no mechanisms for the state to react appropriately to pollution. Only in 2021 did the local court in the neighboring town of Zaječar order the company to pay the state one million Serbian dinars (Đorđević 2021) (approximately 9,577 US dollars/8,484 euros) for the damage, but such one-off penalties could not stop the polluter from continuing to contaminate the town. In the meantime, in 2021, the Chinese headquarters announced that the company planned to build another smelter (Stevanović 2021), this time a brand new one, next to the reconstructed one. The "little wonder" that had promised to deliver ecological "bright futures" was assessed to cost, according to some unofficial estimates, around 350 million euros (Brkić 2019). The media that had freedom to criticize the government announced that "the state in Bor deceived both the citizens and the Chinese" (Stevanović 2020). Long after I left the town, it was still rumored that the smelter was allegedly badly made (just as was feared by many when I was there). The very fact that the smelter did not serve its initial ecological future-oriented goal but made the town even more polluted than before, by reducing significant amounts of sulfur dioxide but increasing levels of lead, arsenic, cadmium and other heavy metal particles brought by significantly increased copper production that came with the new owner, brings into stark focus the staged ecological promises made when I was in the town.

This chapter takes us back to that period of waiting for the realization of the promise of living in "an air spa" (*vazdušnja banja*), which was how many of the performers liked to envision such a life in the future. The ethnographic illustrations of the social fabric knitted around the smoke in this chapter are necessary to fully understand involvements in staging the promise of nonpolluted futures. A great number of studies that have brought insights from communities which contested the toxic conditions in places of mining extraction (Gardner 2012; Li 2015) are undoubtedly useful to understand the political implications of such endeavors. However, the vast focus on social change and social movements has left unexplored what political subjectivities and agency empirically look like in the conditions where such mobilization does not occur (cf. Knudsen 2018), which was the case in Bor. Before illustrating the peculiar conundrums with which I address this gap in the literature, I will first illustrate what kind of political power the (in)famous smoke had and how the smoke became a particular affective force.

Rewind: The Promise of Nonpolluted Futures

In October 2012, the Canadian Ambassador to Serbia visited the reconstruction site of the smelter, where he met with RTB's management. His visit was not surprising, as several Canadian companies actively took part in the reconstruction of the smelter. Export Development Canada (EDC) provided significant loans, and the Canadian company SNC Lavalin was subcontracted by RTB for the reconstruction of the smelter. During the visit, the general manager met with the ambassador and gave assurances that the construction work would finish on time, which was frequently contested in public, and that RTB was sticking to the deadlines:

> I have to emphasize that a complete project (technology, equipment, and knowledge) is provided by SNC Lavalin, the most powerful—and, I would say, one of the world's most powerful—engineering corporations. On the question of whether people from Bor already believe in a cleaner sky, I would answer that the "real" people of this town believed in it from the first day, and the others do not have to believe. Seeing this image [the building site] and such rapid progress of the construction, people believe and live in such confidence (Mitrović 2012).

This and similar performances of promises of clean air left the present pollution to be experienced as something temporary. In the past, there was no such promise of clean air and pollution was rather ordinary. The experience of a "normal life" without the smoke never existed in the past. The general manager's performances usually co-opted people's hope for clean air in his rhetoric and pointed to, but also produced, social division in the public discourse. Through his speeches, such as through his statements given that day with the Canadian ambassador, a division was created among those who "supported" the company project and those who did not. According to such logic, there were two categories of people in the town: on the one hand, those who would refrain from any criticism of the project, and even praise the RTB management and the local politicians, and those who criticized it, on the other.

It is interesting that mobilizing the community occurred through shifting the focus from pollution to the morally and ecologically acceptable technological advancements, rather than from shifting it to, for example, the morality and character of the company (Solecki 1996). It was not that the environmental concerns per se were marked as the enemies of the company (Solecki 1996). Rather, the environmental concerns were very much praised by the company but were acceptable only if they were aligned with RTB's endeavors to tackle the ecological question though the implementation of particular technologies and praising party-political decisions. In spite of the rumors about immense corruption and irregularities that related to this project, for the industrial managers, supporting the new smelter uncritically was the only proper way to speak about ecological futures. By shifting the matter of ecology toward the larger community, the company tried to mobilize a public discourse that implied a distinction between those who were "the real people of this town" (*pravi ljudi ovog grada*), according to the general manager's words, and those who were not. In such discourse, "the outsiders" of the community were mainly those who privately and publicly criticized (pollution, corruption, delays), while the "real" members were those who spoke positively and uncritically about the company and the project. The citizens who would uncritically support the environmental aspects of the promised factory could be the "real" members. Such a distinction was also aligned with the general manager's statement at the local council meeting that people from Bor were divided into "those who criticize" (*oni koji kritikuju*) and "those who build" (*oni koji grade*). Hence, complaints about issues such as corruption, failures to meet deadlines, deferring the building process, or increased pollution were often scrutinized by the company's management and the local politicians, making the citizens who criticized the project enemies of their own communities and even the enemies of their own betterment.

In her account of gold-mining conflicts in Peru, where aggressive expansion and modernization of mining have occurred since the 1990s, Fabiana Li (2015) indicates a similar rhetoric employed in the public discourse. She particularly points to the narrative in which the hegemonic economic model assumed that resource extraction was a necessary path toward "progress" and "development." Such discourse implied that those who "protested against mining development were condemning the country to continued poverty in spite of the wealth of mineral resources beneath the ground" (Li 2015, 13). Although at that moment protests did not exist as such in Bor, the general manager's speech resonated with such rhetoric of the global extractive companies which created mechanisms for those who criticized the activities of the company to be publicly condemned and ostracized from the community. Such individuals were usually portrayed as members who dragged the progress of their community backward. Interestingly, the fault lines were not created with regard to the promise of the potential amount of copper the company had (or could have), as occurred in Peru (Li 2015). Rather, the fault line was created with respect to the promise of modern smelting technologies, which became almost a metonymy for ecologically clean futures. The modern smelting technologies were a suitable material stage for the performances of the promise of ecologically clean futures exactly because technological specifications and their performances sounded very promissory (as an expert investment for the future). They also demanded expertise and knowledge that sometimes created a certain kind of awe. The fact that their specifications could be easily manipulated made the exact possibilities of the realization of the promise less possible to verify, just like the facts of RTB copper production, which I illustrated in chapter 1. Through the creation of this division along such an ecological and technological fault line, the mechanisms of local corruption, nepotism, gray zones, and personal gains were protected from any criticism too. By emulating the rhetoric of the global companies, the responsibility for the potential failure of the promise was deflected away from those who were in charge and responsible for its realization. Since the technological advancements could not be disputed that easily, and due to the creation of political divisions made in relation to them, active opposition to any kind of ecological concern was efficiently silenced. The promises themselves also made the pollution a temporary thing, which made everyone simply . . . wait.

The general manager was not alone in his performances that pertained to assuring citizens that there would be clean air. The Canadian ambassador to Serbia, a frequent protagonist in the company's performances, took the role of a witness to Bor's revival that day at the press conference. While praising the tempo of the construction, he stated: "This project and, I would say, the new birth of 'Bor'[1] set in motion mining in Serbia. Canada is a country of mining in which Serbia has a long history. But we have not only RTB but also other mining companies that are exploring [mining resources] in Serbia, and it is now a trend to renew here local mining" (Mitrović 2012).

While claiming that the revival of Bor and Serbia was approaching, he noted that he had even lost his way when he was coming to Bor because of its astounding revival, which brought the alleged transformation of the town configuration: "When we came to Bor, we got lost because our driver had not been in the town for ten years and later said that he did not even recognize the roads because they are too beautiful and without holes like then" (Mitrović 2012).

Although the holes in the roads had perhaps existed more in the past and there were some investments in the road reparations, the town was never transformed to the point of spatial unrecognizability. In fact, Bor was very difficult to miss when coming by car from Belgrade. There was only one road leading to the town, which was simultaneously its entrance. The exaggerations and dramatizations of the results of the revival were intentional and necessary elements of the performances of the town's revival.

In the general manager's speech, however, there was something very peculiar. Similar to many of his speeches, this speech presented the hope for clean air as a matter of *belief*. It was a belief in the success of the smelting factory's reconstruction, a belief that the project would be completed on time, a belief that the management would have the capacity to deliver it, and a belief in a better future. It was utterly necessary to keep and rejuvenate the need for such a belief, as this very project was, to use Alice Street's (2012) words, "caught up" in the dialectic of hope and potential failure. At that time, the reconstruction site, as a stage onto which the performances of the promises of "ecologically bright" futures were enacted, almost took on the shape of a (quasi-religious) sacral object (Beyer 2015) of nonpolluted futures, where believing in the project was essential to its success. Such a belief in "not yet" (possibly near) futures was supposed to offer a reason for hope and to leave no room for doubt. Having and showing *faith* and believing were important as one was supposed to be uncritical while supporting the company, its management, and the promise of modern technologies. Such conduct was a condition necessary to become a legitimate member of the community, or at least as it was seen by the industrial management. By shaping people's belief, the company, the political parties, and the general manager acquired recognition and legibility. Since there was widespread doubt that such a project would ever be finished (properly), along with rumors of large-scale corruption, lack of respect for legal procedures, and delays, the creation of a "positive orientation towards the future" (Street 2012, 50) was necessary for the company to maintain the residents' hope.

The silences around the potential failures of the reconstruction of the smelter were not only generated by the division in the public discourse. The RTB workers, for instance, also lived in fear because of the consequences they could face if they spoke out. In accordance with a collective agreement, they were not allowed to provide any information that could be considered an insult, a lie, or unreliable or incorrect data. They could be fired if they did not comply with this rule. Sometimes, personal interests might have been at stake, as the general manager had the power to dismiss anybody from any position, as I already mentioned in chapter 1. In addition, the locally sponsored TV station was led by a director who was a distinguished member of the same political party as the general manager and whose TV station received a budget directly from the municipality. Such an arrangement closed down the space for public criticisms, just as much as the particular intimate relationship with the smoke did.

What Are Borani Made of?

There was something peculiar about pollution in Bor. The smoke (*dim*), or "our smoke" (*naš dim*) or Bor's smoke (*Borski dim*), was a local idiom for the polluting smog which frequently "fell" on the town as a by-product of the smelter. As the town developed "under the chimney," the amount of pollution that descended usually depended on the wind and other meteorological conditions as much as on the amount, as I mentioned in chapter 2, and quality of smelted ore. Trails of black, gray, or white smoke could be seen every day and night coming out from the smokestacks. "Our smoke" was also a "microcosm of the periodic table" (*periodni sistem elemenata u malom*), as it contained a great amount of sulfur dioxide but also arsenic, lead, zinc, cadmium, soot, and other particulate matter.[2] The smoke conveyed, awakened, and shaped various kinds of affects—from proud endurance to fear of potential risks. People also projected their affects onto it. They symbolized it, politicized it, projected their own fears, hopes, and anticipations onto it, ignored it, measured it, did not measure it, observed it, remembered it, tasted it, diminished it, described it, neglected it, celebrated it, embraced it, poeticized it, breathed it, got headaches from it, got nauseous from it, bargained with it, got ill from it, despised it, were in awe of it, and even ran away from it. The smoke had its own rhythm, woven into the fabric of everyday life, urban spaces, and bodies. It was an intimate and familiar, yet unpleasant and potentially harmful matter.

The smoke gave me strong nausea and a cough. When I was exposed to it for longer periods, I could sense a shadowy, squeaking feeling in my lungs and felt short of breath for the next half an hour. A couple of months into my stay, my nausea and headaches passed, just as many had predicted, since "one gets used to the smoke," as they explained. I was surprised to learn that many residents found a positive side to that horrendous and nauseating smoke. Svetlana once said to me, when I pointed to the plumes of gray smoke coming out of the chimney, "Shush—while there is smoke, it's good." Svetlana, who was at that time twenty-eight, unemployed, and pregnant, and whose husband was working in the smelter, explained to me that people in Bor lived thanks to that smoke. I met Svetlana long before I came to Bor, when I was sixteen, at a research camp that gathered high school students from all around Serbia interested in science and research. Svetlana and I had maintained occasional contact since we graduated but reestablished it again when I moved to Bor and we spent time together. During our stroll toward the town center, Svetlana pointed to the smoke. She introduced the smoke to me as a sign that the company was working well and that the whole town and its citizens, whether they worked for the company or not, depended on its production. "As long as our smoke remains, it's going to be fine," she finished, summarizing a notion which was folkloric in Bor (Jovanović 2018b, 490). In this often rhetorical articulation, the smoke represented a sign of hope for a stable personal and communal future, which reminded people more of the past futures than of the futures promised by the smelter's reconstruction. For many, there was less hope for the ecological "bright future" offered by the company. The smoke represented hope of not being entirely expelled from the promises of the past futures, hence from the frames of modernity from late socialism that promised industrial, albeit polluted, futures.[3]

The smoke had its own character and evoked a particular sentiment. As we looked at the smoke coming out of the nearby smokestacks, a friend of mine commented, "It's somehow *šmekerski*."[4]

"What do you mean?" I asked him.

"It's like when you smoke a cigarette"—he imitated smoking with enjoyment—"and you look into the smoke and you say '*To!*' ['Yeah!']."

The people of Bor usually represented themselves to me as people who adapted to and endured the smoke while handling well the risks that the pollution carried. Very often, one could hear semi-ironic celebrations of the smoke. Svetlana shared a meme from the website Vukajlija.com, a popular user-generated Serbian urban dictionary and humorous encyclopedia, on her Facebook wall. The meme represented Bor's landscape of buildings, the industrial area behind, and the smoke descending on the town from the smelting factory chimney. Under the image there was a caption: "BOR. Because Fukushima is for sissies" (figure 13).

In this comparison with poisoning from the nuclear accident at the Fukushima Daiichi Nuclear Power Plant in 2011, endurance under pollution in Bor

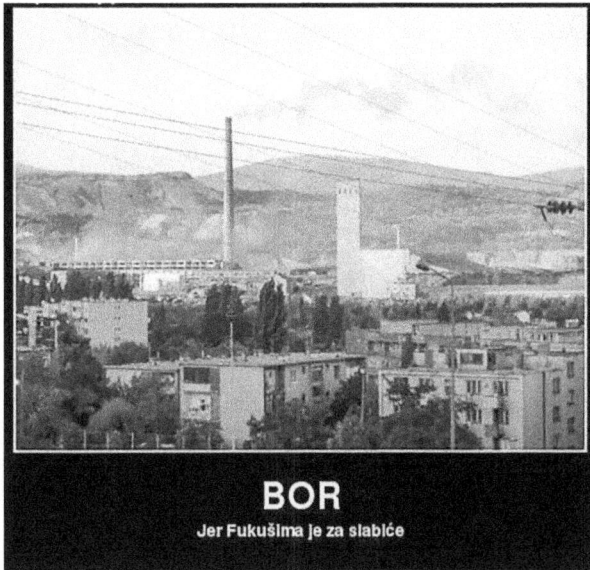

FIGURE 13.   Enduring hazards: "BOR. Because Fukushima is for sissies."
Photo credit: www.vukajlija.com, downloaded in December 2014.

was represented as much more severe and more heroic. People who commented on this picture made jokes on social media about how the citizens of Bor had a particular stamina that stemmed from their poisoning.

Another meme that was adjusted to Bor's context circulated on social media (figure 14). In the cartoon, we can see how Superman is being defeated in an arm-wrestling duel with a skinny young boy from Bor. Superman, his hand pinned down on the table, asks the boy in wonder, "Where are you from, which planet are you from?!!"

The boy answers, "From Bor, you pussy!!"

This illustrates the frequent image of the citizens of Bor as a strong and resilient type with the capacity to endure hazards. There were also stories about the "rough" Borani. While I was strolling down the main street with Jovanka, who was a courier at my municipal office and a mother of three living in the vicinity of Bor, she wanted to show me the smoke coming from the smokestack at that moment. She said that she could recognize that the smoke was a more dangerous kind—according to her, the gray smoke was more hazardous than the white type. Her daughter, who also joined us that evening, told me that she had seen a TV report from a resort at a lake somewhere in Serbia. According to her, people on the TV were making a barbeque and burning leaves that created an enormous

FIGURE 14. The capacity to endure hazards: Superman cartoon. Photo credit: Downloaded from Facebook in January 2014.

amount of smoke around them. When one of the men was asked whether he was bothered by the smoke, he replied: "I'm from Bor, man. How can it bother me?!" Jovanka's daughter recounted the story proudly, smiling, and Jovanka was amused by it too. She explained that people in Bor were tougher since they knew how to bear such poisoning. She referred to the particular image of the Borani who endured under pollution, malleable and even resistant individuals who sometimes had near limitless strength and extreme invulnerability to toxicity and hazards.

What these and similar humorous representations encapsulated was a particular sense of endurance under pollution and a perverse feeling of stamina that people claimed they obtained just by enduring pollution. I frequently encountered such celebrations of individuals who adjusted themselves and endured the smoke heroically. This was accompanied by a feeling of pride and a sense of belonging to such a polluted, toxic environment, sometimes even mixed with a particular ironic enjoyment of such endurance and insolence. How can we fully understand this kind of endurance in the midst of their troubles?

Let me note that endurance under the smoke has had a long history in Bor.[5] Even an anecdote from Yugoslav times brings it to mind: When the Yugoslav president Tito visited the smelting factory in Bor in 1948, many members of his escort started to cough from the smoke while entering and exiting the smelting plant. Tito turned to his escort and said: "Oh, you are all so feeble.... You see how we workers endure it very well" (Radulović 1987, 66). Tito was here clearly making a reference to his apprenticeship to a locksmith and work as an itinerant metalworker before World War II. The leitmotif of endurance is present here, too, but in the context of joint industrial socialist working endeavors.

All these practices were clearly the strategies that Borani used to negotiate the stigma of the toxic exposure of their town (besides defending the modernity of the town) and to deal with the feeling of impossibility of doing anything themselves to change the situation. And the "situation" was not easy. The *šmekerski* character of the smoke and the feeling of stamina that people felt bring to mind what Ghassan Hage calls the "heroism of stuckedness" and a "celebration of survival" (Hage 2009, 101), which he developed in his research on transnational Lebanese migration and white racists in Australia. In contrast to Hage, who uses the feeling of "stuckedness" to explain a sense of "not moving well," the ability of Borani to stick it out, *šmekerski*, with dignity and pride in the polluting setting was a different kind of disposition. The "heroism of stuckedness" rather became domesticated as a significant marker of a particular "mode of life," a lifestyle that contained much irony and tenacious self-enjoyment. Even though *šmekerski* endurance perhaps did not enable one to feel that one was "going somewhere," such a sense of stamina and heroic endurance under pollution speaks about the ways in which such dispositions enabled the condition of grabbing some agency in extremely polluting conditions that the individuals felt they could not solve on their own.

After all the things that the citizens of Bor had lived through, which included the downfall of the company, the dilapidation of their town, a rapid decline of living standards after 2000, a great wave of outmigration, and life in a highly polluted town, I think it was no coincidence that my friend from Bor called his co-citizens "*Borci*" (the Fighters) instead of "*Borani.*" For the people of Bor, heroic endurance under the smoke was one of many social practices entangled with the smoke through which they made their lives tolerable, dignified, creative, poetic, and even amusing in the midst of their troubles.

The Entire Mendeleev's Periodic Table in Our Blood

I met Nevena, a thirty-year-old dark-haired woman, energetic and unemployed, through her mother, who had briefly taken care of my grandfather's neighbor back in Belgrade (cf. Jovanović 2018b). As this coincidence brought us together in Bor, I was frequently invited by her mother to spend some time with her,

Nevena, and Nevena's then five-year-old daughter. I took a stroll later with Nevena and her daughter in the old town center (next to the green market and the smelter) to buy something for Nevena's friend. Suddenly, the smoke appeared. I started to taste the metal in my mouth and could hardly breath. Nevena held her daughter's hand and almost furiously passed me a paper handkerchief to put over my mouth. "Don't breathe through your mouth, only through your nose!" she told me, explaining that that would prevent me from breathing in the soot. She gave her daughter a handkerchief to place over her mouth while holding her sleeve over her own nose and mouth. My eyes began to water while we were trying to reach the part farther away from the smelting plant positioned close by the town's center. A sharp, pungent acidic smell affected my nose and throat and left a bitter taste of corrosive metal in my mouth. While walking quickly toward Nevena's flat, we passed by a dozen people who were standing at the bus stop across the road, calmly waiting for the bus. Only a few of them were holding something over their mouths, usually part of their clothing. Nevena was upset. "This is frequent," she said. She disliked the smoke, just as everybody else did, but she believed, like many, that the smoke "fed" the whole town as well.

After returning to the flat as quickly as possible, we sat on the couch to recover. Nevena was furious. "We have the entire periodic table in our blood" (*Ceo Medeljejev sistem u krvi*), she said affectively. This was a well-known metaphor that Nevena used to explain the extent of her intoxication. The pollution was not only "out there" but also inside her body (Auyero and Swistun 2009). This frequent expression was also used by a substantial number of people to describe themselves as contaminated yet adaptable individuals with a formidable strength that rendered them resistant to toxicity. Such an image of the industrial body, which was a part of the contaminated habitus, was not used as an instrument "of denial" (Auyero and Swistun 2008, 367) of the consequences of pollution. Rather, it implied a confirmation of unknowability and an acceptance of people's poisoning at the same time.

Nevena's mother used to be a nurse. Her husband (Nevena's father) was a miner at RTB who had died very young from lung cancer. She advised me to wash the vegetables I bought at the green market in sodium bicarbonate (baking soda), "just in case." Yet she never did this herself, as she claimed she had probably gotten used to the toxins. She told me that she had heard that the hospital ward for pulmonary diseases and cancer was "packed full" with patients. This was a concealed fact, according to her, because the company's managerial elite, who had a political role in the municipality, had all the power to control both public and private sectors in the town and people's jobs could have been jeopardized. Such precariousness and unknowability of potential risks to health shaped the Borani's world significantly. Their endurance had a potential expiration date, but many could not know exactly when it would be. Many were waiting for the polluting conditions to finally end, for the state or the company to do something about them, and for the new smelting factory to start working.

Despite the semi-ironic celebrations of the smoke as making them particularly well-suited to endurance, my interlocutors did not like the fact that they lived in the most polluted town in Serbia. However, for none of them was it possible to know with certainty or to anticipate the long-term consequences of air pollution for their individual health. The Privatization Agency of the Republic of Serbia, which hired a private foreign company to carry out an environmental assessment of RTB's operations (for the purposes of the potential privatization that never occurred), published a report in 2006 that claimed that the amount of airborne particles in Bor was over the allowed legal limit many times per day. It showed that the pollution could endanger public health, with increasing cancer risk and skin and mucous membrane disease. The report stated that "it is known that it is very difficult to find a clearly defined relationship among disease and pollutant concentration" (The Privatization Agency—Republic of Serbia 2006, 78). While the concentrations of toxic substances in the air were above the permissible limit values for emissions for more than six months of the year (Šerbula 2013), a sociological study on pollution carried out in Bor in 2011 and 2012 showed that air and water quality monitoring was limited. The problem was that monitoring devices often did not work and health monitoring was not comprehensive or systematic, as was also the case for the whole country (Vesković 2013). This problem was caused by a lack of state funds to maintain or improve monitoring and by a conflict with particular interests (Jovanović 2018b, 493). The latter was related to the fact that the public institutions and the municipality which were supposed to monitor pollution were all politically controlled and funded by the state bodies. The executive RTB managers were appointed by the government and were also prominent politicians and members of the ruling party in the local municipal council. Public health institutions were also falsifying the results on air pollution (Vesković 2013). The results they announced—through the state institutions—were dictated as the research institutes made deals with factories that were also their major sponsors (Vesković 2013). There were also stories that the company concealed the data. Even when general practitioners (GPs) (many of them worried that they could easily lose their jobs) wanted to address the extent to which diseases were consequences of pollution (from direct exposure, via the food chain, and so on), they still argued that consequences and causal connections could be known only in the long term and via (nonexistent) systematic monitoring. This lack of data is one of the main reasons why no juridical case based on the health hazard was ever processed in this town. It was only in 2021, thanks to the initiative of one individual from Bor who was engaged in the civil society sector and who invoked the Law on Free Access to Information of Public Importance, that the study of the Institute for Public Health of Republic of Serbia was made public. For the first time in the history of Bor, a study (which would have been kept secret) provided tangible results which showed the high rate of disease caused by contamination and a causal relationship between industrial pollution and health risks. The study revealed a higher risk of mortality in almost all groups for both men and women. The indicators of morbidity and mortality were linked with different kinds of cancers, as well as cardiovascular, respiratory, digestive, and genitourinary diseases (CRTA 2021; Institut za javno zdravlje Srbije 2020).

Back then in 2012 and 2013, however, the impact of air pollution was much contested, minimized, ignored, and relativized. It was also concealed by the press and by RTB officials. Some citizens occasionally wrote letters to the government, to various ministers, asking them to react to the increased pollution, but no one ever did. The expectations that the state mechanisms could and should be sanctioning the company were always present. Nevertheless, people had their own tactics for evading potential hazards and unpleasant experiences. For instance, Petar, the cultural worker, would decide not to take his daughter to her ballet lessons if there was too much smoke in the old town center. Or some people would even act impudently, like the municipal courier Jovanka whom I mentioned earlier. She proposed to me a "hair of the dog" method, teaching me how to light a cigarette to "wash off the lungs" with cigarette smoke, which she usually did if she encountered the smoke in the streets. A seller of green vegetables on the local market from whom I sometimes bought vegetables told me that he often did not tell his customers where he had grown them, because the pollution in his village was so dire that many people would not buy goods from him if they knew their origins. The ambiguities that the context of unknowability of the impact of pollution on health produced through the failure of the state mechanisms, together with the shady deals with the company, silences, and self-censorship, took away the ability to claim for certain that suspected damages were a consequence of the exposure to the smoke.

However, it was not that the smoke was not measured at all back then. The monthly analyses of toxins were produced by the local research institute (Mining and Metallurgy Institute Bor). They were made transparent, published on the municipal website, and printed and hung up on a board in the hall of the public library. These numbers, however, often did not have any significant meaning to either ordinary people or to me. When I saw numbers that showed a great amount of pollution, nobody could know (nor could I know) what it could actually do to our bodies in the long term. The health price of pollution was not known, but people were left to wonder about the noticeably higher occurrence of respiratory diseases, such as asthma, chronic bronchitis, and cancer. Many people knew someone who had died of some kind of cancer. Petar's father had died of cancer, Milica, who worked at RTB headquarter, had lost her spouse, Nevena had lost her father when she was just a teenager, and Svetlana knew people around her who got sick and was very afraid of it.

In spite of anxieties over their health, whose basis in truth the Borani could not prove for certain, many individuals anchored their hope in the smoke, almost equating the two, like Svetlana did. The pungent, toxic, sensorial, and embodied pollution was sometimes expressed as a precondition for individual existence in Bor. When I was discussing the advantages and specificities of their town, Svetlana would usually explain that the company's ethical, social, and even political obligation was to care about the town. This stance was shared by both those who did and those who did not work for the company. In addition, the smoke meant the very existence of life and it was a sign of a common good and progress, both conceptualized as a version of progress in the past. In the shared expressions, the logic of hope was economic: the smoke was a sign of a functioning industry that provided jobs to many, entangled with the notion of modernity from the past. Such sentiment was characterized by a particular orientation to the past's future: "As long as the smoke is out there, there will be money" (Jovanović 2018b, 495). One would hear this saying frequently. This stance resonated with everyone, even with the people who did not work for the company. Everyone knew well and uttered the local folklore saying, "As long as there is smoke, there is hope." The smoke was read as a *sign* (proof) of the energy that the hope granted (namely the fact that RTB was operating). As such, it induced the affect (or ethos) of hope (hopefulness). That kind of hopefulness was directed toward a vision of a stable yet "contaminated community" (Edelstein 1988). The realization of hope for any possible communal or personal future was the realization of the smoke—a precondition and a necessity for the reproduction of everyday lives and the existence of the town in the present. In spite of the fact that I encountered many divergent ideas about the smoke, these understandings have helped me to depict the ethos of hope for the past's futures that was strongly embedded in the community. The particular historical dependency created between the company and the town certainly contributed to the existence of such a hope that was inseparable from the company (and the smoke).

The ontological necessity of the company, fear of the disappearance of the town due to the potential closure of RTB, and the desire to maintain its toxic production despite the hazards are not new. They can be found in many other resource-dependent and industry-dependent places around the world. The most strikingly similar example is the town of Karabash in the Chelyabinsk region of Russia, the copper town "with no future" (Chesnokov 2018). At the end of the 1980s, when there were protests organized by a couple of environmental non-governmental organizations (NGOs), the smelter in Karabash was closed down. Even though the area was recognized by the Russian ministry of the environment as an "ecological disaster zone," in 1998, under pressure from the unemployed local population, the government was forced to reopen the facility, as many of the residents depended on its production (Chesnokov 2018). Today, the privatized smelter in Karabash still works, leaving the town as one of the worst polluted in the world. The inclination to contest the potential closure of the polluting complexes and maintain hope for the past's futures for the sake of the very economic survival, no matter the cost, is most visible in such places of monostructural economies. This is what makes Karabash and Bor quite similar. In Bor, however, there was no opposition to the company that polluted because of the historical, political, and social context in which the company was strongly integrated into the social landscape and how it was seen as "enabling" life itself. The very ecological promises even kept many people engaged in supporting the company in their own visions of ecological endeavors. While they silently waited for the expiration date of the pollution, many imbricated hope with risk (to health) in the ways in which they acted upon their futures. The following sections will give more insight into such imbrications.

The Beehive Case

Every first Tuesday of the month from the end of 2010, RTB held meetings called "Open House" (*Otvorena vrata*) from 4 to 6 p.m. in one of the head offices of the smelting plant.[6] The meetings were an obligation imposed by the EDC, the creditor of the reconstruction project of the old smelter and building of the new sulfuric acid plant. According to RTB officials, the purpose of the meetings was mainly to inform the citizens about the project's ecological aspects and to provide a forum for public participation in the course of the project. The goal was to offer a place where the citizens could make their suggestions and criticisms and ask questions regarding the project, especially about its future ecological aspects. I attended a couple of these meetings, where I met Dragana, a young woman who worked in the Office for Ecology of the RTB headquarters, whom I knew from before. Dragana was a moderator at the meeting. She was well informed about my research and allowed me to attend the Open House meeting. Besides her, only Milan, a man in charge of work safety at RTB and at the smelting project construction site, was present in the role of expert to answer questions. There were supposed to be more people representing RTB, but Dragana did not know the reason for their absence. The meeting started after the arrival of four older men. We all sat down in comfortable leather office chairs around a big black conference table. Dragana introduced Milan to the villagers and myself, and I stated the purpose of my visit. After I asked the villagers whether it would be okay for me to be included in the meeting for the purposes of my research, they said that I should be writing about the town, as Borani faced "tons of problems at every step."

It seemed that Dragana already knew these men from previous meetings. She started the meeting by asking them very politely:

"And how have you been doing? Long time no see. . . . What did you do so far?"

The villagers were tense and eager to start the meeting. By following their conversation with Dragana, I found out that they lived in the vicinity of Bor and had come to address an incident that had occurred nine months previously when the bees in their village apiaries had died. At the meeting, one villager made the accusation that the smoke from the smelting plant was responsible for the damage: "We tried, many times . . . we complained to the municipality . . . because they promised us compensation for the damage. We had an official proof which showed what the main cause of their poisoning is, and our request for compensation was supposed to be sent to RTB."

One man stood up and, in a heightened voice, continued the conversation with Dragana, claiming that the procedure took too long, that their request was deliberately delayed, and that there was incredible corruption of the municipal bodies which were aligned through social, economic, and political ties with the company. According to the villagers, the company's management and the political parties running the town and the company had "obstructed the work of the local board."

It seemed that they had picked the wrong "door" to which to bring their complaint. Dragana said that the Open House served to address ecological issues "*only* in relation to the future smelting plant."

Milan replied to her immediately: "That is the reason why we are here! The smelting plant is an ecological matter!"

One of the villagers raised his voice: "You say that this Open House addresses ecology, so you need to listen to us!" he continued. "What are we supposed to talk about then, if not ecology?" he asked.

"New technologies," Milan replied.

"The bright future," Dragana murmured under her breath.

Milan and Dragana insisted on having scientific facts authorized by the state and the local institutions.

"How do you know it's from the smelting plant, then?" Dragana asserted.

Milan advised them in a patronizing manner to wait and be persistent—but elsewhere. He was occasionally sarcastic and indicated that neither of them had any authority or power to deal with the problem. It was all like a performance: the villagers knew that they could not address their problem at the meeting, but they kept complaining, raising their voices, asking Dragana for help. Milan and Dragana reacted to their concerns but distrusted and relativized their accusations despite the fact that severe pollution was, in fact, the main rationale for the reconstruction project they represented.

"The pollution is so severe that it's absurd!" One of the villagers raised his voice and claimed that the smelting plant was poisoning their land, which was the main source of their livelihoods. Some of them had been recently laid off from their work (they had worked in the bankrupt state companies that were still not privatized) and now they all depended mainly on agriculture. The villagers then turned to me to tell me how severe the pollution was. One of them told me I should note down (as they knew I was doing research and writing down what was said in the meeting) that they had frequent headaches when they spent time in their gardens. The way Dragana was moderating the conversation made it almost impossible for the villagers to claim that it was the company's responsibility. Milan insisted the administrative protocols were *supposed* to work. He emphasized that there were institutional responsibilities and the national and local regulations with which the villagers were supposed to comply.

"Do you know that there is a greater risk of getting cancer from smoking than from the smelter?" Milan asked suddenly.

Such insistence on relativization reminded me of a common practice whereby many polluting companies invest themselves in minimizing or denying the effects of pollution in order to prevent potential mobilization of the polluted population (Markowitz and Rosner 2013) while arguing that the link between industrial pollution and health hazards does not exist (Bryson, McPhillips, and Robinson 2001). This made the performance even cynical, as Milan and Dragana were representing a project that was being built because of severe pollution that was detrimental to health. While the villagers were complaining about the pollution and also about the irreversibility of the damage being done to their environment, one of them contended that those who worked and lived in Bor were willingly accepting the contamination and becoming intentionally contaminated. Milan's and Dragana's high salaries were seen as due recompense for the exposure to toxic contaminants that the citizens of Bor experienced from living in the town:

> When you came here, you came here to be consciously poisoned. You knew that when you came to Bor you would be poisoned; you did not come to a pharmacy. . . . A man is consciously selling his health, and

receives, more or less, a decent salary, but he is aware that he is being poisoned; he is selling his health. And we, who are not employed by RTB, we don't have anything; we are being poisoned for nothing. But you, gentlemen, you have salaries of 700 euros, and the gentleman [he pointed to the other villager] is not working anywhere; he has children; he needs to dress them, to school them; he and his wife need to have some clothes, but it's difficult.

"It's not difficult, it's impossible," the other villager added.

At this point of the conversation, the meeting took an unexpected turn. The ecological agenda suddenly became secondary. One of the villagers addressed Dragana and expressed a desire to work in the smelting plant as a fair compensation: "But what about our health? We are being poisoned every day. In Bor, you are selling your health; you have a salary of 100,000 [Serbian] dinars.[7] Employ at least ten workers from the village in the smelting plant!"

In their further discission, I realized that the villagers had already received an offer from the company to obtain compensation, but through an unofficial settlement under one condition: the villagers could receive the compensation only if they instead asked for a "donation" that would, on paper, support the "development of beekeeping."

"The letter should not contain the word 'smoke,'" Milan suggested.

"Can we still get that chance that was offered to us before and get that promised help?" one of the villagers asked. He said they had founded a nongovernmental organization, registered as an ecological one, which they had recently established for this potential transaction.

"Could you ask the general manager or your other boss if this offer still stands?" one of the villagers asked Dragana.

I was rather surprised by this shift. I sat in silence, waiting for something to be said so I could understand it better. The complaints about pollution looked like an ecological uprising to me but the performance turned out to be an act of bargaining with the company. As the meeting shifted, I realized that the villagers had actually come to the meeting to try to negotiate the alleged consequences of pollution either by asking for a settlement for the damage or by expressing a desire for a job at the source of their contamination. Their initial revolt against the possible detrimental consequences of pollution only existed up to the point at which they managed to ask whether they could still use the offered opportunity to attain the long due offered bargain.

The atmosphere changed. There was less anger and affect in the air.

"Some miserable amount could be transferred," one of the villagers said in a milder tone, while underlining that such amounts could not reflect the real value of the damage.

"We are ready to present the amount as a donation for the advancement of bee-keeping," said the villager who had started off the meeting to Dragana, timidly.

"It will be written and requested as 'help,'" he confirmed.

"I have noted down everything and I will make sure to pass this information to the Director," Dragana said.

The villagers thanked her, and after that, they all shook hands with Dragana and Milan and said goodbye to me. They left the room in a rushed manner. The Open House meeting for that day ended. Dragana told me that there would be no visits. I said goodbye to Dragana and Milan and thanked them for allowing me the opportunity to attend the meeting. After saying our goodbyes, we all left the office.

Imbricating Hope with Risk

What we can see from the interaction that day during the Open House meeting is that while the villagers made their bargains with the representatives of the company in terms of health hazards, the environment was not a category of great significance.[8] It became relevant for the villagers only when used as a "bargaining chip" to improve their near futures vis-à-vis the company (Jovanović 2018b, 500–501). The uncertainty regarding their exposure was seen as an opportunity rather than the responsibility of the company. The toxic smoke that contaminated the villagers' land and bodies was perceived by them as a simultaneous source of hazard, a threat, and a risk in the (undefined) future and a source of money and prospects, an immediate opportunity. In agreeing to represent their request as "help" (and not compensation) and seek that "help" from those who were contaminating them, self-censorship about their troubles with pollution became a viable option. Possible contamination was an acceptable choice in the near future, while they were waiting for a long-term solution to their pollution. As getting a job at RTB had started to become a matter of good connectedness and the source of a decent income for only a limited number of people in the town (unlike in the past when "everyone worked at RTB"), the trade-off with the risks and desiring these industrial jobs seemed to compensate for life in the polluted environment (just like in the past).

During the villagers' interactions with the representatives of the ecological project, different "faces of power" became visible. As I mentioned earlier, at that moment there were no medical and scientific criteria which could be taken as the basis for claiming the harm was due to the pollution from the company. Some legal frameworks did exist, but the villagers emphasized that the state institutions did not work. The failures of the state mechanisms were interpreted ambiguously among the villagers. When the state mechanisms were seen as nonexistent, such inexistence was perceived as an impetus for the company to pollute unimpededly and without any sanctions. At times, the state was seen as an entity which did not intervene willingly due to potential bribery of the relevant state institutions in charge of pollution. What is interesting is that the very unknowability in terms of the potential harms was seen as a product of the state, an entity expected to provide solutions. Such unknowability was a condition which also allowed the company to trump the power of the state and which revealed the inability of the state to sanction the company. For the villagers, the state appeared as an entity that had no authority over the company.

As a result of the lack of alternatives regarding their livelihoods, calculating and commodifying health risks seemed to be an acceptable option for the realization of the villagers' near futures. Such conflicting orientation to the future stemmed from their experiences from the late socialist past, when there was a well-known calculation of the risks: holding stable jobs at the company compensated for the potential poisoning. Smoke was an indicator of money and stability in the past and of the past's future. The risk of losing their livelihoods was valued more than their risk of toxic contamination, while the risk of getting sick was valued less than what they could get from the short-term and immediate compensation. Weighing up, calculating, and accepting risks and hazards that "worked against" them enabled the villagers to attain some tangible outcomes in the near futures. While their goal was to obtain what they could at that meeting, the villagers legitimized the authorities in power—those who made them wait and endure until the expiration date of their pollution. They waited for the company while asking for "favors" from it, which they framed as "help," and miserable amounts of compensatory cash. Hope for a slight improvement of their lives seemed to contain an intrinsic demand for trade-offs (Jovanović 2018b, 499).

What the actions at the Open House meeting illustrate very well is how different scales of futures were present on both sides. On the one hand, Milan and Dragana represented a project that did not yet fully exist but was supposed to instill hope for clean air in the near future. By advising the villagers to be satisfied with an offer they had already received, to compromise, Milan and Dragana were suggesting that they should wait and undertake risks until the new smelting plant started working effectively.[9] This also meant that the "help" that RTB offered implied that the villagers should be covering up the possible hazard the pollution might have caused in the past and deflecting the potential responsibility of the company. The endurance was encouraged by these two actors who provided hope that the "bright" ecological future was almost there.

On the other hand, doubt about the realization of the promised ecological project was not the only reason why the villagers held onto the past's futures and opted for the realization of their hope for short-term compensation. This was also because the promise of the "bright future" excluded the irreversible harms which pollution had produced in the past. The promise of clean air shifted away all other environmental concerns from the ecological agenda. Waste, waste water, or the overall pollution of the environment (all of which destroyed flora and fauna) were absent from the ecological agendas. The practices that I have illustrated in this chapter, from the readiness to bargain with risks to proud endurance, did not consist of orientations to futures that aimed, as Åsa Boholm and Hervé Corvellec assert, to "keep the risk object out and the object at risk in by developing an adequate risk management regime" (2011, 180). Rather, both the risk object (the company that polluted and the relationships with the managerial elite) and the objects at risk (health, livelihoods, jobs, communal good, environment, and villagers' children) were navigated without "expelling" any object. The mutual imbrication of hope for more immediate compensation that attached to the past's futures with risks to health that attached to the unknown futures prompted the acts that managed to translate indeterminacy into a set of possible gains sooner in the future.

So far, sociocultural examinations of risk have characterized risk, to a large extent, by its negative value and have observed how individuals and societies secure protection from it (Douglas and Wildavsky 1983; Giddens 1991; Beck 1992). In contrast to such approaches, the ways the risks were navigated by the villagers and those who heroically endured under the smoke resonated more with Zaloom's (2004) idea of risk in its active and productive forms. It seems that the villagers knew ways to use limited channels of only seemingly democratic participation (imposed by the foreign investor), where it was possible to show up and, by acting, turn the risk of exposure into a more immediate resource. A similar aspect of risk has been delineated by the classical account of the aftermath of the Chernobyl disaster by Adriana Petryna (2013, 116–17), who argued that those who knew the ways to complain in Ukraine rendered the exposures to risk visible, through which economic survival and even profitability were achieved. Although there could be a big difference between exposure to risks from Chernobyl and in Bor (but we cannot know that for certain), for the villagers, exposure to risk was something which was not limited or simply denied. Rather, it was "turned into a resource and then parceled out" (Petryna 2013, 117). The value of exposure to risks which was then always very difficult to prove was part of a well-known calculation with risks which could be traded for a job. Trading it for some "miserable amount," in fact, speaks to how such socially, economically, and culturally defined acceptable risks were commodified, with their transactional value determined within the wider frames of contemporary capitalism. As Arjun Appadurai (2016) pointed out, capitalism always "requires its subjects, as *individuals*, to operate on hope, aspiration, and images of the good life while its financial, actuarial, and algorithmic instruments increasingly render us *dividuals* who are indexed by our profiles as bearers of risk, disease, debt, or dysfunction" (emphasis in original). While such navigations were clearly noticeable among the villagers too, their navigations consisted of assessments of particular scales of futures to which hope and risks attached. Thus, such assessments created particular subject positions of those who calculated and commodified risks and thus made the near futures a bit more possible. In an environment in which the simple choice of "either/or" was a rare instance, just like it is for a great number of individuals who make their futures possible within a wider landscape of capitalism, ambivalence seemed to be an unavoidable future orientation that enabled some scales of futures (the near futures) to be made more possible than not (cf. Jovanović 2016).

Ecological Quandaries at the Semiperiphery of Europe

Many readers could, perhaps, interpret the strong desire for the state-supported environmentalism that I depicted in this chapter as a heritage of the paternalistic state during Yugoslav times. I have to note that such an explanation cannot explain the practices I have described in this chapter. During socialism, when "everyone worked at RTB," the paternalistic role of the state was to provide jobs, flats, good salaries, and comfort and not to protect against the health risks that the rapid industrialization brought as the collateral damage of socialist progress. In that period, social stability was maintained by means of economic benefits (e.g., jobs, cheap electricity, writing off taxes, provision of mineral water and milk in the toxic factories, and sending the workers to the local spas and seaside) to compensate for the negative environmental impacts of the industry (Špirić 2018; cf. Oštrić 1992). Since the 1970s, the subversive potential of ecological concerns (because they jeopardized unimpeded industrial production) that entered the public domain has been tamed by bureaucratizing ecological concerns through particular bodies. Introducing severe ecological standards in industry would be regarded as being against industrial growth (Špirić 2018; cf. Oštrić 1992). Protection of the environment had to become an integral part of the planning of social development during socialism, but it was only pro forma grafted onto extremely polluting developmental strategies and projects in the industry. This reflected the fact that Bor was physically planned and expanded around the smelter. Most of the investors and planners avoided procedures related to environmental protection.

Today, the practices of engagements with risks in Bor speak about a particular continuity with socialism, which indicates that environmentalist actions did not (and, sometimes, even should not) address the work of the main polluter. When I was in Bor, there were only a few active environmental organizations and they had only commonplace ecological themes on their agendas: the promotion of recycling of paper, tins, and plastic, neutral discussions of global climate change, promotion of sustainable tourism in the vicinity of the town, celebration of natural resources, engagement in reforestation, and the promotion of green areas. Just like during socialism, all the environmental actions carried out through them were mostly disconnected from addressing what had been the main source of pollution in the town for decades—the industrial company. The idea of investing in ecologically greener life without addressing the main polluter in the past was also reflected in the way in which urban planning was carried out in Bor: planting trees in the town and making green areas in front of and between almost every building block was a counteraction against severe unhindered pollution.

The relationship with hazards and ecological harms in Bor complicates the perception of environmentalism-as-opposition today and the common image that environmentalism has been state-supported during socialism in Eastern Europe. The popular discourses about environmental mobilizations in post-socialist Eastern Europe today frequently frame the emergence of new ecological movements as a result and expression of democratic freedoms, which Larisa Kurtović and Azra Hromadžić (2020) insightfully noticed. They argued that such engagements are usually seen as an opposition to "the state," which the citizens should have allegedly got rid of after the end of socialism (Kurtović and Hromadžić 2020). In contrast to such perceptions of environmentalism-as-opposition to the state, the desire for state-supported environmentalism was very much present in contemporary Bor. As I have shown in this chapter, hope was located, for many, within the frameworks of the state (Jansen 2015) to regulate the environmental hazards and to find the solution to pollution. The idea that the society could not exist without the regulated and regulating company and the state, which I explained in the previous chapter, certainly contributed to such orientations. The ambivalence I found, which resulted in bargaining with risks, thus complicates how we understand the environmental engagements in post-socialist Eastern Europe.

Certainly, the situation of dealing with double-bind conundrums (cf. Eriksen and Schober 2018), which entail navigating risks, could be found at many other sites of industrial disasters (Fortun 2009; Petryna 2013). Bor shares a common trait with them as much as with many lived experiences of toxicity and exposures (Allen 2003; Auyero and Swistun 2009; Little 2014). The anthropological literature has also extensively addressed the dilemma of risk of toxic contamination caused by the same instances that provide livelihoods on an everyday basis (Nash 1979; Phillimore and Bell 2005). Bor resonates with these other ways in which industrial pollution was caught up in the mutual imbrications of hope and risk. As such, this example supplements the anthropological and sociological studies of industry–community relations. In contrast to studies concerned with risks in other industrial settings (Edelstein 1988; Zonabend 1993; Tilt 2013; Little 2014; Mah and Wang 2019), the practices of heroic and enjoyable proud endurance under pollution together with the practices of bargaining with risks depict specificities formed through the intimate social and historical intertwining with the company (and with pollution).

This chapter has shown how dealing with ecological hazards was set in the discourse in which ecological solutions were required to be more holistic. The ecological projects offered in this late-industrial town provided only partial approaches to the overall pollution. Often the environmental promises were seen as theatrical ways in which very short-term benefits were made possible. The villagers were ready to take part in staging the promises of nonpolluted futures—they were willing to camouflage the harms by calling the compensations ecological contributions and to play-act accordingly. The ecological promises and the gigantic investments in futures were also often seen by many of my interlocutors as a frontier of the enrichment and proliferation of party-political power, which could be gleaned from the villagers' statements that day at the Open House meeting. As they were embedded within the circulation of global capital, ecological harms were seen not only as sites of intervention and remediation but also as lucrative sites that could offer opportunities for short-term deals. Even though such understandings of ecological practices may be found in other parts of the world (Knight 2020), Bor offers an example where such reflections were very prominent.

The engagements with risks as "a locus of production of self and space in contemporary economic and social life" (Zaloom 2004, 384) also tell us how risks were commodified and how they became opportunities for (individual) profitability and chances to make the present and the nearer future possible. The proud endurance under the smoke, enjoyment in hazardous conditions of risk, and opportunities to trade risk exposures for some benefits fit within the landscape of commodification of risks under global capitalism. In contemporary Serbia, durable and more holistic approaches to long-term visions of ecology (in distant futures) were severely limited and oftentimes seen as less probable. Such myopic temporalities, together with the smoke as the "vibrant matter" (Bennett 2010)—a life-giving and life-taking substance—make us rethink how the biopolitics of exposure to industrial pollution, as well as practices of embracing pollution, bargaining with risks, and the embodiment of toxins, might be a new register for (ecological) citizenship in deindustrialized post-socialist towns like Bor.

In the light of the failure of the promise of ecologically clean "bright futures," we can better understand the urgency of the villagers' participation in the performances when they were acting to produce some more immediate effects. The process of balancing environmental sustainability with economic growth in Serbia was in the past very much determined by the implementation of EU standards. This was part of the process of accession of Serbia to the European Union at that moment, when the state was a guarantor for the colossal loans (Jovanović 2015). As the pathway of joining the EU market inextricably required the fulfillment of EU ecological standards, Serbia, with its underdeveloped industry and economy, was unable to adjust to such demands without taking out colossal loans. However, the loans for "the biggest ecological investment" were then used as a good investment for getting a good deal with the new buyer. It thus served the Serbian government to get rid of the ecological burden by making the product available through use of the rhetoric of the EU environmental standards (Jovanović 2015). The sale of the company steered the economic and political futures of Bor (and Serbia) in a surprising socioeconomic and political direction. Apart from the fact that the holistic long-term goals to alleviate the heavily polluted environment were never envisaged by this project (and perhaps never will be in the future either), for the citizens of Bor yet another double-bind continued to linger in their still heavily polluted air. The citizens of Bor obtained an extremely expensive ecological commodity that served to attract Chinese capital rather than to protect them from pollution in the future. The stage of the reconstructed smelter where the (failed) promise of an ecological "bright" future was performed was turned into a site of the triumph of Chinese state capital, which would be redistributed elsewhere, no matter the ecological and social price, in the imminent and unpredictable future.

(DIS)CONNECTING
Infrastructures and Thermopolitics of Hope

So far, I have provided a sense of what the surfaces and the air in Bor feel like. Now, let us go a bit deeper underground to see how the heating pipes carried warmth but also hope and politics straight into people's homes. Heating was a proper "hot stuff" in the town. The flat where I lived in the neighborhood called Peta Mesna, in the Fourth Kilometer, had five big radiators that were piping hot twenty-four seven during the winter. When the radiators started working at full capacity in the heating season from late October until April, I would wake up in the middle of the night almost gasping for breath. My landlady, who was in her seventies and used to work in the kitchen of a socially owned company in Bor, lived for years in the flat I rented from her. Her late husband had obtained the flat through his work (self-management system of distribution) at Mining and Smelting Combine Bor (RTB) during socialism.

During one of our regular monthly meetings, while sorting out the utility bills and rent, I complained to her that I had not been able to sleep the previous night because of the extreme heat. She mentioned that I should know that such district heating meant it was a good neighborhood with solidly built flats. Then, she told me that she loved the fact that she could walk about in a T-shirt and that such a sensation was, for her, a sign of "normal" and "good" provision. "Keep your kitchen window open during the night," she advised me, adding that I should perform regular cool-offs by opening the windows throughout the day. People often echoed what my landlady advised me to do, many of them praising the constant heat. What made us keep our windows a crack open on cold nights in Bor? What was the rationale behind such excessive heat? I was puzzled throughout my stay.

As I grew up in a flat in Belgrade attached to the centralized heating grid, the provision of abundant district heating was not unusual for me. My mother, who lives in Belgrade, adores the district heating. She always praises the fact that the heating radiators allow her to be in the flat with her cardigan off during winter. Because I grew up in Belgrade with such abundant heating, I was constantly cold in places where I lived, such as Manchester and Utrecht, where I had to control (and pay more for) the heating myself. I also had to learn to remind myself that I should turn it on only when it was necessary. The very idea of comfort connected to the embodied sensation of (uncontrolled) warmth was undoubtedly connected to the way in which district heating was built in Yugoslavia to provide an equal and abundant amount of heat.

The excessive heating to the point of boiling, "blazing all the time" (Fennell 2011, 41), is not something that is merely a distinction of post-socialist towns but can be found in other places, too. Maria Şalaru (2018) described an experience of abundant district heating in one block of flats in the aging and shrinking town of Piatra-Neamţ in Romania, while Catherine Fennell (2011) illustrated similar issues in a low-income social welfare residential block in Chicago. The excessive heat in the Romanian block was a consequence of the energy transition. It was also a technical matter, as the pressure of the new centralized heater (adjusted from the socialist times) could not heat up the higher floors equally (Şalaru 2018). More heating was thus required on the higher floors, leaving the lower floors to seek salvation by opening their windows. The process of individualization of consumption of heating that occurred in this region had to do with transforming the energy-inefficient systems. This was, according to the European energy-efficiency and environmental agendas, in line with the neoliberal prescriptions warranted by supranational frameworks (Şalaru 2018). In the Chicago case, however, the abundant heating was also provided by design miscalculations that had not accounted for the heat-retaining capacity of concrete (Fennell 2011). In spite of the difference, what these two examples share and have in common with Bor is that, through the heating configurations, a promise of modern and comfortable lives, and of welfare and care provided by the welfare states had been made in the past and was expected to be delivered in the future. This promise was what my family in Belgrade and I had experienced, too.

However, what made my experiences with heating in Bor peculiar was the curious case of the equal *nonstop* heat in a substantial number of flats, making it quite different from these and other ethnographic explorations of heating systems (Humphrey 2003; Johnson 2016). In the whole of Serbia, including Belgrade, only rarely was there twenty-four seven delivery of heating, which occurred mainly during holidays. This was usually at Christmas, over New Year's Eve, or if the temperature dropped below −10°C/14°F.[1] The way in which the incessant super-heating was praised by the residents or how such abundant heating was in complete opposition to the energy-efficiency policies and energy sustainability made the heating quite interesting to explore. However, what made the case distinctive was the fact that the solution of maintaining the warmth twenty-four seven was an outcome of maintaining an extremely faulty and rundown technological system.

The public relations (PR) officer of the public heating company, with whom Janko from the administrative headquarters of RTB connected me, was kind enough to explain to me the puzzling logic of the overheating. He clarified that equal twenty-four-seven heating was mainly a "technical necessity." The system was over-dimensioned, prone to frequent breakdowns, and had not been properly maintained in decades. The heating capacity was only 46 percent. This meant that around 70 percent of households were overheated while 30 percent were heated to below 20 (±2)°C/68°F (±35.6°F). This was the temperature prescribed by the legal obligations of the heating company, which was still a municipal public institution. The heating installations were too old, the terrain was very hilly and rough, and the continental winters could get severe. The average winter temperature was around 0–2°C (32°F to 35.6°F), but it could fall to −15°C (5°F). Sometimes, the town was covered in snow for two months. Equipping the heating substations with thermoregulatory valves that could help the equal distribution of the heat would solve some technical issues, but not entirely. The system was too old, inefficient, and required specific technical measures. According to the PR officer, the delivery of a constant and equal amount of twenty-four-hour heating was introduced as a "less costly measure" that prevented fractures and breakdowns of the whole system. The decision to keep the pipes warm twenty-four seven was there to control and deal with technical defectiveness. This apparently technical measure that served to avoid potential calamities in fact maintained the volatile, fractured, and derelict infrastructural system.

In public, the overabundant heat was always camouflaged and performed as an incredible success and a proof of the potency of the municipal governance and the company. In those camouflages there was no mention of the underlying cause and faultiness. While proving the competency and extraordinary functionality of the heating system, the message was that those who governed it were so successful in their governing abilities that the system even produced an excessive amount of heat! The abundant twenty-four-seven heating system was a piping-hot stage for the performances which not only promised infrastructural provision but also served to perform the successful governance of the town and company. The audience of such performances, the users of the heating services, were tightly connected to the system. It consisted of pipes with a total length of around 225 kilometers, built during the late 1960s and 1970s. It was unusually special as it had the largest number of households in Serbia connected to only one source, covering up to 95 percent of all the households.[2] This was one of the reasons why the encounter with the district heating radiators in barns in some villages near the town was not surprising at all.

The material engagements with the performances of promises of care and welfare that were played out onto such a physically pervasive stage were in this town unavoidable. Enthused by the growing literature on infrastructures that delineate how hope and anticipations (Reeves 2017; Enslev, Mirsal, and Winthereik 2018), desires and dreams (Edwards 2003; Dalakoglou and Harvey 2012; Larkin 2013; Jensen 2017), and promises (Schwenkel 2015; Anand, Gupta, and Appel 2018) are evoked with encounters with infrastructures, I here look into how people's engagements with the heating stage made this system an object that configured dynamic relations between the state, the company, and the heating users. The thermopolitics of hope among various actors will enable a better understanding of the critical role that the materiality and the management of the infrastructural futures had in navigating everyday life and in maintaining authority and power. Before I delve into these matters in more detail, let me first provide some insights into the history of the pipes and how they assembled materially, politically, and socially (Collier 2011) to bring warmth into people's homes.

Infrastructuring the Futures: Making of the Social Contract

The district heating in Bor consisted of a system of pipes connected to one main source of heat—the heating power plant. The plant heated the water, which was then brought by a system of pipes into people's radiators in their domestic spaces. The district heating was technically constructed in Yugoslavia in such a way that the pipes ran vertically through the apartments, linking them successively rather than in loops, making it almost impossible to provide an individual supply. At the time when I was in the town, the residents could not control the amount of heat brought into their flats, just like during socialist times, nor could they turn it off whenever they wanted. The bills were equal throughout the year owing to the cost distribution, and the heat was calculated and charged for by the square meter.

Due to its material obduracy, which reflected the way in which it was built during socialism (Tuvikene et al. 2020; Collier 2011), the residents were literally tied to the piping-hot stage. Heating started to become expensive and volatile and was not equal throughout the town. The residents could not physically disconnect from it. For this reason, it became a source of anxiety and frustration for many. The provision would sometimes be interrupted due to fractures in the network or sometimes even due to stealing of copper infrastructural parts (cf. Jovanović 2021). The heat, the windows that needed to be open when it was too hot, and the excavated streets when the pipes needed to be repaired were the sites of obscure and uncertain responsibilities for the infrastructural fabric.

The municipal heating service was provided on the basis of the universal rationale of uniform coverage by a single source and provider. Such provision of heating was part of what Stephen Graham and Simon Marvin defined as the "modern infrastructural ideal" (2001) of integrated planning of unitary networked cities of social, economic, and political coherence, which was also visible in the modern urban planning of Yugoslavian cities. As the basis of modernist European planning, which tried to unify and homogenize urban space and promote cohesive city-building, Graham and Marvin (2001) argued that such provision of public services became the foundation upon which European welfare states were constructed and sustained. The material building of the town, which included building of urban infrastructure, was also supposed to reflect the ideology of an egalitarian, classless society based on the ideals of working-class emancipation, and on the idea of withering away of the state (as an attempt to differentiate from state socialism), which was not different from other modernist tendencies at large.[3] In Bor, this "modern infrastructural ideal" as a "bundle" regulated by the state institutions (municipality) was simultaneously integrated into the socialist idea of the provision of the "minimum living standard" for the workers by the state. Within such arrangements, the workers were allocated the right to use socially owned flats plugged into a centralized heating provision.[4]

During socialism in Yugoslavia, district heating (like other infrastructural services) was never provided as a consumer good in the way in which other goods, services, and experiences were available and consumed.[5] They were also not provided for free. Embedded within market socialism, they were supposed to deliver a modern standard of living to its citizens. In her study of district heating in Belgrade (Serbia), Charlotte Johnson (2013) argues that the flats with all the modern conveniences (mod cons) that make modern life more comfortable (such as district heating) were offered "as the reward for citizens who were contributing to the socialist pursuit of modernity" (Simić 1973 in Johnson 2013, 146). She explained that "district heating was a system that helped construct such privileged comfort" (Johnson 2013, 146–47). Even though "district heating brought a vision of Yugoslav consumerism into the home and made it material" (Johnson 2013, 147), it was very much linked with the moral project of the Yugoslav state as urban planning echoed the aspirations of socioeconomic development (such as social ownership, equal access to jobs and housing, satisfying a minimum of living standard) (Đurašović 2016, 107–108). By using their flats, and through the pipes, the citizens entered into a "contract" (Johnson 2016) with the Yugoslav state, which ought to provide heat (and welfare and care). Through collective, social, material, and political efforts, infrastructures had a role in being themselves socially transformative—socialist citizens should have fulfilled their part of the social contract through labor (as producers) and, in return, expected the socialist state to deliver the promise of modern housing as a reward. It was not an accident that the heating system mattered so much among the residents of Bor and why it was used for staging the promises. Precisely its promise of comfort, well-being, and care given in the past (for the future) through the pipes and warmth provided by the socialist state made it relevant for the inhabitants of Bor, more than any other utility provision. Other infrastructures and utility provisions mostly only became visible through their mere physical destabilization, such as on the occasions when the water was not drinkable or when the public enterprise in charge of dealing with water utilities was put in charge of the street lighting, which was frequently made fun of.

RTB played an important role in building the district heating system, first directly through pipes and then indirectly through a system of Yugoslav socialist self-management. The district heating system developed from RTB's power plant, which produced electricity for industrial needs and for a few apartments in the surrounding areas, as a part of the RTB smelting factory. Instead of being directed into the industrial turbines, the steam from the smelting factory was channeled to a newly built heating station and hot water pipeline. The district heating network started to be built in 1973, with the rapid urban development of the town, and was finished in the 1990s. Therefore, it could be said that RTB was an enabling element for the heating provision and that the community was assembled through an "enterprise-centric social modernity," as Stephen Collier (2011, 101) suggests in his analysis of the city-building of Belaya Kalitva, a mono-industrial aluminum-processing town in Russia. However, the introduction of district heating in Yugoslavia was not a centrally planned realization of an ideological idea like in the Soviet Union. Some architects were hired from Belgrade, but the local construction was realized through a self-managed *komuna* that consisted of councils and delegates chosen through elections in the local community.[6] Yet, clearly, the introduction of electricity and housing was a part of the ideology in Yugoslavia that aimed to secure general conditions for industrial progress, leaving the workers to maintain their control by self-management through bodies such as the local community office (Golubović 1978, 1979; Cocović-Krstić 1990). In this way, the self-managed socially owned urban infrastructure connected residents to the local urban heating network, while making tight connections between the company, the municipality, and the citizens.

District heating was a par excellence post-socialist infrastructure that was ubiquitous in everyday life. The fact that almost the whole town was covered by this system reflected the fact that the socialist urban planning was carried out more holistically in Bor than in many other Serbian industrial towns. This was because this Yugoslav mining and copper-processing working town had great importance in building and maintaining the socialist system. For that reason, providing the workers, the carriers of such a system, with material care and comfort was extremely significant. As the network expanded, the heating capacity also increased.[7] For a couple of decades, the heating was maintained by both the industrial and the heating power plant, until the heating plant took over the management completely. The heating company was disentangled from the ownership of RTB only in 2002 and emerged as the independent, state-owned public enterprise Toplana Bor (Heating Plant Bor), a municipal public company.

Bor in 2012 and 2013 provides an example of a place where the heating infrastructure was still a "bundle," to use Graham and Marvin's (2001) expression, by which they refer to the ideas of the unitary provision or "wholeness" of both cities and urban infrastructure networks. As privatization did not occur, the heating infrastructure was provided by the state-owned public enterprise in a highly monopolized market. The introduction of thermoregulation equipment and valves into households under EU policies and regulations that would allow billing according to the amount of heat consumed rather than per square meter (as a part of environmental protection action and improvement of energy efficiency) was on the agenda for the future. This started to be implemented only after 2014.

Behind the Scenes: Making the Heat Flow

Being highly problematic, oversized, and prone to frequent breakdowns, the heating network was not just physically but also economically difficult to maintain. The provision of heating was possible only through sustaining the unsustainable economy of heating. The heating enterprise was indebted (just like RTB) to an already indebted municipality. The citizens were also indebted to the heating enterprise, as the heating prices were still unaffordable for many. The heating company operated in such a market regulated under conditions of monopolistic provision of public utilities as governmental bodies, with enormous losses. The public enterprises also had too many employees in Serbia. This was a product of the fact that employment at such enterprises served the ruling political parties to employ their voters and political-party members, family, and friends, usually in return for favors and their political votes and support. The utility companies, most of which were state-managed and state-owned companies, would usually receive substantial direct subsidies from the state and local subsidies from the municipality, which contributed to increasing public spending and the fiscal deficit (Lazić and Pešić 2012). This was the reason why one could occasionally hear in the media that millions of euros were being "irrationally" wasted by the local public enterprises in Serbia. This seemingly "irrational logic" had a quite "rational" short-term political outcome: the economy of exchanges and favors that made the public institutions work fulfilled its social function of providing heat in the end. This also helped maintain the party-political power, which was crucial in the regulation of everyday life. The quality and malfunctioning of heating, the contracts won through setting up the public procurement, successful or failed investments, accusations of who managed to profiteer from public procurements, and which director and political party could provide better, more efficient, and less costly heating were all topics discussed at the local public assembly. Such heated debates served politicians when dealing with political opponents and making claims about the (dys)functionality of the ruling politicians (e.g., RTB managers).

The decision to maintain the capacity of the heating system by making the system work twenty-four seven was in complete opposition to the energy sustainability agenda and the energy-efficiency regulations. The heating plant was a polluter as well. Working twenty-four seven was a "quick fix" that enabled the heating system to deliver the heat only in the near future. This was because such a "quick fix" would make the system even more prone to breakages in heating delivery. Apart from the technical factors which kept the unsustainable network going, it was important to provide an immediate sense of abundancy of heat because such embodied sensations also enabled desired electoral outcomes. The heating was an important PR device for political engagements. As no one could predict whether the same political party would be managing the heating plant in the next three years or even less, the abundant immediate effects were necessary and more desirable. As the management of the plant changed continually due to party-political alternations, there was no interest in repairing the system in the long term. This was because the political parties would not be able to claim success of their heating if they were not in charge of it anymore. Hence, big potential investments in the sustainability of the system (and investment in fewer breakages) would probably take time and would become visible in more distant futures. Such temporality of the system's transformations would bring the danger that some other political party could use the potential transformations to claim someone else's achievements as their own. These calculative political dynamics resulted in opting for short-term infrastructural planning in this town.

As a result of the logistical, political, and financial volatilities, the heating was always on the verge of being late for the winter season. Obtaining coal was the direct responsibility of the heating company and indebted municipality.

The public procurements of coal, which fueled the heating system, were frequently problematic for this indebted company. It was always uncertain whether the heating company would obtain a sufficiently large amount of coal to start the heating season. It was not unusual to see the general manager of RTB assisting (financially and/or logistically), directly and indirectly, through personal connections and his influence, in the acquisition of coal. What is more, he was also a director of the executive board of a smaller coalmine in Serbia. If the usual provider for the heating plant (Kolubara, located in western Serbia) failed to deliver the coal for any reason, the smaller coalmine would sometimes suddenly appear as a helper in the midst of the coal crisis. The fact that the general manager was on the board of this smaller mine was a public secret. In the case of delayed delivery of coal, RTB would sometimes help out the heating plant from its own supplies of coal until a delivery eventually took place. This was possible because Energana, the part of RTB which supplied the industrial area with energy, used the same fuel for industrial heating and for the preparation of sanitary hot water for RTB. Because of this, RTB was a long-term business partner of the Kolubara coalmine, one of the big suppliers of RTB's industrial requirements. A rumor circulated that RTB was able to negotiate the prices of coal with Kolubara and, for this reason, the municipality could allow lower prices for heating and subsidize it heavily. No matter whether the subsidies were secured or not, they enabled Bor to have the lowest heating prices in Serbia (until 2015). Such circulatory politics of coal and mutual logistical help based on personal, business, industrial, and party-political interests enabled the heating to work as quickly as possible. Through such temporality of actions, RTB emerged as a significant support for the municipal institutions that had power to enable the future of infrastructural provision in times of its uncertainty.

Sometimes the quick fixes were not possible, especially when the heating broke down severely. Nevertheless, while awaiting these fixes, the public performances of care, specially performed by the company (and when it could not speed things up), were not infrequently seen. Although many performances could illustrate such occasions, the most illustrative happened in December 2017. Due to a very harsh winter, the hot-water pipeline broke down and the town's center and the First and Second Kilometer were left without heating for three days. It is not only that houses and flats were left without heating. The main institutions like the Music School (the theater which was not one), the Police Administration, the Old Post Office, and the hospital were also affected. The hospital made appeals on the second day of the heating outage as the temperature outside dropped below zero, which made the conditions critical. RTB Bor was first to "come to the rescue," as the media reported (*Telegraf* 2017). The general manager and the director of the Bor Copper Mine (one of the companies of the holding group) visited the hospital and the patients bringing heaters, blankets, and quilts as a stopgap solution and an act of care. The general manager performatively made a statement while visiting the hospital:

> We cannot allow patients in the children's ward, surgery, and any other ward to freeze, and RTB reacted as soon as we learned that the hospital was without heating. . . . We have provided 45 heaters, 310 blankets, and 80 quilts from our funds and with the help of friends such as Mr. Stanko Popović within two hours, and during the day we will see what else can be purchased.[8] But regardless of that, the heating in the hospital must be enabled as soon as possible and all the conditions must be provided so that such things do not happen again. As a human being, I am indignant because of this and I will personally insist that everyone in the chain of responsibility bears the consequences (*Telegraf* 2017).

Apart from the media coverage, the pictures of the general manager talking to and shaking hands with the patients and the pictures of the medical staff with whom the general manager, the director, and the mayor were talking were also added to the general manager's Facebook profile and circulated in the media.

It was through the pipes and performances through infrastructures that the power of particular individuals and the power of the political and industrial configurations were brought to myriad private and public spaces. Such "infrastructuralization of power" (Mann 1984) also occurred illustratively one winter's day in the library. That day I had a meeting with the director of the public library to discuss the potential project in which I was supposed to participate. After I had spent some time in her office, it became extremely warm. The director took her cardigan off. I commented on how tremendously warm it was in there and started waving my hand to cool off a bit. Then she touched the radiator behind her and said to me cheerfully, "*Sosa ga baš ugrejao!*" (Sosa really warmed it up!). This was a good joke, so we both laughed. In such a material site of accountability and delegated responsibilities, the pipes, radiators, and the whole heating infrastructure enabled the performance of political (and industrial) power. Sometimes it was perceived as communal/political care provided by Sosa, who was sometimes seen as "the state."

The ways in which party-political power games interfered with the functioning of the infrastructure were certainly not new. For instance, Caroline Humphrey's (2003) classic account of the great freeze in Russia shows that as well. While this situation might be common for post-socialist transformations due to the particular material post-socialist obduracy (Tuvikene et al. 2020), which played a great part in political transformations, Bor's specificity was that the management of the industrial company overlapped with running the heating. Here, it was not only that the state power was "infrastructuralized," to use

Julie Y. Chu's expression (2014), which she developed from Michael Mann's (1984) notion of "infrastructural power." In fact, simultaneously with the "infrastructuralization of state power" (Chu 2014), the company's power was "infrastructuralized" as well. The affective efforts to keep the rooms overheated, which were at the same time party-political and an RTB campaign, were shaped around the collective ethics of care around infrastructure, which stemmed from the reminiscence of the futures promised in the past. In this way, the heating became entwined with the redistribution of moral and political obligations to the power of the company and they were mutually dependent and entangled.

The simple lack of thermoregulation devices in the heating network, a technical and a material thing, managed to materialize the power through the pipes twenty-four seven as an abundant embodied sensorial experience. As such, the district heating became a site where physical sensations of thermal comfort were made possible through technical, physical, material, industrial, historical, economic, and political assemblages, which made this system work. The laws and documents which regulated the comfort, the coal deals, the technical reparations, and the "sensory politics" (Fennell 2011) had a specific political and technically unintended outcome: a "regime of comfort" (Shove 2003) that domesticated the power of the company and its management and brought such configurations of power straight to our homes.

Even though there were a great number of people who found the heat in their flats excessive and some had to open the windows to cool off (like I did), due to the technical impossibility of keeping the heating equal everywhere, it was not equally distributed to everybody. Those who were not among the lucky ones whose flats could not be overheated were not content, nor were those whose bills became too high or who were simply displeased with the frequent breakdowns and political marketeering. Many of them had hopes of disconnecting from the heating system and that they would be able to delimit the political power felt through the heating stage. The hope for disconnection and unbundling from heating was most visible among those who commented on disconnections caused by *havarija* (calamity) and among those who had substandard and unaffordable heating.

The Audience of the (Broken) Stage

Havarija: I am Disconnected!

Excavated streets were a frequent sight during and after the heating season, when the heating power plant tried to patch up the leakages, damages, breakdowns, and fissures in order to sustain the provision of heat. When serious breakdowns occurred, the RTB workers (such as welders) were sometimes sent to the field site to fix the pipes. There were great demands on the workers when the heating plant worked twenty-four seven, especially on those who maintained the system. *Havarija* (calamity, accident, crash, damage) would usually happen due to leakage from heating pipes and many other breakdowns that were caused by the old, worn-out system. When *havarija* occurred, the heating would not be delivered for a couple of days in some parts of the town. In the beginning of 2013, one of the *havarija* occurred in part of the system network. The citizens started to complain on various websites and on social media about the dysfunctionality of the heating system and many criticisms targeted the ways in which it worked or, rather, did not work. I watched the local news on Bor TV station, on which the heating company announced the problem and said that the citizens would remain without heating while the outside temperature was −5°C (23°F) for several days. Then the official announcement read by the speaker emphasized that everyone should remind themselves that heating in the town had worked twenty-four seven without any outages over the past hundred days consecutively. They reminded the citizens that abundant and twenty-four-seven provision was still rarely seen in Serbia and should be considered an achievement.

As I spent time in the local community office (*mesna zajednica*) following up the town's governance on a microlevel, I regularly attended the monthly meetings where we discussed issues such as leaking rooftops, maintenance of shared corridors in buildings, and similar communal issues. Spending time there offered me insights into the issues around urban utilities. In this local community office, as I already mentioned, I met Katarina and the courier Jovanka, as well as their families. At the time when *havarija* was happening in winter 2013, the local community office had one of its regular monthly meetings. The problem was raised at the very end of the meeting. One of the elderly men commented on the news that other parts of the town were again struggling with heating delivery. He mentioned that in spite of "their efforts to create an image that the government (*ova vlast*) is taking care of the citizens day and night, the residents pay for cooling instead for heating."

Another man who worked at RTB added that we all knew that the whole system was worn out and that in "sixty years nothing has been repaired," so no one should wonder why it did not work. A man who had been reading the newspaper up to that point became interested in the discussion and added that everyone had the right to their own opinion but that no one wanted to be a prisoner of the heating plant: "I do not want to justify the excuses for the dilapidation of the distribution network . . . but we need to know that this is happening because some irresponsible people from the heating plant . . . instead of reconstructing the network, repairing boilers, and heating . . . they spent money on various embezzlements, for which no one has yet been held accountable." He argued that instead of processing the responsible institutions and individuals in court and paying compensation for the damage, the heating prices would go up or some loans would be requested for further investments in the repairs.

What struck me as I listened to their conversation and took the minutes of the meeting was that the whole discussion raised the matter of responsibilities, and in particular, how the management of the allegedly corrupted state overlapped with the responsibility of the company and "the state." Some of the attendees claimed that it was the responsibility of the general manager to punish those who did not work well at the heating plant: "It looks like he managed to discipline them, but I am not sure if this will last when he goes home." Everyone laughed.

The daughter of my interlocutor Milica and one other woman strongly reacted to this discussion, saying that no matter who forced the heating plant to work properly, the party-political games were stopping them from receiving a proper service. The paradoxical fact was that most of the people who were in the local community office were actually active members of the ruling party, the same party whose local branch president was the company's general manager. The lack of investment in the heating system was seen as a strategy of the political parties to only patch the leaks but not to substantially repair and invest in the system in the long run, because they were, allegedly, involved in corruption. A blonde woman in her fifties said that she knew a lot of people who could not afford the heating and that something needed to change very soon. The man who had protested against corruption joined the discussion again, adding that it could get extremely warm and comfortable but that it became very expensive, so "that's why we need to have the freedom to disconnect, but they are not letting us go."

While the councilors from the local community office stated strongly that the utility users should become proper consumers and spoke about the overlap between the authorities over the heating, the heating provider in Bor was never clear about whether its services were a commodity or not. This was noticeable especially in the way in which the utility provider advertised its services. As Javno Stambeno was highly indebted, it was significant for the company to remind the users to pay their bills. On the local TV station, a short advertisement showed images of running water, radiators, corridors, and communal spaces in buildings, with a voice-over saying: "We kindly ask you to pay the bills on time, so that everyone will be better off." The billboards throughout the town (figures 15 and 16) also asked the citizens: "I paid my utility bills (*komunalije*), have you?"

FIGURE 15. Billboard reminding citizens to pay their *komunalije*. Located in the Third Kilometer; the billboard was attached to the newly renovated building. Photo credit: Taken by the author in 2012.

FIGURE 16. Billboard reminding citizens to pay their *komunalije*. Located in the old town. Photo credit: Taken by the author in 2013.

This kind of "responsibilization" of the users (Collier 2011, 8) relied on the notion that individuals were responsible for the collective good (which utilities could secure) through regular payment for utilities. The logic was that a responsible citizen was one who paid bills on time, which was supposed to make a better life and conditions possible for all. Not paying the bills could jeopardize the well-being of the whole community. For the people from the local community office, however, paying did not guarantee customer satisfaction with the quality of the services provided, and they demanded fairer calculations.

I will stop here for a moment to provide another example of hope of unbundling, to provide more details on the example where certain individuals not only wanted to disconnect completely from the heating but at the same time saw through the performances that were happening on the heating stage. After that, I will come back to these joint desires to attempt to delimit political power, experienced through the pipes.

I Want to Disconnect!

I have already introduced Katarina, a woman in her thirties who, together with her partner Kosta, affectionately pointed out the superficial and insufficient repairs done in the town in chapter 2.[9] As I mentioned, I met Katarina at the local community office, as she was a member of the office's council. Katarina was not present at the meeting that day when the councilors discussed the matter of heating. At some point during her engagement at the local community office, she started feeling that the meetings were pointless as, according to her, they merely served party-political interests. She saw that she could not influence anything through her involvement at the place as she had hoped. Katarina also had problems with district heating, like many. Her desire to disconnect from the district heating was a telling and illustrative example of a situation that was very common in Bor. Focusing on her experiences, which reflect those of many others, will help us to understand more closely the hope of unbundling. Katarina lived in one of the blocks of buildings that was slightly higher up in the hill, so she belonged to the 30 percent of people for whom the twenty-four-seven heat was not efficient.

Katarina was upset when I came to see her at her flat. Yet again, she had received a letter from the public utility company Javno Stambeno (literally translated as "Public Housing"), a final notice before a summons to pay a debt of nearly 1,700 euros. We sat down in the living room of her flat, obtained by her father through his work in the late 1980s at the factory, which used to be a part of RTB and which was privatized in such a way that many workers were laid off without receiving any redundancy payments. Her father was laid off as well. She lit a cigarette and showed me a list of alleged debts from 1996, including periods in 2002, 2003, 2008, and so on. She was trying to find the receipts for bills that had already been paid, which her father kept in a pile of unsorted documents. She claimed that the debt seemed to be much bigger than what the household actually owed and that she knew it should be around 1,200 euros. On a piece of paper, she ticked off the bills that her father had already paid off. She scattered her father's archive around the room while taking documents out of a chest of drawers in the living room. A quick look through the pile evoked Yugoslav and Serbian history, which intersected with her family's past: her father's university library fine from 1987 for three books he had borrowed (*State and the Revolution* by Lenin, *Manifesto of the Communist Party*, and *About Marx and Marxism*) and electoral flyers for the (nationalist) ruling parties during the 1990s. There were newspaper clippings about the war in Bosnia and extensive correspondence between her father as the president of the worker's union in his factory and the state bodies regarding corrupt privatization and the bankruptcy of the factory from which he had been laid off in 2008. Katarina explained that her father had taught her that it was important to always keep some written documents in correspondence with state institutions. This was significant because such records could save them from being deceived by the state. The higher amount on the bill than the family actually owed, she said, was an example of such an attempt by "the state" to extort more money. Katarina had been born and bred in Bor, pausing her final year of law studies for many years, and was unemployed. At that time, her parents were living in a village, trying to survive after both losing their jobs in a privatized RTB factory and leaving Katarina to deal with the family (utility) debts on her own.

The public utility company Javno Stambeno, which was threatening to press charges against Katarina's family, was run by the state municipal bodies. Its main jurisdiction was payment for municipal services. So-called *komunalije* (utilities) were charged through a combined bill for different public utilities issued to each household or business unit within Bor's jurisdiction that was supposed to be paid by the fifteenth day of each month. The bill was addressed to the owner of the flat and monthly payments were equal throughout the year. It covered rubbish collection, building maintenance, and so on, but the biggest item among Katarina's family debts was for the district heating services provided by the heating company. Javno Stambeno had introduced a measure to allow citizens to set up a payment plan, which was supposed to allow Katarina to pay the debt with interest in installments. Should Katarina not accept this offer accompanying the final warning, her father's pension would be suspended for a while (so-called *administrativna zabrana*), which would enforce the payment of debts until they were paid in full. If he did not have enough means, he could be summoned to court, their belongings could be confiscated, and the whole family could be left without any income.

Katarina claimed that "the state" always found something that one had already paid and sent a bill while relying on luck that one would not find a receipt for it or on the fact that nobody checked it. "This only exists in this country!" she said. She claimed that such "extortion" and almost legal stealing existed to generate extra money that went straight into the budget of the political parties that were in charge of the public utility companies to finance their own political activities. The director of Javno Stambeno was always a member of a ruling political party and so the money went there, she explained. "I am not so uneducated," she said, claiming, "Only in this country can such negligence happen, and nowhere else!" She consulted a lawyer, a family friend, who told her to get a document from the local court to prove that all debts became obsolete after ten years by law. Many people did not know how to read their final notices, but Katarina knew how, she said. "These people, politicians in the municipality, they only argue over who should become a general director of some public company, while the people are being robbed and they do not even want to know how we live." She spoke about the state as a "usury state" that extorted money. And because of that, she had to go around to various public institutions and queue at the counters. Every time she went to the counters in some public institutions, she became stressed "just by entering the room." Her experience told her that there would always be a paper that she did not have, one extra document to "chase" and hand in, and another municipal tax to pay for their services. She would have to go from one office to another. "I'm sick of it!" she said. The person at Javno Stambeno had even said to her impolitely that instead of going on vacations she should have paid her bills. "Can you believe how impudent they are? And I have not been on vacation since 1996," she added.

Another paper came out from the pile that she was furiously going through. It was her father's documentation of substandard heating delivery services and his request to Javno Stambeno to disconnect his flat from the district heating system. "Argh! I'm so looking forward to disconnecting from them!" Katarina commented on the letter that I had started reading.

"Can you really?" I asked, because as far as I knew one could not easily disconnect from the district heating. Katarina believed that one would be able to disconnect from it, but in the near future. However, first she needed to repay all the debts to the heating plant. In addition, physical disconnection was difficult, as the system was still new to finding ways to disconnect the users due to its obduracy. She said that the district heating was a service and that the cheating company should offer and sell good services. As the service was bad and not reliable, she hoped that her family would manage to disconnect from it very soon.

I looked again at the letter, which was stamped with "October 9, 2012," the date of receipt, in the right corner, written in a bureaucratic and very straightforward way, well explained, and bullet pointed. Two reasons for their request to disconnect were stated. The first was the provision of "inadequate heating." The second was their "difficult financial situation on the verge of poverty." The problems with the inadequate heating, according to the letter, dated back to the moment when the family had moved into the flat during the 1980s. The temperature of the flat never rose above 16°C (60.8°F) during winter, and the company was, as I mentioned, supposed to guarantee 20(± 2)°C (68°F ± 2/35.6°F) by law. This had been confirmed many times by the workers from the heating power plant who came to measure the temperature in the flat. Due to this fact, Katarina's father argued in the letter, the family was forced to heat the flat by using another source of energy, such as electricity, which resulted in extra costs. The letter also elaborated on the financial situation of the household. Four household members, it said, lived off only the father's pension of 28,000 Serbian dinars (314 US dollars/245 euros), which was 7,000 Serbian dinars (78 US dollars/61 euros) per person per month. Until 2009, Katarina's father had been able to pay for the heating services even though they were not adequate. Because he and Katarina's mother, along with other workers, had been "thrown onto the streets" after her father was illegally laid off by the privatized factory, further payment for the district heating would lead the family into a greater "depression" (*dubioza*). The letter ended in a poetic and convincing tone: "By respecting the old saying, 'The wise person is not the one who distinguishes good from bad, but the one who chooses between the lesser of two evils,' I judged that the lesser evil for my family would be to disconnect from the district heating system rather than to become evicted from my flat due to enormous debts."

At the end of Katarina's father's letter, it was stated that a copy of this request had been sent to the Ministry of Social Work and Social Policy and to the prime minister of Serbia. Katarina explained that the letter had not actually been sent to these recipients but that the statement made the letter sound more important. One week later, I found that Javno Stambeno had written off the obsolete debts and acknowledged the retained receipts. Katarina only had to pay the amount that she was certain about. She still thought that the whole attitude and attempt to obtain repayment of the obsolete debts was a deception.

The transformation of the "modern infrastructural ideal" (Graham and Marvin 2001) or rather, in this case, the transformation of the relations between Katarina, her family, and the state was made visible. This further opened an issue of responsibility which became murky and unclear. For Katarina, the consequence of not paying bills was a moral dilemma between two bad choices that demanded a compromise. Of course, the topic of moral dilemma is not something new in the anthropology of post-socialist infrastructures. As Catherine Alexander identified in the case of privatization of the public sector in Almaty, there was a production of "a new kind of a moral citizen: the consumer citizen" (Alexander 2007a, 83), where the local government (e.g., the municipality) started to be the carrier and the manager of the urban infrastructures. Such social dynamics are also in line with what Caroline Humphrey showed in the case of Ulan-Ude, in Eastern Siberia, where the citizens experienced a "moral harm" after the failure of district heating (Humphrey 2003). Katarina's example brings a new aspect to these perspectives on infrastructures from the post-socialist settings. The principle of the lesser of two evils was different in Katarina's case, as her position was a product of the situation of being a captive (dependent) customer of the centralized provision, which obliged the family to choose between either having inadequate heating that they could not afford or living in a cold flat. Since the family could not be disconnected from the system at that point, the debt became so high that heating began to seem like a bad "connection" and a bad choice, or rather it could be said that no good choice was available. Faced with such dependency, Katarina and her father became morally righteous citizens on the basis of knowing how to distinguish between and navigate scales of what they considered to be "evils," which produced the ambivalence they navigated in their everyday life. A solution to their troubles was seen in making conditions (hence, disconnecting) in which Katarina would become a fully entitled consumer, like the councilors insisted that winter day at the local community office meeting.

The Captive Customers: Hope of "Unbundling"

According to Charlotte Johnson's ethnographic study of district heating in Belgrade (2013, 2018), the inability to disconnect from the heating system among her interlocutors created a problematic relationship between households and the state. Her interlocutors saw themselves as captive customers of an effective monopoly and others saw themselves as beneficiaries of the Serbian welfare state (Johnson 2013, 2018). Johnson explains that "the captive client of the heating system was produced through the principle of supply-side management on which the city's system was designed" (Johnson 2013, 159). The individuals from the local community office and Katarina felt exactly like captive customers of the state (cf. Jovanović 2019). This similarity with Johnson's study speaks about the specific post-socialist political and material configurations which made possible the utility provisions in Serbia.[10] The daily contentions around such thermopolitics of hope are illustrative examples of the hegemonic discourse of transformations of a household in Serbia. This is very visible because there was a state monopoly on infrastructural provision (Lazić and Pešić 2012) from which it was very difficult to become disconnected due to material post-socialist obduracy (Collier 2011). Through people's desire to have the heating regulated by the state and through their hope of sustaining their everyday lives comfortably, the state, RTB, and the heating plant were seen as the frameworks for the regulation of everyday lives. While the citizens embedded hope in the idea that the state and the company should provide infrastructural provision in the future, those who perceived themselves as captive citizens asked to be granted the right to become customers (Jovanović 2019).

The very enchantments (Harvey and Knox 2012) with this mod con that stem from the socialist promises set up the conditions for prospective disenchantments that I found among my interlocutors. The reason for such dispositions was precisely because the district heating offered the promise that the past care and welfare would be delivered in the future. Such disenchantments brought to the fore what these individuals saw as "the state," which was sometimes the utility company and sometimes RTB's management. For them, this was also a mundane encounter with fraud and theft and "with a fragmented state" (Harvey and Knox 2012, 530). The very failed attempts to deliver the promises of care and welfare and the ways in which "the state" was seen through nontransparent combined bills constructed the notion of a nontransparent state which was no longer just a service for heating but was also seen as a vehicle for corruption. The very performances of welfare and care that the company and the utility company enacted through the pipes were an occasion when the "incapable" state appeared. The encounters with the heating system were always occasions for rumination over expectations and the failure to provide. As the company and the municipal authorities, as I previously explained, made the infrastructural futures possible in the near future with short-term, performative quick fixes to immediately achieve a sense of warmth consequentially made the infrastructures even more prone to frequent breakdowns. Such outcomes further induced hope of unbundling from the heating system among the heating users and, at the same time, underpinned the political order that maintained it.

Even though good district heating was, for many, still an indicator of a normal, comfortable, and good life, as it was for my landlady, Katarina, and for some individuals in the local community office, the heating was not only occasionally substandard but also unaffordable, which could lead to a greater debt. This experience is shared with many inhabitants of post-socialist countries across (post-socialist) Europe (Kovačević 2004; Bouzarovski 2007, 2018) and beyond. Many residents lived in energy poverty, which also entailed a condition of living in inadequately heated homes (Buzarovski 2007). The heating was no longer an asset (*komfor* in warm flats), which had been the case in the past. In Katarina's case especially, the former socialist mod cons were part of Katarina and her family's social standard that her father had obtained through his own work during the 1980s. Today, such infrastructural connections contributed to lowering their social standard, by making them even more indebted because of the impossibility of disconnecting. Moreover, the desired disconnection would allow her family's relationship with the state to be reconfigured. During socialist times, such a relationship used to promise entitlements such as a job, a warm, comfortable flat obtained through self-managed funds (through her parents' work), health care, and more. The betrayals of these expectations were visible in the case of her parents being "thrown onto the streets," as well as in the case of the provision of the heat that was expected to be delivered.

Katarina's expectations and subsequent disenchantment came precisely from the enchantment of the past generation of her parents, when there was an investment that structured such expectations (Jovanović 2019, 49). The situation she faced also speaks about transgenerational consequences of such enchantment. As the enchantments from the past (generations) did not live up to the expectations of the older and new generations, it was now Katarina's task to disconnect the family flat from the same pipe that her parents had built through their own work (and the work of their co-citizens). Hence, her example reminds us how the consequences of post-socialist transformations are not just gendered or classed (Einhorn 1993; Watson 1993; Pine 1998, 2002; Galbraith 2008) but also transgenerational. For her, the connection with heating was a transgenerational burden and a source of anxiety and worries.

Yet we can see that the audience of the heating stage rather saw themselves as captive "consumers" of a public company who believed that the state, the municipal bodies, the political parties, and the company were responsible for the heating provision. They all embraced the care that was promised through the performances and by keeping their flats warm. All this was expected by the same people and institutions in power that were allegedly involved in shady businesses. From the users' point of view, the heating infrastructure was clearly seen as the responsibility of the heating company and even the responsibility of the industrial managers and politicians. According to the users, the logic of payment for services denoted a particular understanding of a contract with clearly delineated responsibilities: customers were paying the municipality for services, and such payments should guarantee the certain, stable, satisfying, and constant delivery of heating.

After the decline of socialism, the municipality remained the provider, while not being entirely able to offer the citizens the option of becoming fully fledged consumers of heating (like in the case of flats, which were turned into commodities).[11] This was impossible partly due to the pre-neoliberal material specificity of the heating system, which somewhat constrained the reforms, as in other post-socialist countries (cf. Collier 2011). This post-Yugoslav infrastructural legacy, which became a space for moral ruminations, was the root of my interlocutors' frustration precisely because it relied on the material obduracy of infrastructures (Tuvikene et al. 2020). The heating did remain determinant of everyday lives (Humphrey 2005), but not as a part of people's integral development like during socialism (Krstić 1982). It was rather a part of their deprivation, a space for the production of inequalities. It was a space where the "ordinary" site was turned into a site for greater indebtedness and into an unjust matter.

Since those who had power to provide heating could not offer the old relationship and provide heating as a social good in the future, and when the users could not physically disconnect for any reason (in the near future), my interlocutors found a solution in both yearning for the (welfare) state that ought to provide heating (just like in the past) and for a "proper" capitalist state. They expected a solid, constant service, which, if and when it was paid for, was supposed to provide value for money, with fair calculations of the amount of heat delivered. Katarina, for instance, used the rhetoric of individual consumer choice that assumed that the family had a right to spend its already extremely limited income in a way that would maximize the total effectiveness derived from utility services consumed. The possible choice of paying for heating as a properly calculated commodity would enable her to change the relations with the state in the long run. Interestingly, the heating system as a "modern infrastructural ideal" (Graham and Marvin 2001), constructed on a premise of universal, equitable, and public provision of basic services, was challenged by the citizens. They tried to delimitate state power by insisting on a more liberal doctrine of individual choice and their right to disconnect. By reiterating such logic of the individual rational choice, which all my interlocutors insisted on, hope of unbundling from the infrastructural stage seemed to be working to produce a feeling of liberation from being a captive client of the state. In practice, they remained even more indebted to or dependent on the state provision.

As I already mentioned, the dynamics of transformation of social relations configured through district heating, which was regarded in the past as an "ordinary" provision to the "ordinary" people (the workers) and was still remembered as an extraordinary provision of comfort and care, rendered not only moral reasoning and "ordinary ethics" (Lambek 2010) visible. What these dynamics also rendered visible was how this "ordinary" provision became less accessible and more unequal. This indicates a transformation to a far more fluid scenario in which the relationship between the people and their state had to be made anew. Having a consumer choice was the way in which these individuals attempted to make the social contract anew. Paying for services guaranteed delineated responsibilities in the future: the customers were supposed to pay the municipality for services, and such payment should have guaranteed certain, stable, satisfying, and constant delivery of heating. Unlike during socialism, when socialist morality was inextricably linked to ideologies of labor and where the moral ("ordinary") citizen was considered to be the producer, my interlocutors constructed the moral citizen as a consumer. Having consumer entitlements was perceived as potentially bringing a sense of a greater capacity for decision-making, which seemed to offer a sense of justice. They also held the state, the company, and the heating provider accountable to the ethics of provision and maintenance. They simultaneously criticized these authorities in power and asked them to enable the conditions in which they would become consumers in the future. This situation resembles what Marina Simić (2017) found in her exploration of cosmopolitan yearnings in Novi Sad (Serbia): in order to become consumers, whose rights would be guaranteed by the market, the citizens felt that they first needed to become individuals whose rights would be, again, guaranteed by the state (Simić 2017, 26). As I described in the previous section, the individuals desired the state to be the main regulating framework which also had power to delimit the citizens from those who were considered as corrupted and incapable managers. Yet, at the same time, the users accused the authorities of being insufficiently involved in such governance, and the state was also seen as a failed authority.

The encounters with the heating performances of the promise of care and welfare that I have described in this chapter show how post-socialist transformations of infrastructural provisions created new forms of political subjectivities (Fennell 2011). In fact, what they show is how privatization of infrastructures provision (and its parts) did not have to be the *only* economic, political, and social condition under which the moral citizen as consumer would have appeared, as ethnographies of post-socialist infrastructures have pointed out (Alexander 2008; Humphrey 2003, 2007; Collier 2011). In Bor, the process of individualization of the heating consumption and the emphasis on becoming moral citizens as consumers all indicate a specific neoliberal governmentality when infrastructure was still, to a great extent, a "bundle." This points more to an emergence of what Nikolas Rose (1999) has referred to as "advanced liberal" political subjectivity endowed with the cultivation of self-management techniques (see also Fennell 2011). Hope of unbundling, therefore, speaks about the ways in which the neoliberal individuals may even surpass the full realization of neoliberal policies, impeded by the given post-socialist inflexible material qualities of the heating infrastructure and significant debt to the utility companies. Such political subjectivity, built on "free to govern" values, in this late-industrial town was formed through people's engagements with the performances that promised short-term infrastructural futures. At the same time, they remained dependent on what the party politics, personal connections, the industrial management, and the state were able to make possible.

Infrastructural Conundrums and Infrastructural Visibility

As we can see, the ways in which performances were carried out on and through the heating pipes also inflected the ways in which the publics were formed around these materials and infrastructure. Through the performances of the promise of care and welfare that were supposed to be provided in the future through heating, the conditions for making the infrastructure visible in everyday life were made. What the engagements of individuals that I have described in this chapter also revealed is how the visibility of infrastructures was not *just* achieved through their mere physical breakdown. There is a widespread assertion in scholarship that infrastructures are usually "taken for granted" (Humphrey 2003, 93) and inflexible and invisible (Furlong 2011) and that they only become visible upon their physical breakdown (Star 1999, 389; Humphrey 2003) or when they are repaired and maintained (Graham and Thrift 2007; Barnes 2017). What I have shown here is that the heating infrastructures became visible *also* through a shared sense of the *broken promises* of modern and comfortable lives, welfare, and care that were supposed to be carried through the pipes (cf. Jovanović 2019, 50). The infrastructure, thus, became significantly visible (Sneath 2009), which was necessary to persistently renew its thermopolitical effects in the present. The pipes, the radiators, the nonexistent valves, the lack of thermoregulatory elements, the coal as a fuel, the material and sensorial properties of abundant heat, and the very performances of the promises and their contestations together made the heating system prominently visible. Moreover, they played an important role in reordering the relations between the state, the company, and the citizens.

As it turns out, the environmentally degraded infrastructure was suitable for the performances of infrastructural futures. It maintained not only hope among the residents but also political dynamics. The energy-inefficient, volatile, and dilapidated post-socialist infrastructure became a vital material for performances where the power of particular individuals and institutions was generated. While one "economic corpse," a remnant of the socialist past, was helping the other, RTB and the heating company configured themselves as the state powers. In this process, the heating infrastructures became not only entangled with but also essential for the business of the industrial company. The performances enacted on the infrastructural heating stage made it possible for the technical and material accretions to work. It is exactly through the engagement of bodies with this contingent, disordered, unruly, and unstable object (Kallianos 2018) that the dynamics between the state, RTB, politicians, the heating plant, and the residents became configured. Through the embodied experiences of the performative outcomes, the heating infrastructure became considerably mobilized in everyday life, becoming crucial for maintaining authority and power in this town.

Part III

HOPE FOR POST-INDUSTRIAL FUTURES

.

5

PRETENDING
Making Post-Industrial Futures through Handicraft

In the previous chapters, I have dealt with situations in which the presence of the governing powers was utterly important for the regulation of everyday lives. The reader might wonder by this point: Was there any part of everyday life in Bor that was not pervaded by the company? The answer would be: hardly, but yes, there was. In contrast to previous chapters, in this chapter, I explore the conditions in which Mining and Smelting Combine Bor (RTB) stopped being the caring "state" for particular individuals. I focus here on the handicraft organization that I call EthnoCraft[1] in order to offer insights into a group of older women who had been laid off from privatized daughter factories of RTB. These individuals became engaged with the promises of the possibility of realization of their own futures away from the prospective ones that RTB could offer.

In October 2012, I got in touch with Mirjana, who was in her mid-sixties at the time we met and who was recommended to me as a person who had very successfully managed to transfer the skills she had learned at one of the retraining projects provided by RTB. Mirjana had been made redundant and received a redundancy payment in 2006, after approximately thirty-five years of service in the administrative sector of the RTB headquarters. This occurred in the "gray" and hopeless period of the town, when redundancy was offered to many workers on a voluntary basis. Many individuals, including Mirjana, told me that the redundancies were not as voluntary as they were proclaimed to be, as significant pressure was exerted on them to leave, giving them almost no option. Many argued that the workers were told that getting a redundancy payment was a one-off chance that could easily slip away tomorrow. After she took the offer, Mirjana participated in one of the projects offered in cooperation with the National Employment Service (NES) and the Center for Transition of RTB workers, established to successfully provide new chances for the future to the laid-off workers. These trainings were enabled by financial assistance from a World Bank project. They offered the workers help to overcome the troublesome period and to become more employable after losing their jobs. Among the variety of courses offered by the RTB Center for Transition,[2] Mirjana believed that the handcrafting course would help her enhance the skills she already had. She had hopes of meeting other women in the course and potentially starting a new initiative together with them.

In 2011, Mirjana registered her own nongovernmental association for handicrafts, the EthnoCraft, whose activities I followed from late 2012. The projects were financially supported by the municipality budget, the United Nations Development Program (UNDP), some foreign embassies, and certain ministries. There were usually two official objectives of the projects. First, EthnoCraft was "the keeper of folk tradition" and represented itself as such to potential donors (the ministries, municipality, civil society sector, tourist office, and so on). EthnoCraft's primary goal was to keep the traditional crafts alive and to save the national and cultural heritage of Eastern Serbia from oblivion and extinction. The second goal was to alleviate poverty and address unemployment among socially deprived categories of people (women, youth, and people with disabilities). The products that these women made were not meant to be distributed on the market to promote social entrepreneurship, or at least not explicitly. The organization's official goal was to help them become more competitive on the market by providing a place where they could learn and realize their potential.

At the time I joined, the group consisted of approximately ten women who had been laid off from various factories. Among them were also some younger women (in their early twenties) who had no experience in paid employment. Mirjana was the president of the organization and the facilitator of the group. Jelena, Zagorka, and Danica, with whom I became close, were in their mid-fifties. They all needed around ten years of work in order to retire. Mirjana, the facilitator, was lucky in a way since she had managed to obtain a redundancy payment of almost 4,000 euros (5,038 US dollars) from RTB. This was a product of her higher position within the RTB structure. She had used the amount to "patch" the gap in working years that she needed in order to retire. Unlike her, due to the opaque and suspicious privatization of their factories, Jelena (age fifty-four), Zagorka, and Danica had been laid off without obtaining any benefits or redundancy payments. They were still awaiting the court's decision regarding whether they should receive ten monthly salaries and other benefits that the privatized firm had never paid them. Jelena was married and the mother of one teenager and one twenty-three-year-old. Zagorka (age fifty-three) and Danica (age fifty-four) had grown-up children. These women all had families to support and husbands who worked in the private sector but did not make enough money to secure their livelihoods.

Through their activities, the women mastered embroidery, knitting, and weaving and made products mostly for tourism retail. EthnoCraft was not very different from myriad other handicraft organizations in Serbia and the Balkans that had the goal of preserving this traditional occupation and national tradition. Sometimes such organizations included a therapeutic element and aimed to help women regain some kind of "normality" through their creative engagements. For instance, today there are many women's organizations in Bosnia that offer handicraft as an occupational therapy for women victims of war and use handicraft as a tool for making peace and for reconciliation (Pupavac 2010). Ethno-Craft officially offered opportunities to enable the unemployed women to adapt as workers to the new conditions of the market and to get them back to "normality" by providing new knowledge and skills.

What made me initially interested in following their engagements was the emphasis on their investment in their own futures, which was also a question of self-crafting and rendering themselves into flexible transformative subjects (Kondo 1990; Dunn 2004; Dunk, McBride, and Nelson 1996; Pine 2002).[3] By learning new handcrafting skills, other than industrial ones, they self-crafted through their involvement in such practices while awaiting the realization of the promises for their own futures, held both by the state and by the group facilitator. Looking at the temporalities of the women's actions in this chapter helps me to explore gendered and classed aspects of hope more deeply than in the other chapters.

There are a couple of additional reasons why I focus on these women. As a woman in Bor, a lone young female researcher, I encountered many situations in which the basis and expectations of relationships with men as potential interlocutors became unclear. This was reflected in the fact that during the course of my fieldwork I more frequently established relationships imbued with trust with women, with whom I felt more comfortable and to whom I found it easier to relate. Of course, this did not apply to all my relationships with my male interlocutors, as I managed to establish rapport with many of them too, and they found their place in this book. The reason is also political. As a place centered on extractive and heavy industry, Bor's social landscapes were significantly gendered, like many other industrial places worldwide (Ong 1988; Fernandes 1997; Mills 2003; Kideckel 2004; Matošević 2010). At RTB, for example, there was a disproportionate gender ratio of 1:5 in favor of men, due to the "nature" of the jobs, and this contributed to unequal access to available jobs.[4]

In addition, the privatization of the parts of RTB, similar to many other factories in the former Yugoslavia, was marked by "shady agreements, mismanagement and corruption" (Bonfiglioli 2014, 9; cf. Potkonjak and Škokić 2013). Many women were laid off from factories in Serbia when they were in their fifties and sixties, like Mirjana, Zagorka, Danica, and Jelena, and they belonged to a generation that had faced many (structural) problems. This has been documented in the whole region of the Western Balkans, where "entire generations lost their industrial jobs without being old enough for retirement and are at great risk of poverty" (Bonfiglioli 2014, 18). In addition, scholars have also pointed out how gender represents one of the main social axes along which social inequalities are constructed in post-socialist transformations. The studies especially showed that labor during socialism had its gendered component, and that women were more vulnerable to losing their jobs. The allocations of redundancies were also gendered as women frequently had lower educational levels, lacked certain skills, had time-consuming responsibilities around families, and so on (Gal and Kligman 2000a, 2000b). My decision to illustrate the social dynamics among the older women within EthnoCraft addresses all these social and political concerns and reflects my own position as a researcher. Of course, I address here only one of the possible ways in which gender inequalities were reproduced. The following ethnographic illustrations from the wool-felting course I attended at EthnoCraft in 2013 will best serve to introduce the women and their engagement in learning the new skill.

Wool Felting at EthnoCraft

An intensive wool-felting course, financed by Bor's municipal budget allocated yearly to nongovernmental organizations (NGOs), was organized by the national handicraft umbrella organization. EthnoCraft was a member of this organization, through which it had the opportunity to sell its products. The felting course was held in EthnoCraft's small workshop on the ground floor of an apartment block. We spent every working day in the workshop, from 8 a.m. to 3 p.m., for four weeks. Our two tutors, women in their early fifties, were hired by the handicraft umbrella organization and were from a neighboring town, 50 kilometers southwest of Bor. They were licensed tutors who ran their own handicraft organization.

Raw combed wool, in colors of dark brown, gray, and white, was delivered in big plastic bags by post. Since the material did not arrive on the first day, we just met our tutors and had coffee with them in the workshop. Mirjana introduced me to the tutors as "the doctoral candidate (*doktorantkinja*) who writes about us." Each tutor worked for a fortnight and they registered our attendance in their diaries. They also had a course manual with instructions for wool felting and products envisaged by the course, used only as a memory aid by the tutors. Our tutors acted very formally regarding the structure of the course and took their responsibility seriously. They earned 25,000 Serbian dinars (291 US dollars/223 euros) in total, per person, for their engagements. The tutors thought it was a decent payment considering that other women worked seven days a week as shop cashiers for the same amount, "plus you get to do what you really like." During the course, Mirjana was not always present as an attendee, but she occasionally helped us make the products. She was already familiar with felting as she had attended a course in 2009 and had the status of an official tutor of the national umbrella association of handicrafts.

During the four-week course, each of us made a couple of bouncing balls, one round sitting mat, one pair of slippers, a hat, and two kinds of ladies' bags. The larger bags were our "final projects," which Mirjana sent by bus to the Belgrade headquarters of the umbrella handicraft association that organized the training. I did not hear about the outcome of these examinations while I was in Bor, and we did not get a certificate, at least by the time I left the town. All the product was made out of one piece of raw wool that we rubbed in soap and hot water with our hands while transforming the amorphous raw wool fibers. We also used a plastic bag to cover the wet wool so we could press it firmly and rub it with our hands. The more we rubbed it, the more felted the wool became. Fifty repetitive strokes, which consisted of simultaneous vigorous rolling and pressing of wool placed within a bamboo mat, were necessary to get a proper felting effect (figure 17). Persistence and patience were essential in order to reach the point at which the product would look satisfyingly firm and properly felted. The tutors tried to encourage us when we started to complain about how monotonous and tiresome the work was. They insisted that only through practice would we master the technique.

Very few resources were necessary to produce one product: the room, electricity, the tables, our own bodies, soap, hot water, and raw combed wool. As we did not have any hot running water in the workshop, we took the water from the bathroom tap and heated it in a white metal pot (one-liter size) on a small electric hotplate placed on the floor in one corner of the room, next to the toilet. The women made sure that we never ran out of it. The hotplate was working during the whole time we were there. As a backup, we also used one plastic electric kettle (called a *kuvalo*), usually used for making Turkish coffee. The kettle was very old and slow, so we relied more on the hotplate. We would hold the handle of the boiling-hot metal pot with cotton cloth and pour the hot water into plastic bowls that we had brought from our homes. We were supposed to buy our own bamboo tablemats with which to roll the wool. Some women

FIGURE 17. The process of making felted products during the training. Photo credit: Taken by the author.

complained that they could not afford the mats from the local Chinese shop, as they were too expensive for them.[5] Our tutors brought their own big brass trays in which the wool was felted and for collecting the soapy water that came out from the soggy wool. We would pour off the soapy water into a red plastic bucket, and when the bucket was full, we would empty it outside the workshop into the surface water drain. The room was always sultry. The windows were steamy and would not open. Condensed water dripped from the windows, through which we could barely see. The workshop did not have any source of heating, so we used a fan heater, which we had to turn off when there was too much water on the floor, as a precautionary measure against electric shock.

The days were all much the same. After the second week, we were all already exhausted from the repetitive and monotonous movements of our bodies. We spent forty hours a week working, and women complained they could not manage to finish their household chores. I also struggled to manage to write down my fieldnotes, as I would return home completely worn out, my whole body aching. My hands became wrinkled from keeping them in hot water for too long. My back hurt from the strong constant pressure that we had to exert upon the mat. Regardless of the difficulties we encountered during felting, we all did our best to make the work as fun as possible. We made a lot of jokes and helped each other whenever possible. We laughed and made fun of the fact that we looked silly while felting and how tired we were. Danica, a former worker at the factory, who usually wore a woolen pullover and big glasses hanging on a neck lanyard, had a very entertaining sense of humor. Together with Jelena, she would make us laugh, and taught us some words in the Vlach language.[6] Together we spoke about daily news, national and local affairs, politics, and anecdotes from our lives, and we got to know each other very well.

While we were inside the workshop, most of our conversations were monitored by Mirjana, who would sometimes interrupt my discussions with the women, trying to push forward her answers instead of theirs. The women were also very careful about what they said in front of her. The most informative discussions for me happened outside the workshop when Mirjana was not around, usually during our break at around 12 o'clock, when we drank Turkish coffee. During these occasions, I found out that the older women did not particularly like Mirjana, especially her "personality." One of the women claimed that Mirjana was taking their products and using them to bribe her doctor at the health center. They complained about the lack of transparency regarding the donations that the organization was receiving and that Mirjana was getting money from the projects while other women did not receive anything, not even payment for their personal expenses during felting. The women were very polite to Mirjana but gossiped about her a lot behind her back. Something was wrong in the atmosphere, I thought.

Learning the Skill While Awaiting Something Else

During one of our coffee breaks, I was surprised when Jelena, who enthused me with her energy, started talking slightly bitterly about her engagements in the organization. She looked at me and told me she did not see a future for her engagements at EthnoCraft. She thought that the products they made were not competitive on the local market and that the power relationships in the town were not in favor of them. I asked Jelena, "And what do you do with the products?"

She answered: "Nothing! Last time we made products for a 'public work' project, they distributed them somewhere. . . . Our products went to the Ministry of Foreign Affairs; they gave them away as gifts to the officials. And we gave away the products to the zoo, to our tourist office."

"Did you sell anything?" I enquired.

"The tourist office does not have its own proper shop window in the town, and nothing was sold!" Jelena replied. "And even when we manage to sell products, like in Banja [a nearby spa village] and in Hotel Jezero,[7] the municipal tourist office takes 30 percent of the price."

Unlike Jelena, Mirjana, the facilitator, was much more optimistic about the future prospects on the local market. She hoped that things would get better when the products became more visible on the Internet and when the application for online shopping on the EthnoCraft website started to work. None of the other women showed any particular interest in learning how to place their products on the Internet when they attended a one-day course on this given by Mirjana's acquaintance. Mirjana persistently argued that "today you need marketing for everything" and that EthnoCraft's main flaw was the lack of a marketing strategy and of enthusiasm among the women.

Danica was determined that she would never use the felting technique in the future, since it required too much physical energy. She regarded the work as too monotonous and said that too much was invested in the products for too little gain. All of the women agreed on one thing: the time and labor invested to make one product was not worth the effort. Felted wool products were supposed to have a higher price on the market,[8] and no one could compete with the low-quality and cheap products from the popular local Chinese boutiques, they argued. Felted products and other handicrafts were more luxurious goods and women thought it very unlikely and uncertain that somebody would actually buy them: "Who can afford it in Bor?" Danica asked rhetorically, almost pointing out the absurdity of her own work. Mirjana, on the other hand, claimed that the higher prices were not relevant as they already had a target group—the RTB workers, who had good salaries. She blamed the lack of "culturedness" and ignorance of people who did not appreciate good quality products and "our own tradition."

Jelena took the opportunity to talk to me when Mirjana was not present and expressed her doubts regarding the future of her engagement at EthnoCraft:

"How can we make a living out of this when we do not have anywhere to sell it? Nothing will come of it."

"Of what?" I asked.

"From all of this." She pointed with her finger to the workshop where we felted. "Felting, knitting. . . . We are just wasting time with all of this."

I was always puzzled as to why the women then stayed on the course for hours, completing their daily tasks, felting diligently and persistently, and investing their emotional and physical resources, even sometimes pretending they were interested in learning the skill, if they all found the skill tiring, tedious, and monotonous and thought that their overall engagement at Ethno-Craft would not lead them anywhere. They thought that they were only wasting time, that their wearisome work would not pay off, and that it placed them in an unequal relationship with the facilitator. If it was not about the particular felting certificate and not even about getting an opportunity to spend time with each other (although they did enjoy each other's company when Mirjana was not around), what was it about? While I was engaged in the drudgery of felting, I kept asking myself these questions over and over during the first two weeks of the course. Then I realized that it *was something else* that they oriented their futures toward:

"We are waiting for the 'public work' project, but nothing is known," Danica said to me once. The "public work" project (*javni rad*) was the state's program offered by the NES, which was the state's incentive for employment. Its aim was usually to engage long-term unemployed citizens in participating in work that contributed to "public benefits," such as taking care of the elderly, building infrastructure, maintaining utilities, and so on. This work was supposed to be nonprofitable and nonmarketable and would be offered as a short-term, six-month state job for a minimum-wage salary. EthnoCraft, as a civil society organization, would be able to apply as an employer. Through this scheme, the women would be able to become self-employed and get the opportunity to obtain what they lacked: six months of health insurance and six months of service. Unfortunately, this would help them to accrue only a portion of the years that had to be accumulated to finally retire.[9] Mirjana hoped that the state would make a new call for applications for the projects again.[10]

While they were learning to felt, the women were actually waiting to be selected by Mirjana to take part in the state's potential "public work" project that Mirjana intended to apply for (but still did not). No one mentioned that particular project and goal throughout our engagement with felting. What I found was that through learning to felt, they wanted to make sure that they were in Mirjana's sight when she decided who would be selected to take part. Felting was supposed to be a technique that could potentially be included in the public work project and could expand EthnoCraft's product assortment in the future. As a technique, it was not essential for the realization of the new potential public work project, and it did not appeal much to the women. The women were there just to spend time with Mirjana and to prove themselves as diligent and interested workers, worthy of being included in a potential project. During the felting course, it was still uncertain whether any call for applications would be issued, since the state at that moment was nearly bankrupt and certain austerity measures were announced (Petrović 2012). It was also uncertain how many women would be employed even if this organization were to be awarded the project at all.

Waiting: Pretending and Brokering

In the practices of learning a new skill whose official aim was to help the women return to the job market, we can see how, at least partly, there was an entrepreneurial logic that led them to feel that their time was wasted: time was money, and according to their cost–benefit analysis, they saw that the investment was bigger than the profit, which made their investment less valuable. According to such logic, they invoked a particular temporal understanding of their actions through which they assessed what was worth doing and more worth the investment of their time and energy. "The fragile hope in need of permanent rekindling, that one is moving forward" (Jansen 2014b, S75) was not corroborated by any kind of tangible proof for Jelena that could offer her a sense that her engagement with EthnoCraft would enable her to feel the move forward. Jelena did not have any hopes regarding the potential of EthnoCraft's products on the local market or in the felting technique itself. She saw the obstacles as external, especially because of the disadvantages faced by their products on the local market. The women in training also assessed the productive use of time and calculated their costs. Here, time appeared in relation to their productivity, especially in relation to the market. Their waiting on the public work project was a "generalised resource" (Schwartz 1974, 843) which could have been "expended productively or wastefully with respect to the acquisition of other, more concrete advantages" (Schwartz 1974, 843).

Through their engagements in the felting training, the older women crafted their selves, their sociality, and the social hierarchy within the group. As the temporality of waiting was always defined "around expectations of who will wait for whom" (Bryant and Knight 2019, 68), the particular distribution of time coincided "with the distribution of power" (Schwartz 1974, 867).[11] Their waiting on the state and successful brokerage that Miljana could achieve affirmed and reinforced unequal power relationships within the group and implied a particular circuit of and reproduction of dependency. The women perceived themselves as having a specific twofold role. On the one hand, they attended and complied with a position of being clients, "surrendering" their agency to Mirjana while accepting the position of being exploited by her. They wanted to *appear* genuinely interested in learning to felt and as though they were dedicated to the organization. The older women were acting *as if* they were interested in mastering the skill that was officially intended to help equip them to become competitive on the market. On the other hand, they gave Mirjana the position of a broker whose task was a common one: to bring the state's short-term project "to the waiting room." As we saw, Mirjana was in a quite different and contrasting social position to the other women. While she had been offered a redundancy payment that she was able to allocate to her retirement fund, other older women had been laid off from the factories without being given the opportunity to obtain redundancy payments that could have helped them to do the same. For them, navigation of their relationship with Mirjana and pretending that they were on good terms with her was an act of investing themselves in the potential possibilities of obtaining short-term employment.

There was a lot of concealment of expectations among the women, especially regarding the navigations of the future-oriented "ends" of their engagements. According to J. L. Austin (1958), at the heart of the acts of pretending there is always a certain kind of concealment, where "the pretender must be present and active in person to effect the deception by dint of his current behavior" (Austin 1958, 276). Of course, it was not that they were pretending to "be" someone. Rather, they crafted themselves in specific power relations (cf. Kondo 1990) while they were "pretending to do" (Austin 1958). They performed to be eager to learn to felt, and they actively went to the workshop, where the potential promises were given to them every day. This placed the women in a situation in which, by expressing willingness to wait and stay at EthnoCraft (and to wait to be recognized by Mirjana and by the state), they showed particular deference to Mirjana. They were doing things so that Mirjana would take them into account. They complied with such positions while at the same time furthering the interests of Mirjana. They praised her handicraft skills, which were truly fascinating. She was able to do something for them. Nevertheless, they did not like the way she treated them. They complained that they sometimes felt humiliated but also claimed that they "got used to it." Through their engagements, their agency was minimized and centered on perseverance and on the imperative of movement forward, which "functioned simultaneously as comforting (perhaps tranquillizing) demobilisers" (Jansen 2014b, S82). A common saying in Serbian, "Shut up and suffer/endure" (*Ćuti i trpi*), which Zagorka used to interpret women's positions at EthnoCraft, exactly reflects a discourse that served as "a governmental tool that encourages a mode of restraint, self-control and self-government" (Hage 2009, 102).

I noticed that during the course, any idea that the women could be doing anything else by themselves (beyond EthnoCraft) was prevented by Mirjana before it was even discussed between the participants as a possibility. While we were felting, I began to tell the group about a project that a friend of mine had started. She had a social enterprise that gathered different women's organizations to sew linen bags for corporations in Serbia. When I mentioned this project to the group, while rolling the wool with the bamboo mat, Mirjana immediately said that she had already heard about it and, in quite a convincing tone, added "It's not worth it at all—you only earn 3,000 Serbian dinars [35 US dollars/27 euros] a year." Examples such as this were many, and they illustrate how Mirjana subtly impeded the possibilities of enhancing women's potentials. In fact, Mirjana needed the women as "the welfare cases" (*socijalni slučajevi*),[12] as she sometimes referred to them when talking to me and in interviews at the local TV station. She needed skillful women who could knit and produce and to whom she could provide protection and provision as a broker. In this way, Mirjana distinguished herself in relation to them and in relation to the public (which included a performance in front of me as well) as a sacrificing patron who took care of, as she called them, "poor women."

The group consisting of socially deprived individuals was suitable for Miljana to apply for projects on their behalf. The financial rewards for her endeavors as a coordinator and a facilitator were always calculated in the expenses of the project. At the same time, Mirjana maintained, confirmed, and enhanced her own social status while keeping the women together to craft the objects (with no financial compensation) so that their time was completely occupied by training. Her capacity to make other women wait was embedded in the property of her role of broker, assigned to her. In the end, she managed to manipulate the women's time and to provide points of access for future opportunities. Her power was also derived from her access to women's resources and skills. Governing access to such resources through "modes of soft domination" (Bourdieu 1990) allowed Mirjana to continue to be a broker of short-term state projects. She needed the women who could and had to wait (and wait for her as a broker) and who were skillful. She needed them throughout the whole year, while taking donations only for herself, winning the prizes at competitions, and applying for more donations. She offered hopes that maybe, someday, their products would be sold and that the public work project would appear, which was what kept the women in this organization. With such practices and through the announcements of the possibilities in the futures, the "waiting room" was fabricated. In addition, the women's dependency was crafted, too. The waiting room further enabled Mirjana to use the women as a tool and a product that could be further "sold."

While the women were yearning to move forward and invested themselves in the waiting room, their subordination was constituted through Mirjana's ability to make them wait by giving them reasons to hope. They were, in fact, leaving space for "the perhaps," which was an important part of their expectations. As Bryant and Knight (2019) argue, "the perhaps" and "the maybe" are parts of the expectations that are open to the possibility of surprise (Bryant and Knight 2019, 55), to the unexpected and open-endedness, while they awaken "the sense of how things *ought* to be, given particular conditions" (Bryant and Knight 2019, 58). Pretending while waiting enabled the women to keep the future open, to expect and to feel that they *had* a future (cf. Bryant and Knight 2019). While they were anticipating a sense of "moving forward," the acts of pretending seemed to be a *vehicle* that could allow them such movement, at least for a short period of time. Their practices and engagements in this group, however, were also structured by the expectations posited as normative on the basis of what they had come to experience as familiar (that is, as "normal" life in the past). What is interesting is that the women hoped for different kinds of futures than EthnoCraft could have offered. In fact, their engagement at Ethno-Craft was their plan B. They desired plan A, which was more distant and less probable in the future.

The Substituting Futures: Post-Industrial Handicraft as Plan B

One day, after we had finished the felting session and mopped the tiled floor of our workshop, Danica and I headed toward the bus stop in the Fourth Kilometer together. She expressed her disbelief that any kind of activity with Ethno-Craft would work out and said that she could not see herself making a living from felted products. She also said that she would hate selling them by herself on the market. The problem was that she would be exposed to the public: "We do sell cheese, milk, eggs, but people come to our house to buy them—they know that we are selling them!" She explained that she was not the "type of a person" who would go to the market and sell things. Immediately after this, she compared a potential future in the business of wool felting with the job she used to have in the privatized factory: "That was a job, Deana! Everything you had was safe and certain!" She used to work on a production line in the factory. Her task was to lift up coils of copper wire, put them back on the production line if they fell down, and transfer them to another line. The copper coils were extremely heavy: up to 25 kilograms (55 pounds). I asked her whether she had found her previous job tedious or exhausting. To my surprise, she said that felting was much worse but that she intended to continue with it.

Like other women who had been laid off due to privatization of their factories, the rupture had come surprisingly and suddenly for her: "Well, I would have slapped you in your face if you had told me that it [being laid off] was ever going to happen." She said that if she got any other opportunity she would immediately leave EthnoCraft so she could have a "normal job." Later on, while we were felting, she explained that a "normal" job could be as a cleaner in a primary school, where she could get work benefits and a minimum-wage salary of 18,000 Serbian dinars (209 US dollars/161 euros), or as a "coffee lady" at RTB for as much as 400 euros (512 US dollars) per month.[13] For Danica, such job positions would bring stability, which was especially associated with permanent jobs in state firms. All the women complained that to get a position in a public firm nowadays, one needed a connection, to bribe someone, or to be connected with people from influential political parties that controlled such positions. Hence, they lacked not only qualifications and skills (and their age and gender could have been obstacles as well) but also the "proper" social capital required to obtain what were considered as more secure jobs.

Danica's story is representative of those of all the older women (except Mirjana) with whom I spent time on the wool felting course. Their engagements at EthnoCraft, including their engagement in learning skills and crafting objects, and their desire to participate in the "public work" project were actually a *substitute* for what they desired, their plan B. They wanted *something else*: a permanent job in the public sector or in a state company, which was almost impossible to achieve (again). Compared to Danica's previous experience at the factory, EthnoCraft could not offer stability and predictability such as she had experienced in the past. Plan B was considered a suitable compromise due to its resemblance to such an arrangement.

Even though their engagement did not lead to a particular yearned-for goal, they still persisted in crafting objects and attending training as an investment in their substitute plan, which had the potential to eventually connect them, if only briefly, to the state, through the public work project. All women, including Mirjana, hoped that they would attain some opportunity from the NES before it was too late. Women were investing in a precarious, contingent future led by fragile hope that "a few dinars will drop." The temporality of their expectations was quite particular. On the one hand, women engaged in plan B in order to at least open a potential route to plan A. Therefore, plan B potentially brought plan A nearer to them in time. On the other hand, their plan B further *deferred* their plan A, because it prevented them from engaging in direct attempts to realize plan A. All the time invested in learning wool felting was not invested in applying for jobs or gathering finances and connections to increase the chances of success of any such applications. They accepted this kind of tension because of their subordinate social position.

Women's expectations of the state and labor stand in a particular relation to a sense of legitimate entitlements regarding labor experienced during socialism in Yugoslavia, where employment was a constitutional right and became a vital means of accessing wages, social insurance, health care, cheap housing, and paid vacations (Bonfiglioli 2013, 5). Such employment defined identities, social status, economic interests, and the "political loyalty of Yugoslav citizens" (Bonfiglioli 2013, 5). "One's place of work was the centre of one's social universe" (Woodward 2003 in Bonfiglioli 2013, 5). Job security was a crucial feature of this system (Potkonjak and Škokić 2013).[14] Studies also show that engagement in workplaces provided a sense of contribution to the Yugoslav state through labor (Vodopivec 2012; Kirin and Blagaić 2013). Nina Vodopivec (2012) provided an insight into how the process of transformation since 1989 affected women's lives in Slovenia, one of the former Yugoslav republics:

> Work is conceived of as a right, and an important role is attributed to the state, or more precisely, to the way workers imagine its role. They expect the state to assume responsibility and guarantee work; they expect to be treated as active citizens, entitled to certain rights and not just passive recipients of the state welfare programs. Work is considered a right that should be made available to all. To have work is related to a notion of dignity. Rather than being about receiving support, work is all about the contribution and the sensation of being needed. Such a perception relates to how workers perceive their relationship with the state (Vodopivec 2012, 626).

The public work project only resembled a normal job, being a mixture of employment and welfare that the women desired. However, what Jelena found to be important about the work on public work projects resembles Vodopivec's account. She thought that the public work could bring the "freedom to work whenever you feel like: you can go out whenever, to have a weekend for yourself" because in the private sector "you won't have any of that." Yearning for and expecting the public work project was their struggle to retain some kind of freedom to dispose of their own time, with dignity, in order to avoid the harsh conditions that existed in the private sector. What is also worth noting is that women remembered having had more dignity while working during Milošević's period when they still had their jobs in the factory, not quite emphasizing the rupture in the early 1990s (even though conditions in their factory became worse back then) but locating the rupture in the first decades of the 2000s.

Furthermore, older women's hope for public work was framed in relation to their experiences of the state during socialism but also by the lack of choice of having any decent employment in the private sector in Serbia in that moment. Selling the products on commission was uncertain and could not provide them with any sustainable income. Such engagements would not be a job with work benefits and a possible pension. Work in the private sector, such as being a seller in a street kiosk or fast food stand or being a cashier in a shop or supermarket, which were the only viable options, would only bring them hard physical work without any breaks during the day. This would be work without any weekends off, unpaid overtime work, no work benefits, and no vacation, for a maximum of 100 euros (130 US dollars) per month. Zagorka had once worked as a cashier in a shop, and she complained that her experience had been so dreadful that she would not recommend that job to her "worst enemy." That was why the public work project provided more dignity than the private sector and was a more desirable route for them. This was also the reason why it was worth enduring and waiting for the state projects. They saw possibilities of future brokerage on the horizon as well as some approximation of a normal job, which was an approximation "of the normative good life" (Berlant 2007, 277).

Crafting Objects, Selves, and the State

On EthnoCraft's agenda, learning and applying the skills to traditional hand-crafting was officially conceived as an investment in women's empowerment in order to activate them as self-employed ethno-entrepreneurs in the future. Even though they expected something else by learning and concealing some of their expectations, the women not only officially preserved the national heritage through their handicraft. With their engagements, they also reconstituted patriarchal gender-based roles through training, crafting, and engaging in a highly gendered traditional occupation. Handicraft in Serbian tradition (knitting, weaving, and embroidering) was regarded as an exclusively women's craft that added more value to women's qualities as daughters, wives, sisters-in-laws, and so on. The products were mainly made for the household. Young women used to make products as a part of their dowries, and as a traditional gendered craft. This activity was mostly associated with the rural economy and areas. It was also primarily regarded as an activity of women and girls that was done at home during their leisure time (hence, not even leisure time was idle or work-less).[15] Training in such tasks was a result of the association of women with "nimble fingers" (Elson and Pearson 1981). Because of the naturalization of women's domestic work in the private sphere, these skills were assumed to be "natural" and the work was described as "unskilled" (Bonfiglioli 2013, 10). Today, the handicraft products also have an artistic and traditional folk (and national) connotation.

In practice, these women, who used to be part of the former Yugoslav working class, engaged themselves in lowering their social aspirations through engagement with such nonindustrial means of creating a sustainable living. For them, becoming a cleaner in a public institution was considered superior to being a self-employed artisan. It appears that the trainings did not recognize their class by equipping them with nonindustrial skills, which could also be one of the reasons why the learning activities within EthnoCraft did not appeal to them. The women were mastering crafts associated with pre-industrial times as a post-industrial strategy for their futures. After two generations of women had been offered waged work and obtained access to permanent employment and emancipation through labor in the public sphere (in Yugoslavia), what these women were offered today was an endeavor that in the long-term future lacked the employment security and benefits attached to salaried state employment which they used to have. Such handicraft activities had no major prospects on the market and were unlikely to empower or create a sustainable living. Even though the handicraft promoted tradition, which could be seen as "a return to an idealized past, informed by Western consumer society's post-romantic yearning" (Pupavac 2010, 490), in this context, it still "echoes traditional images of the virtuous woman with her needlework" (Pupavac 2010, 490).

EthnoCraft particularly illustrates the retraditionalization of gender relations that Chiara Bonfiglioli (2013) identified in her study of textile workers in the Balkan region. She claimed that retraditionalization is not only a consequence of nationalist discourses but also a direct result of "transformations in social citizenship which occurred during the post-socialist transition" (Bonfiglioli 2013, 1). Bonfiglioli (2013) further argued that "the overall deterioration of labor and welfare rights in the region had major consequences on women's position as workers and citizens, producing the demise of the 'working mother' gender contract which existed during socialist times" (Bonfiglioli 2013, 1). Even though the socialist agenda of achieving women's empowerment through labor contributed to what feminist literature calls a "double burden" (women as workers and as mothers/carers), it also contributed to a mass entry of women into the public sphere and thus into politics through self-management (Denich 1977). Underpinned by an increasingly withdrawing state but still waiting for it to appear to provide short-term welfare, the handcrafting in EthnoCraft retraditionalized gender roles, lowered women's expectations, and reinforced the traditional division of labor.

This makes us think about women's process of *learning* in their trainings. What else were women equipped with while being involved in the future-making practice of learning the skill of felting? In her analysis of apprentice-style learning among the mat weavers in Pattamadai in south India, Soumhya Venkatesan (2010) asks a similar question which is relevant to women's engagement at EthnoCraft. As learning is a socially embedded process, Venkatesan argues that the mat weavers in India reconfirmed, negotiated, learned about, and accepted their social position, gender roles, ethnicity, notion of their own possibilities, and agency: "when people learn craft skills in a socially embedded setting, they also learn how to think about the work this enskillement will enable them to do" (Venkatesan 2010, 173). Similar to this and to what Michael Herzfeld (1997) found in his study of apprenticeship in Rethymno in Crete, the women at EthnoCraft associated handicraft with a lack of enterprise, ability, and opportunity (Venkatesan 2010, 166). For them, it represented a choice among an already limited number of choices. Through learning, they adopted the unequal power relations between women and incorporated dissatisfaction, pain, and physical exhaustion. They incorporated the fact that the handicraft was a potential impasse. Through learning a skill and through crafting the felted objects, the women learned about and confirmed the unequal power relations which lasted over time and which they saw as inevitable. Learning and making objects were done in the function of concealment of expectations and in the function of waiting. Hence, they revised their knowledge of how to endure in such power relationships in the waiting room, in which they crafted their selves. It was through such temporal understandings of their actions that were shaped in regard to their (substitute) futures that gender and class inequalities were reproduced, normalized, and legitimized.

Betrayed by RTB, which, for them, used to be "the state," after losing their jobs, these older women immersed themselves in new "ways of being related" (Pine 2002, 104). This new position also generated a new awareness of the state as being dispersed and mobilized (and neoliberalized) through the regional NGOs. While their engagement enabled them to potentially reach their plan B (public work and their engagement at EthnoCraft), the relationship with the facilitator also minimized their agency to invest themselves in the realization of the expected long-term plan A. Hence, in practice, the project that offered an incentive to entice them to become self-employed ethno-entrepreneurs and to incorporate them into the national and global economy "closed the door" to new options for these women. This time, after losing the dependency on the company, other kinds of dependence were reproduced—they became even more dependent on the state and on Mirjana's brokerage.

However, it was not that the trainings were completely unsuccessful. The facilitator had the role of state broker and was supposed to bring the work benefits to them for a very short period. Moreover, the projects offered to them were not feasible for these women because they did not fit into what they considered to be a proper way of securing an income (a salaried job, preferably in a public company) and because they did not recognize such engagement as a sustainable option. They were looking at their engagements through a certain entrepreneurial logic while at the same time also looking for brokerage to the state *and* they demanded that the state "fulfil its part of the deal" (Vodopivec 2012, 627). The "awkward deal" was precisely an action which was a product of how they reasoned about their futures, while they persistently engaged in evaluating the scales of futures that could be possible.

As the effective broker "who knows the way through the political-bureaucratic labyrinth is central to a certain regime of power" (Nuijten 2003, 3), Mirjana played a role in the fantasies of state power and operated as an intermediary who seemingly worked on women's behalf and to whom other women surrendered their agency. Therefore, all women were implicated in the construction of the "idea of the strong state" (Nuijten 2003, 15–16) and crafted themselves as state subjects in the waiting room. Their waiting and their engagements at EthnoCraft made women learn the opposite of citizenship (Auyero 2012). By pretending and by being patiently engaged and obedient to Mirjana, they learned to be what Javier Auyero calls "patients of the state" (Auyero 2012). They learned how waiting was a crucial experience of the remaking of being a citizen after the protection of the welfare state and of the company had been withdrawn. Becoming such a citizen, as this chapter has shown, occurred through micropower gendered relationships, which included an intermediary who made the other women wait on her behalf to bring the future promises closer to the present. It is through such practices of navigating different kinds of scales of futures and making their near futures possible through enduring in an exploitative relationship that social inequalities were produced. Interestingly, this brokerage had a specific scalar geography. On the one hand, the town had Sosa, the embodiment of the state who ought to regulate the heating, contribute to the renovation of the buildings, or bring clean air to the town. On the other hand, the women had Mirjana and her brokerage skills. It seems that the brokerage "worked" almost fractally and was thus unequally distributed in this town, yet involved in the reproduction of gender and class inequalities. In this example, the unequal redistributive role of the state was clearly visible. While the company at that point was a redistributive niche supported by the state, which I described in chapter 1, in the EthnoCraft workshop, the state was withdrawn and appeared intermittently while offering only limited possibilities.

If anyone were to ask the older participants on the training course what the proclaimed revival of the company and the town had brought to them, they would probably say very little or nothing. Even Mirjana felt like she was acted upon by RTB, as she calculated that she would have still been employed, enjoying a good salary like the rest of the workers, if she had not accepted the redundancy offer in the past. Unlike other women from EthnoCraft, she was more motivated. She hoped that due to RTB's revival, some other projects might work, that some connections to secure more funding would succeed, but her expectations were limited. The following chapter will illustrate how the immediate effects of staging the promise of the company's success were felt differently among some younger individuals who had more social capital than the women from EthnoCraft. In contrast to the story I have related in this chapter, younger individuals were equipped to embrace presentism to obtain employment at RTB while the high salaries at the company still lasted. The temporality of speeding up and acting faster in order to obtain good job positions certainly contrasts with the temporalities that the women from EthnoCraft had at their disposal. The drastic difference was created exactly because of their younger age, higher class, gender (mostly male), and/or social capital, which would enable the youth to experience the effects of their future-making practices sooner in the future.

ACCELERATING

"Get It While It Lasts" and Obtaining Jobs at the Company

In September 2012, I went to do my regular grocery shopping in the local supermarket. On my way to the shop, I decided to buy a freshly printed copy of *Kolektiv*, the Mining and Smelting Combine Bor (RTB) newspaper, from one of the kiosks on the Fourth Kilometer, across from the Sports Centre. As I bought the magazine, I took a look at the front page, which featured a picture of big copper cathodes in the factory. The title was optimistic and had a celebratory tone, announcing that the company made 17 million US dollars of profit in the first six months that year. As it was nice weather, I sat on the bench in the midst of an informal green and flea market stretching along the pavement of the main boulevard, where some citizens sold vegetables and second-hand goods on the improvised carton stalls. I started looking through the newspaper and somewhere in the middle, an article under the tagline "Note: Bor—a chance for young people," caught my attention. The title of the article written by the RTB public relations (PR) officer was "Better to Be First in the Village Than Last in the Town" (*Bolje prvi u selu, nego poslednji u gradu*) (figure 18).

The article stated that Bor represented "a chance for young people" who were suddenly coming back to Bor to work at RTB after a period of severe outmigration (Tončev-Vasilić 2012, 11). Bor was an advantageous environment for young people, the article suggested. The popular saying "Better to be first in the village than last in the town," frequently heard in Serbia, used the notion of being "first in the village" to indicate that in spite of the fact that Bor was smaller and a provincial town, it offered more chances for individuals to excel in comparison to the chances they would get in the bustling bigger town. This success could

„БОЉЕ ПРВИ У СЕЛУ, НЕГО ПОСЛЕДЊИ У ГРАДУ"

FIGURE 18. "Better to Be First in the Village Than Last in the Town."
Photo credit: Kolektiv, September 17, 2012.

mean that the environment of the smaller town might be far less prestigious but more attainable. A young electrical engineer, thirty-one years old, who could be seen in the picture, was represented in the article. He was someone who after two years of "wandering around Serbia in search for better life, returned to his own town" (Tončev-Vasilić 2012, 11). Driven by "hope for normal and comfortable life," as the news reported, he moved to the capital city. According to his story, he went to try to find a "better job and life" in several other bigger towns. Now, he had found a job as a head manager of electrical maintenance in one of RTB's mines. He was happy to come back to work in "one of the best companies in Serbia." He expressed his satisfaction that he was "first in the village" because, despite being a provincial town, Bor was, according to him, very advanced in comparison to other towns in Serbia. According to him, the town "lived through its revival in the last couple of years, young people have somewhere to go out, the surroundings are way prettier, and people have smiles on their faces. In Belgrade, I could never live well as here" (Tončev-Vasilić 2012, 11).

This article mentioned one woman from a smaller town in Serbia who claimed that the prospects of Bor were incomparably better than other towns and that one needed to give the town a chance. In Bor, she had also found her future fiancé. The general manager was also quoted in the article: "Bor is becoming increasingly interesting, and young people and those who are a bit older see it again as the town of the future. Well, it is enough just to pass through its streets and see those smiling faces" (Tončev-Vasilić 2012, 11).

The newspaper featured an image of three painted buildings in the old town center (under the heading "New Face of the Old Center") and emphasized the great increase in salaries at the company. It claimed that, for all these reasons, many expressed a desire to come back from all over Serbia and even abroad. It also included one person from Greece who wanted to learn to speak the Serbian language and immediately start working at the company with good prospects. The news concluded that Bor offered a chance to repopulate the town and bring torn-apart families back together at last.

On my way back with the groceries, I started thinking about the issues around the opportunities for employment in this town. This was a recurrent trope and a storyline used in staging the promise of the company's success and its promise of the revival that targeted the "youth." In this narrative, the employment of the youth also meant rejuvenation of the workforce, which promised to provide greater efficacy of work and increased production. As such, it was tangible and immediate proof that RTB was a successful company, which also contributed to creating an impression that hope of a better life could be realized in this town. In fact, many individuals known well to me, as well as their families and friends, often looked for opportunities to find a job at this company, since many of them still considered that there were "good conditions" at the company, even though they were considered to be potentially temporary. Some even immediately started searching for a "connection" rather than for a job.

The stories of how *kumovi* (godparents), parents, family friends, neighbors, members of political parties, and colleagues of the local business partners of the general manager were all good connections for employment at RTB were a common trope. Securing what was usually short-term and only sometimes long-term employment at RTB usually depended on the strength of the connections one had. The *RTBovska plata* (RTB salary) became synonymous with a high salary. It was a motive for those who were looking for employment to get *any* position at the company as soon as possible, regardless of their qualifications, education, and job preferences. Suddenly oversized salaries were perceived by many as "artificial" (*veštačke plate*). Interpreted as a potential attempt to secure political votes, the jobs at RTB were still a highly desirable goal for some.

During my stay, I had the chance to spend time with individuals in their thirties who had obtained jobs in this hasty manner. I met some of them through Katarina and Kosta, while others were Kosta's friends, with whom we all occasionally spent time. Being young in Bor was a flexible category. Those who were in their thirties considered themselves to be young. Some of them even drew my attention to the fact that under Serbian Youth Law, "youth" was defined as between the ages of fifteen and thirty years old. Although some of them were perhaps one or two years older, their jobs at the company were their first jobs. I was eager to understand their experiences better, as they were exactly the "youth" onto which successful futures of the company were mapped. I wanted to know more about the widely felt and socially ingrained sense of urgency among them. By looking in more detail into the stories of three individuals who best captured how the "work of kinship" worked for them, here I consider how social capital worked differently for them. Through their stories, we can also get a sense of how this next cohort of workers, of the generation that experienced work during socialism at RTB, narrated and experienced the specific meaning of the revival and of their work at this company.

The "Work" of Kinship

A Deceit That Worked Out!

It was 6 p.m. on August 4, 2013, two days before Miners' Day. That day was extremely warm, with the temperature reaching almost 40°C (104°F). I was watching the news on the local TV channel. Nor surprisingly, one report was about the beautification of Bor and the significant transformation it had gone through. A voice-over introduced the topic: "Perhaps those who left for abroad a couple of decades ago, aspiring to a better life, know best how significant the refurbishment of the town is and how much positive movement forward is noticeable. One of the former workers of RTB Bor who left for Australia is in Bor again, and thanks to one slightly unusual letter, she found herself at a reception at the RTB headquarters."

The next thing viewers could see was the general manager (Sosa) who started his speech. He said that "there was the lady" who had worked at RTB until 17 years ago in one of the mines, performing a very difficult job. Sosa, at first, did not give away that the woman he was talking about was the person whose words the voice-over introduced. Speaking about her in third person added some suspense in the reportage. Then he read out loud the letter written by the lady, which he held in his hand. The letter was also shown enlarged in the background:

> Mr. Blagoje, I did not manage to reach you, though I tried many times. I am going back to Australia and I am sorry we could not have a coffee together. Everything I have seen so far in the town of Bor, in *banja* [spa], and on the lake amazed me.[1] You made a miracle out of a dead town. I do not know if others can see it, but I had to tell you this. I enjoyed a meal in the restaurant at the lake where the members of staff are very polite and the food is delicious. Thank you so much for everything that has been accomplished, and you should know that Melbourne is not much better arranged with restaurants like these. Kind regards.

Then the woman who had written the letter appeared. She was sitting on a sofa, looking slightly uncomfortable, slowly reading from a note she was holding in her hand:

> I left seventeen years ago, but Bor stayed in my heart. I left one dirty and disorderly town, but now newborn children will have something to look forward to. The *banja*, the lake, the town itself—everything is so nicely done. Whether all the citizens can see what has happened to their town . . . I am not sure. Probably 70 percent of them can, and 30 percent can't. But it seems that it is necessary to step back from the town and from the country in order to see and learn to appreciate what one has.

We will return to this TV report in a bit. Keeping in mind the lavish praise heaped on Sosa by this lady, we now turn to the story of Nevena. In chapter 3, I spoke about how she and her mother navigated the risks of pollution. When I met Nevena in 2012, she urgently needed a job, having been unemployed for a year already. She was a woman with strong temperament and short dark hair, divorced and thirty years old at the time, with a five-year-old daughter, as I already mentioned. The father of her daughter sent her alimony only occasionally, and she rarely received any help from him. She had been living with her mother and daughter since the divorce.

No jobs were available for Nevena. There were only informal ones in the retail sector, where the salaries were 100 euros (130 US dollars) per month, which was three times lower than the average national salary. Her experiences were that one was forced to perform very heavy physical labor for twelve hours a day or more without receiving workers' benefits. She had previously worked for a private health and beauty retailer (similar to CVS in the United States or Boots in the United Kingdom) for two years, where, she told me, she was exploited while working overtime and not being paid. This job prevented her from spending time with her daughter. If she had not had her daughter, she said, she would have tried to go abroad to earn some money, but she did not want to go too far away. She had relatives in Australia, but she did not want to go there even though Bor was *vukojebina* (a godforsaken town, a remote and hopeless place). Nevena had a university degree in management from a private university, which did not have any credibility compared to a diploma from the state university, but she did not care.[2] She said she had just wanted to get any diploma, "just in case." Yet now she was disappointed that this diploma was not a guarantee of getting any job.

"In this town one needs to know the general manager to get a job," she told me bitterly. "All the job positions are set up in advance," even in public and state institutions outside RTB. This, she said, was because Sosa and his political party, but also other political parties that collaborated with Sosa, controlled and allocated jobs to their friends and families and the loyal party members. At RTB, she claimed, regular job advertisements were rarely issued. She badly wanted a job at the company, as the salaries were extremely high at that time. "What I would do with *RTBovska* salary, man?! It would solve all my problems immediately," Nevena smiled. She wanted to move out from her mother's flat and buy her own. Since "Sosa came to power," things had gone very well for the town, she thought, but she did not know anyone who could find her a job. Neither her mother, who used to work at RTB in administration but had been laid off, nor Nevena knew anyone who would "get her in." She said that two years ago her mother had lobbied a very influential person, "close to RTB management," for her brother. Eventually, he was awarded a temporary contract for three months at one of RTB's open pits. The three-month contracts, which were subject to renewal, were the only way in which the company was allowed to employ new workers. During restructuring, state companies could not legally employ anyone permanently, so the precarious short-term contracts were usually issued at that point. Her brother moved out from their family flat and did not lend her any money. Nevena was even prepared to drive a mining truck if only they would give her the job. I asked her once why her mother did not "pull some strings" as she had for her brother. She said that her mother had asked once, but the man who had employed her brother said that employing women was not their priority. This was not (only) due to the "nature" of the jobs. There were various positions at RTB, from administration to some easier jobs, she said furiously. After that, her mother decided not to "bother" him anymore.

After not seeing Nevena for a couple of months, I met her on Miners' Day at a free concert by the former Yugoslav popular pop band *Parni valjak*, arranged and funded by RTB. Nevena was there with her new boyfriend, who became her husband some years later. She told me she had finally got a job and was really excited about it. It was a temporary administrative job at the RTB hotel at the lake, which had been recently renovated. I had never seen her look so pleased and content before. She told me then that I would not believe the crazy story. "Oh gosh, how I got that job is hilarious, a farce! You won't believe it—so crazy! You can't believe what she did." She told me that her aunt had just returned from Melbourne, Australia, to visit. "She is so crazy, bloody queen!" Her aunt, who turned out to be the lady from the TV report, had "fixed" her a job by taking part in the appraisal of the company on the TV. "Finally!" she smiled. "It's so awesome!"

Finding a job at RTB was a pressing matter for Nevena. She needed a job immediately in order to move out from her mother's flat as soon as possible. She did not always get along well with her mother. They did not have enough means, as they all lived off her mother's pension. She wanted the job immediately while the salaries were still high at RTB. She had no preference regarding which job position would be appropriate for her education, age, or gender. Any kind of job at the company would be satisfying, even the lowest position, which required almost no qualifications. Nevena did not have very strong social capital that could "fix" any kind of employment for her at RTB, and her gender was a disadvantage. She was not an active member of any political party, and she did not know anyone in the management who could do her "a favor." As I already mentioned, her father, who had worked as a miner, died when she was seventeen.

With the help of her aunt from abroad, who obviously had her own way of doing this for her, Nevena's pressing wish became a reality immediately. Through a performance on the TV, her aunt became involved as an actor on RTB's stage, where she publicly praised the good management, the town's revival, and the company's success. Nevena's aunt had given the dramatic performance on the TV in order to be able to organize job prospects for her niece. Nevena, like many others, also thought that such RTB propaganda contained much deceit, as the representations did not actually match "reality." Nevena did sometimes feel, however, that things were better in the town than before, but not as fascinating as the company made them out to be. With her aunt's performance, Nevena turned the possibility into reality. The kinship ties had "worked" for her through a performance. Becoming a part of the company's staging sped up her chances of obtaining such a job. This involvement and the investment of her aunt compensated for the disadvantage of her gender and other kinds of more powerful social capital that would have been necessary to obtain such a job earlier. Nevena was very much aware that the "positive" prospects in terms of salary or available job positions might not remain for long. In contrast to Nevena's example, the next examples will indicate slightly different positions of two men, also in their thirties, illustrating how kinship ties worked for them to secure jobs at RTB. As they were male and had different social capital, they had more secure ways to get access to RTB.

Inheriting a Job Position

I met Jovan at the time when he got a job at RTB. He was Kosta's old friend from high school and Katarina's friend. A man with dark hair, Jovan was thirty-one years old and had just come back to Bor from Belgrade, where he had studied for a bachelor's degree for a little longer than it usually took—around ten years. Jovan was very open with me and wanted to share his story. He was not in a hurry when he was studying, he said. He came back because he knew that he had better chances of finding a job in Bor than in Belgrade. In fact, he was certain that he would get a job at RTB. Jovan's father had just retired from RTB, where he had worked his entire life. He retired because he made a deal with the management that promised that Jovan would inherit his position at RTB. Inheriting the job position of one's parent was not an unusual practice at RTB, and this company was not the only place where it occurred. For instance, it was a widespread practice that existed in many public and state companies in Serbia.[3] Jovan explained that the children of parents who were still working at RTB had priority for employment upon their parents' retirement. When it came to recruitment, the priorities for the enterprise were the workers' children, Jovan explained. If someone retired, their child would replace them, as it was company policy, he said to me. He added that the inheritance of parents' job positions after their retirement was even guaranteed by a collective contract with RTB.

This did not come as a surprise to me. Some of my older interlocutors who worked at RTB had mentioned to me earlier that either they had already been offered jobs for their children by management (especially if they had worked for the company for a long time) or they were lobbying for them. Since they used this possibility to employ their children, they sometimes referred to RTB as "a family firm." In this context, this expression did not have a negative con-notation. Unlike them, the people who did not work at RTB and/or whose chil-dren were not employed at RTB may have used this expression to refer to nepotism and unequal access to employment at the company. However, the for-mer workers who were engaged in the practices of finding jobs for their chil-dren often thought that it was "normal" and "logical" to pamper the children of the workers like that, and they usually referred to the "family firm" as "a social welfare company." Jovan, for instance, saw this employment practice as "a logi-cal step," just like his parents did, as he said. He eventually got a job at the smelting factory, where he managed the transportation of copper into the old smelting factory. He was certain that he would continue doing that job in the future for the new smelting factory when it started working. At that moment, he was working during a probationary period, and he hoped that he would get a more permanent contract after that. Perhaps in other circumstances this would have been a near certainty, but now, since the company had entered the process of restructuration, it did not have permission from the government to issue permanent contracts. Jovan was hoping that when the company finished the restructuration, it would be able to employ him on a permanent basis.

His job position did not suit his university qualifications, as he was an engi-neer with a university diploma. The requirement for the position was only a high school diploma. Nevertheless, he did not feel that this position devalued his education or qualifications. He considered that the university had merely enabled him to "expand his horizons," while the work itself could have been done easily without any university knowledge. "The concept of studying is a bit weird anyway," he said, while commenting on the incoherence between the requirements of his job and his university knowledge and qualifications. Every-thing he needed to know he had learned from a person in his office, a technical production preparation manager. It was merely a coincidence that he had a diploma that matched that position. He explained that the people who hired him had probably tried to get a match with his diploma, which meant they would have searched for a job that would suit Jovan, but luck had played a sig-nificant role too. The job Jovan was doing was "extremely easy," according to him, and the salary was "absolutely great." He said to me that he had a lot of spare time on his hands while he was at work, which allowed him to do things for himself. He managed to write stories, which he wanted to publish. He was also developing his own board game at work. He claimed that if one actually counted the effective work he did, it would come to a maximum of five days in a month. He kept smiling slightly while being ironic about the whole situation. "Sometimes I am embarrassed about how little I work there," he told me. This was, however, very convenient for him as well.

The job Jovan obtained enabled him to have a secure and very comfortable life. He still lived in his parents' flat and spent most of his salary on himself, which he considered an advantage. With this job, he saw his future in Bor and was happy to be back with his friends from high school, many of whom had come back to try to find jobs at RTB, too, through their parents. Jovan's family was one of those families that was strongly "connected" with the company. For instance, all the male members of his family worked at RTB. Jovan's grandfather had been a miner and had died very young, at fifty-six, before Jovan was born, due to the harsh working conditions in the mine. His father had a secondary education. He had first worked as a miner as well and was then transferred to the other part of RTB. Jovan's younger sister also managed to get a job, although in the other factory that was no longer owned by RTB. She obtained it through a job advertisement, but their father had lobbied for that as well. Jovan commented on this: "You have to remind other people of the favors you did for them." Nepotism, personal and political connections, and bribery were a "public secret" in Bor, Jovan explained. Someone who did not have "a connection" could pay 5,000 euros (6,525 US dollars) to someone close to management, but they would still not be certain how long the employment would last. This was an insecure way to obtain employment, since the ruling political coalitions changed very quickly in Bor. Therefore, it could not be guaranteed that one would be able to keep the job position in the future. Jovan saw all this as "an investment for the future." The bribes paid for the purposes of employing women were as much as twice as high, he said. His family had learned this from their own experience. According to what he had heard from his father, in order to get employment for one's son in the company, the requirement was that one parent needed to retire. For a daughter, the rule was different: usually, both of her parents needed to retire (if they both worked there). He thought that what his sister had experienced was "a complete injustice," especially when he compared it to his own experience of getting a job. "It is the worst discrimination," he said, but explained that it was probably due to the fact that women took maternity leave and had children, which employers did not like. He was strongly against this and wished the whole "system" would change, but he believed that one had to navigate such an unfortunate situation in order to reach one's goals.

Punished with a Good Salary

Pavle, whom I met through a mutual friend, had an interesting and sarcastic stance toward his job at one of the RTB factories. I already mentioned him in the introduction, when I illustrated the ways in which he believed that better futures of this town were made through "fake it till you make it" logic, through which the proclaimed futures had a chance to become a self-fulfilling prophecy. Pavle was in his late twenties and was a lively person. He was trying to entertain me with the story of how he had got a job through his father, who worked in a senior position at the company. He had a great sense of humor, so we both laughed at the anecdotes, which he told in a nonchalant way. He explained to me that his father was "some sort of big shot around there" (*tamo neko mudo*) and had managed to get him in. Pavle had studied the management program at Bor's university for a long time;[4] he had been a bad student and was never interested in the subject. His mother did not work for the company but for a public institution, while his father had always worked in the factory in various important managerial positions. His father had the power to make decisions about who could be employed, and he had decided that Pavle needed to finally start working because it had taken him a very long time to finish his studies. Therefore, as Pavle said, his father had placed him "in the worst possible place you can imagine"—in a dirty factory—to punish him for being a very bad student, he said humorously. He interpreted his father's decision to employ him there and not somewhere "nicer" as being due to the fact that his father needed to have a "clean conscience" when he eventually transferred him to a better (and cleaner) job position upon his graduation. This was the only way he could justify the decision to the other workers and to the other people in this town, as some would "kill" for a similar position, he thought.

Pavle made fun of the work discipline at his job at the plant and how his colleagues in the factory were drunk throughout the whole day at work. He told me anecdotes about how some workers rejected retirement and wished to stay in the factory forever. Pavle was cynical and made fun of his own presence in the factory, presenting it to me as a paradox, a comedy, and "an adventure." He was underlining the fact that he did not belong to that "world" in terms of his education, occupation, and interests and therefore, perhaps, even his class. But he was not making fun of the workers. On the contrary, they were not the target of his jokes and cynicism. Rather, he made friends with them and talked very fondly of them. He found their characters and lives so interesting that he wanted to write a book about them. He talked about the job at the factory as an opportunity to meet various interesting and funny people and to listen to their stories. For Pavle, it was rather the whole discourse and the "system" that allowed the politics of employment to exist as such. The fact that no particular work was required for the amount of money he received made his whole presence in the factory subject to his cynicism. Pavle even gave me a tour of his workplace a couple of months later, as he was eager to illustrate what he was talking about (figures 19, 20, and 21).

FIGURE 19. Pavle's tour of the plant. Photo credit: Taken by the author in 2013.

FIGURE 20. Pavle's tour of the plant. Photo credit: Taken by the author in 2013.

FIGURE 21.   Pavle's tour of the plant. Photo credit: Taken by the author in 2013.

Pavle hoped, at that time, that he would still manage to graduate from the university. He expected to receive some reward by being transferred to a better (and cleaner) office job, which would be in the administration in another part of the company. He was supposed to get a promotion based on his university qualifications. Eventually, he got this promotion while I was still in the field. Even at his new job, nothing in particular was supposed to be done, as in his previous position. Over a coffee, before he got the new job, he explained to me the "upside down" situation at RTB and how the wrong values were appreciated there:

> The system is like that . . . and I cannot fight for something better with my abilities. It's impossible. You cannot progress at RTB. Perhaps it was possible before, and now it's like that—an absolutely stupid person can be your boss. It's not like that where I work. But I know a lot of people who work in low positions with university degrees. I know a guy who finished economics in Belgrade and works in the RTB warehouse, lifting boxes, while somebody else who has a degree in management does his job in a financial department. . . . That's the situation.

While Pavle was strongly against such unequal and unfair distribution of jobs and of the potential of young people, he used his own presence at the factory to make a lot of jokes about the politics and about a situation that he could not even have imagined a couple of years ago. In the midst of his sarcasm and irony, there was a sense of optimism, which all these individuals shared. It was a kind of what I call strategic optimism, entangled with the particular temporality of urgency, deeply embedded in their engagements with their futures. I will expand on this in more detail in the next section.

Temporality of Urgency and Strategic Optimism

What we can see so far is that these three young individuals with whom I had the chance to spend time perceived formal employment in the company exclusively as waged work, a practice with exchange value. The jobs were desirable foremost because young people received good money for little work and because they allowed them to afford independent lives. The jobs, according to them, provided "good conditions" (*dobre uslove*), by which they meant a salary, the health insurance one received with formal employment, and years of service toward a pension, which were not always promised by the jobs offered in Serbia, especially in the private sector. The work of social capital and using kinship ties helped speed up their progress toward the desired goals and produced immediate effects. Their actions resulted in achieving (to a certain extent) the stability that employment promised, while the chances to obtain jobs seemed to be continuously slipping away. In spite of their deeply ingrained cynicism toward the staged revival, their optimism was strategically used to produce desired immediate effects that they struggled to obtain.

There were different kinds of social capitals that became important at different stages along their paths to employment at RTB. Before they had started looking for jobs, long before employment at the company had become desirable (and during the 2000s, it was seen as completely unpredictable), these individuals had had a specific reasoning about investment in education. Their education and qualifications, as daughters and sons of the former socialist working class, surpassed those of their parents. Education was not relevant for them at the point when they got jobs. For them, the types of job positions were not so important (even though they always desired better ones), and studying for a particular profession was not seen as an investment in a particular job. Rather, studying was chosen as something that was good to do "just in case" (Nevena) or to "expand one's horizons" (Jovan). It was also seen as something that might retrospectively look (through a kind of luck) as though it matched one's job position (in the case of Jovan). There was a sense of arbitrariness not only in relation to the types of jobs in which these young individuals were interested but also in the ways they invested themselves in their postsecondary education and professionalization, since they could not and did not foresee the long-term future at the time when they were supposed to choose what to study (Jovan in 2000, Nevena in 2001, and Pavle in 2004, all in RTB's dark years). Further education enabled Pavle to "hang out" and do other things. Nevena almost forgot about her diploma, and Jovan gained an opportunity to live in Belgrade. Jovan told me that at the time when he had had to decide what he was going to study, an industrial job was not a well-paid one. He had never thought he would come back to Bor, as people were "running away" from the town back then. The experience of unpredictability in the past determined even more the temporality of urgency that they were all enacting when it came to obtaining jobs. In addition, arbitrariness was a constitutive part of such temporal aspects of their actions. The opportunities and probabilities emerged chaotically and quite unpredictably, while the work of kinship and the work of deceit enabled more certainty.

Furthermore, what they emphasized was the value of the company and/or its contribution to the state and economy through natural resources, rather than valuing their own labor at the company and for the company. They saw that the maximum profit was made for their own personal interest produced though the smallest possible investment of their labor. This kind of engagement, on the one hand, was seen as an asset. On the other hand, such a situation was subject to mockery and cynicism. Nevena, Jovan, and Pavle all emphasized the "irregularity" that had actually been "allowed" by the politicians and the company, by which they meant bribery, nepotism, autocracy, partocracy, or gender inequalities. They also perceived that immorality and corruption were part of the "system" they criticized. However, they praised the conditions of work and salaries that that "system" could provide. Jovan disapproved of the "autarchy of one man," the administrative inefficiency of the company, and obstacles to employment for women.

Nevena, Jovan, and Pavle may have criticized the way in which the company and state institutions worked and considered them to be ultimately "out of order." However, they also presented themselves as "making the best of" this imperfect situation. They were adapting to the ways of the world and even being "caught up" a little in the situation. As they reflected on the conditions of work at the company, they claimed that the way everything functioned was "abnormal" yet favorable in the present. They themselves even became objects of their (self-)deprecating humor. They were all involved in mocking the political system and how the company worked, through which they legitimized their moral selves. All these stories of how they saw their own involvement included their positioning of relative moral noncontamination (Rajković 2018a) (of being able to see it for what it was, at least). Through such a community of complicity (Steinmüller 2013), they accelerated their chances at the right time in order to obtain opportunities, by attaching their hope for such jobs to immediate futures. Hastily "going forward" toward the random jobs was not a temporality of "pattering in place" (Jansen 2014b) or spinning in a circle (Spasić and Birešev 2012), the temporal reasonings of stalling, waiting, and/or "not going forward" that a great number of ethnographies of former Yugoslavia have detected. The different temporality that could be detected among the young individuals in Bor existed because they were engaged with performances of the revival that instilled hope for them. Acceleration of the opportunities before they disappeared was employed as a strategy to make their immediate futures a reality, in spite of the fact that the opportunities they strived for could be short term. They also did not take into account more distant futures nor even consider them in their actions. The temporality of urgency to get job positions with good salaries *while they lasted* was conditioned by the specific potential expiration date of the revival that lingered in the air, which further prompted their actions. They worried that their salaries might go down suddenly or that there was uncertainty about the very favorable constellations that maintained the high salaries at that point. The personal connections that one might have could potentially expire tomorrow. These individuals were no longer in waiting. In fact, there was no ambivalence among them in terms of attaching hope and its opposite to different scales of futures. Only cynicism existed. The workings of hope and optimism together with scoffing and derisiveness, however, were not so much conflicting orientations. Nevena expressed faith in a better life in Bor with a sense of withholding. She told me that it was not possible that the good moment would last for long, as it was not possible to predict the volatile political situation. Perhaps the company would be privatized or perhaps the copper price would drop. Jovan was an optimist without any reservations, also uttering what I called the paradox of insufficiency in chapter 1: "I'm not sure how long it's going to last. There are many rumors. . . . I believe RTB is only going to develop even more. But the governing structures need to go. I mean, maybe it is only my hope . . . I don't know. . . . We have natural resources, but nothing is of good quality or efficiency any more . . . but everything is improving."

For Pavle, as I mentioned already in the introduction, the revival of Bor was only "a marketing trick," but he hoped that the belief in better futures and such a marketing image could itself produce the very revival. While the expiration date was always present, their hope was guided and shaped by the performances of the company's success (and the hope that it would be successful in the future) and brought benefits based exclusively on the workers' self-interest.

The copper price, natural resources, and PR marketing of RTB were certainly not the only reasons for their strategic optimism. The state protection of the company and the importance of RTB for the state played an important role as well. They were all proud that RTB had built their "whole town." The state-privileged status of the company, which provided the conditions for experiencing a good living standard of the workers as part of the staging of the promise of successful industrial futures, was also justified through a wider political imagination of Bor and of its immense contribution to the state-building projects over time. They regarded the ease, comfort, and good living standard that one salary could offer at that moment as something that Borani "deserved," as many other fellow citizens did too. This was not only because such a privileged position of the company in relation to the state was seen as compensation for social suffering and the "emptiness" (Dzenovska 2020) felt in the previous decades. Rather, it was also because they saw how politically and economically important RTB company was for the whole country (see chapter 1). For instance, all of them believed and always repeated that "Bor built the whole of Yugoslavia." Jovan mentioned a widely shared notion that Bor's gold was the main factor in stabilizing the hyperinflation during the economic crisis in the 1990s. He also thought that the town has been placed on the periphery because Belgrade, the epitome of the state, had been capitalizing on and taking the profit made by Bor on behalf of Bor's greater urban development. Believing that Bor was cast to the margins, Jovan thought that the moment of the revival was the moment in which Bor could get back what it had lost and yet deserved. This historical reservoir and particular political economy of Bor's simultaneous centrality and peripherality in relation to its importance to state-building (in the past) played a great role in how these young individuals oriented to futures and how they integrated the temporality of urgency in their everyday lives.

The Performers of Industrial Work

Let us go back to the work of kinship and the meaning of the work at the company, which was an important aspect of the ways in which these young Borani made their futures. Jovan's example illustrates the phenomenon in Serbia in which job positions in the state companies became almost like an asset that could be passed onto one's children through kin relations (especially from father to son in the industrial context). The right to work in such an example took the shape of some kind of hereditary right that was encouraged by the company, where the managers themselves offered to employ workers' children and asked for their retirement in return. This arrangement enabled rejuvenation of the workforce and loyalty to the company but also the maintenance of power. In addition, RTB faced a situation in which the workers sometimes calculated that it would be better to stay at work (when they still could) even when they could have retired in order to receive a much higher salary in comparison with their future pension. The management's "deal" was their solution to this issue. Jovan's example shows how such semiformal practices turned a job position at RTB into social capital that remained in the family for sons (for which families struggled, networked, and lobbied). This was used strategically to make some of Jovan's longer-term future plans possible. In fact, all three examples show how their families became the managers of their futures, struggling to provide access to security and secure job positions. Their parents and relatives were grabbing the moment for them too. However, the positions that Pavle and Jovan obtained were more stable than anything that Nevena could have obtained at that moment—partly due to gender and class inequalities and partly because Nevena's connections were weaker than those of Pavle and Jovan.

Obtaining jobs through kinship and other kinds of social relationships, the low work activity in the factories, the informal economy in the plants, and clientelistic relationships were not new topics in Bor. In fact, Rory Archer and Goran Musić (2017) identified similar practices in their study of the history of socialist factories in Yugoslavia. Similar to what Vodopivec's (2012) study of textile workers in Yugoslavia indicated, which I referred to in chapter 5, Archer and Musić (2017) argued that the workplace in a factory was deeply embedded in the welfare regimes of state socialism as the provider of social services guaranteed by the state. They emphasized that the industrial plant served as a site of political agitation and a cultural hub and that there was a great sense of identification with the companies. They pointed out that the narrow understanding of social ownership contributed to the fact that the workers in Yugoslavia felt that only a small part of the factory was indeed "theirs." Such understanding impacted, inter alia, a common practice within the factories of favoring the children of employed and retired workers and pensioners when hiring new workers. According to them, this contributed to spreading of the informal practices that were widespread in the plants in the past. This characteristic, they emphasized, is also common among other socialist Warsaw Pact members, while Yugoslav socialism distinguished itself by self-management from the 1950s onward. In this light, we can better understand the historically formed concept of the "family firm," in which the continuum with the socialist past is embodied.

Taking into account such historical layers and economic and political configurations of the company while I was in Bor, I wondered what was actually new in this setting, then, if the practice of looking for "connections" was not a new way in which people were acting in order to achieve certain goals (and get jobs) in the future. I believe that what was particularly transformed, apart from the social and economic relations, were exactly the temporalities of actions undertaken by individuals like Pavle, Jovan, and Nevena, who desired to attain the objects of their hope (job positions) and to make their futures a bit more of a reality. The temporality of obtaining the jobs at RTB *as soon as possible* was something new. Such temporality of urgency was particularly structured and framed in relation to the company's performances of the promise of its successful future perceived as artificial and/or potentially fleeting from the company's stage. The urgency and the hasty (and, perhaps, sometimes even random) attempts to subject the future content of the progression of time to their agency (Ringel 2016, 26) points to tremendously transformed sociality and temporality in this town. Interestingly, recent literature on austerity also points to the temporality of acceleration, but of a different kind. Paul Stubbs (2018), for instance, pointed out that there is a continual frequent need for indebted countries "to 'act swiftly' on austerity reforms, that there is 'no time to lose,' or the belief that austerity measures can turn things around in a short space of time" (Stubbs 2018, 26). In Bor, it was not primarily that the capitalist logic of profit-making induced the temporality of acceleration. Rather, such temporality was induced by the perception of uncertain durabilities of the conditions that the very performances could have offered in the present. The understanding that "time is of the essence" (Stubbs 2018, 26) was practiced by them but only to obtain the benefits of the performances while they were happening.

In her study of youth in Bosnia and Herzegovina, Vanja Čelebičić (2014) found that estimation of the speed of an effect following one's action can be significantly shaped by the experience of waiting. Such was the case for the Bosnian youth in the town of Bihać explored by Čelebičić, among whom the estimation of the immediacy of effect of one's actions was important in their reasoning about their futures. Čelebičić (2014) contended that such orientations both shaped and were shaped by many other practices, relations, and engagements with the futures. This resonates with what I found in Bor, only with a significant difference of temporal understandings of actions. While Čelebičić's interlocutors' hope was embedded in waiting and being "stuck," more like the women from EthnoCraft in the previous chapter, among the younger individuals there were no practices of "timepass" (Jeffrey 2010). For Jovan and Pavle (but not for Nevena), the only time that was supposed to "pass" was the one that was about to elapse at the workplace at RTB. By condensing waiting time through the immediate effects of their engagements and by "tricking" the indeterminate futures (Ringel 2016, 29), they directed themselves toward making their desired outcomes more probable (hence, making chances work faster). Such practices were defined also by their experiences of the recent past, when their future vocations, education, and future diplomas did not make any sense in the present (the element of arbitrariness). While witnessing the demise of the Yugoslav working class, when the working conditions of their parents also deteriorated significantly, these individuals got a chance to not delay anything any longer like their parents or the older women from EthnoCraft had to.

Apart from the temporalities of their actions through which these younger individuals took part in the staging RTB's promise of its successful future, what was also new in Bor were the ways in which the meaning of industrial work was framed. The peculiar ethos around the quest for a random job at RTB that I described in this chapter, which required ridiculously little work for a good amount of money, came as a surprise to me. Usually, labor in industrial and mining areas is associated with heaviness, exhaustion, skillfulness, dullness, repetitiveness, and/or hazardousness (Nash 1979; Fernandes 1997; Ashwin 1999; Kideckel 2008). Of course, praise for this unexpected and unusual standpoint did not apply to all positions available at RTB. All of these individuals would always emphasize that many workers performed extremely hazardous and difficult jobs in this industrial complex that were *supposed* to be well paid due to the risk the work carried. Everyone highlighted the importance of the work for the overall production and the importance of the skills, knowledge, and expertise. This related especially to the endeavors of mining (at that point there were approximately five hundred miners in the company) or to the engineering tasks, which demanded particular expertise and experience. In fact, they all shared a particular awe toward such professions.

Many scholars (High 2003; Mah 2012; Strangleman 2013) have criticized studies of deindustrialization and representations of "smokestack nostalgia" by arguing that insights into the continuing struggle over the meaning of industrial work and its loss may reveal unresolved social, cultural, and political tensions that were often significantly omitted. If we look at these young individuals from Bor and the particular political and historical moment in which they lived, they did not speak about themselves as "displaced" or "dispossessed" workers. There was no "smokestack nostalgia" for the (socialist) past nor much longing for the past's future. Moreover, they did not get engaged in struggles to attain better conditions of work that used to be provided in the past to their parents during socialism. The past existed in their narration, but only as a legacy that enabled strategic usage of their kinsfolk in relation to obtaining the job positions. Rather than cherishing the ethos of hard work, there was rather more sarcasm. The fact that they could do little work for a very good amount of money could also be seen as "logical," as the increased number of workers in the company indicated "a social welfare" company that employed more people than it needed to (or maybe even than it could afford) in order to maintain "social peace" (see chapter 1). They were also guessing that maybe the outcome of having less to do had something to do with the fact that, perhaps, there was not much work at all for some. Ironically, the ways in which these young individuals articulated the meaning of their labor could even be related to a sardonic idea that I mentioned in chapter 1: that the industrial production was being performed by producing something out of "nothing." Once the epitome of socialist hard work, where the RTB workers, especially miners, at least performatively played an important part in building the state, today the work itself was seen as something that was performed. It was an image of the production. These workers became the performers of work (cf. Rajković 2018a). While positioning themselves as such, they became complicit in staging the promise of the prosperous and successful futures of the town and company, and they tried to use the conditions created by those performances while they still could. Their agency was allocated in the very process of acceleration of their chances. By engaging themselves in such staging, they enthused the power of the company as well. These young individuals did not see a direct link between their practices and such political and social consequences. In fact, such decisions and acts not only reproduced age, class, and gender inequalities but also potentially precluded their friends' and co-citizens' access to similar kinds of jobs. They were the performers of work but also of the company's success. They were taking up the position of becoming the proof of the performed success of the company and remained hopeful that the revival would last at least a little longer for them. It remains to wait and see what the forthcoming future will bring for this next cohort of workers.

CONCLUSION

Staging the Futures

The sale of Mining and Smelting Combine Bor (RTB), the former Yugoslav "giant," was a major point in the reconfiguration of the social and political setting of the town. With this change, the promises of revival made by the politicians and the industrial elite simply disappeared from the horizon. Sosa, the prominent performer, stepped away from the scene, never to return to it. With the arrival of the new Chinese owner, different kinds of futures and uncertainties appeared. The new management of the company had very little reason to provide care for the town in the way RTB had done. A sense of uncertainty lingered in the air. There were no strategic legal documents that could predict the ways in which the company intended to operate and expand in the future. Worries emerged that the company might only remain temporarily until the gold and copper reserves were all taken and then the exploited town would be cast off. The new owners, at least by the time of completion of this manuscript, had not given any public assurances to the citizens to assuage their worries. The most concerning issue was the detrimental accelerated expansion of the new mines that had already started to operate prior to obtaining official environmental impact assessments. The increased amount of mining copper and gold ore, whose quality was impossible to verify, had the potential to significantly jeopardize the environment. Anxieties over worsening of labor working conditions and land-grabbing due to uncontrolled expansion of mining arose. While some workers at the company still enjoyed the perks of having well paid jobs and many new job positions were opening up, others were publicly engaged in myriad conflicts over potential relocations (of the villages in the vicinity) and over low compensation for the expropriated land.

The ethnographic details of future-making practices that I have illustrated in this book remain as evidence of everyday life in a moment that now seems to reflect on Bor's past promises of future revival, developed in between the Yugoslav socialist past and the transnational capitalist future. The moment this book describes is the ultimate space-time of post-socialism that might have been gone by now.

In this book, the analysis of the revival and the performative promises of something better that was yet to come, enacted by the Serbian industrial and political elite, the town's authorities, and certain individuals, has employed the lens of staging to examine the temporal, material, and political effects of staging of the promises. While looking at what the staged promises "did" for and to certain individuals and how the engagements with them shaped the experiences of the present (Bryant and Knight 2019), I have provided fine-grained ethnographic details of the performative processes through which temporalities and power relations were remade. The ethnography in this book has shown that the "social dramas" (Turner 1986), which entailed the promises of the revival, welfare, and betterment, produced particular social relations, possibilities of certain scales of futures, and different "faces of power." I emphasized that, through the repetitive performative repertoire of promises and through people's engagements with them, the staged promises became a dynamic force which caused particular temporal, social, economic, and political effects in this town. In this conclusion, I will first elaborate more on some of the book's main arguments about the temporal effects and then I will address the ways in which power was produced.

The Temporal Effects of the Staged Promises

As the chapters have illustrated, the very negotiations with the performances of the promises of coveted futures and welfare in this town enabled the residents to decrease the indeterminacy and openness of the futures in order to steer the potential futures toward more desired ones and away from the dreadful ones experienced in the more recent past. Although, perhaps, the staged promises had the intention of bringing the particular futures closer to the present and of changing the way the present was experienced, it was the aspect of indeterminacy of the very outcomes of the performances and relationships established by them that also, among other things, made the performances vital to their success. The chapters in part 3, in particular, augment anthropological studies of hope as they have pointed to the classed, gendered, and generational dimensions of hope.

As mentioned, the focus on staging enabled the performative enactments of promises of revival, welfare, and betterment to be situated within a contemporary moment when performative practices played an important role in reconfiguring social and political relations. The very temporal transformative effects are visible in the chapters in two ways. First, the performances which I have described in this book *shaped* the present and also the ways in which the individuals who encountered and engaged with them contemplated and acted upon the individual and collective futures. The encounters and engagements with the promissory performances had a critical role in making particular *scales* of futures possible (only immediate and near futures) while creating a general shared sense that Bor and its residents had a future. It was not only that the past haunted the citizens through the ruinations from the past which shaped the present and the future. It was also that the futures were projected onto their revival that significantly shaped the inhabited present.

Second, the book has illustrated that the promissory performances significantly shaped the very temporalities of actions of those who engaged with them. The chapters have shown the ways in which different individuals were mainly preoccupied with how their engagements with the performers and the performances could be effective (and culturally acceptable) vehicles to obtain certain opportunities. In the situation in which the performed promises of possibilities, opportunities, and/or ideas about possible better futures were considered to be less of a "real thing" by the residents, the performances carried out by the general manager (of the then still state-run) company, local politicians, infrastructural managers, and particular individuals with power were creating "reality effects" (Ezrahi 2012, 2). They, thus, managed to capture different audiences (consumers of heating infrastructures, residents of the town, workers, the youth, those who sought pensions, and so on) who hoped for the realization of the promises staged for them—for reindustrialization, better lives, clean air, or higher salaries at the company, infrastructural care, and so on. The "reality effects" were drawn from the repertoire of narratives, which included different actors, material props, and stages that were meaningful for this late-industrial town and its destiny. While they enmeshed the experiences of late socialism (past future promises) and promises of near futures, they were there to do the work of the suspension of the ingrained widespread disbelief in the possibility of realizing the promised potentials.

While the promised transformations were presented as they were happening in the *now* or were "just around the corner," Borani assessed the temporal aspects of such promises. They asked themselves whether the opportunities offered by the "reality effects" would be *durable*, such as, for example, "artificially high salaries" (chapter 6), abundant heating (chapter 4), or the repairs of their town (chapter 2). While struggling over such questions, there was an apprehension that the performances offered some opportunities but were merely short term, provided in and for the nearer futures. As I have shown, this situation shaped people's actions and motivated them to ask themselves *how quickly* one should act to obtain at least some of the possibilities that the performers offered. In fact, the book has shown how the staged futural promises charged the present with demands to act more immediately and has indicated the differential possibilities inflected by age, gender, and class that structured the unequally distributed ability to act accordingly. Such temporality of immediacy reflects not only the populist "chronopolitics" characterized by prompt mobilization (cf. Taş 2022). More broadly, it also reflects how social relations and actions are temporally experienced in such industrial, post-socialist peripheries of global capitalism. In places like Bor that depend on their extractive resource potential (cf. Ferry and Limbert 2008) and whose future prospects are severely jeopardized by various crises caused by the process of deindustrialization and post-socialist transformations, the temporality of urgency and immediacy seem to be today even an imperative for the individuals who live there. Being a citizen of a town where the possibilities in the present are severely curtailed today means having the ability to act quickly, which might allow the individual to feel some effects of their actions in the near future.

The book has shown that the performances of promises had also caused not just geopolitical but also economic effects in the present. For example, even when the futural promises were never realized, their performances still managed to produce some powerful effects in the present, even long after the performances were finished. Chapter 1 has described the remarkable geopolitical and economic effect of the performances. As I have argued, they paved the way to configuring particular political structures that eventually resulted in the sale of RTB, the state's asset and a burden, to the multinational Chinese company. In the global landscape of capitalism, Bor represents a site where the presence of extractive mineral resources was not adequate for the town's and the company's independent survival on the global market and for the structural difficulties in reindustrializing caused by the lack of continuous investment necessary to keep the metallurgical and mining industry profitable on the global market. Having a lack of possibility of making the economic choices on their own terms, the performances of the promises of revival were necessary elements to create the possibility of imagining the possibilities of reindustrialization and acting upon them. Bor needed to "fake it till you make it" to realize some of its potential and to continue the extraction of the resources. The "reality effects" were needed both for the "faces of power" in this town and for its citizens to make the nearer futures a little more possible in the present in an environment where many disadvantaged structural positions shaped their living conditions.

After the 1990s, when both capital and people left the town, the decline of living standards occurred in parallel to the collapse of industry, and a feeling of neglect or abandonment could be perceived in the town. For some, it conveyed a sense of betrayed expectations. As a result of such historical embeddedness, the ethnographic accounts in this book offer an insight into the afterlife of what Dace Dzenovska (2018, 2020) called post-socialist "emptiness." Being peripheral at both national and global scale, the town tried to (again) become part of the circulation of global capital as it used to be during late socialism. Staging the promises of revival, of welfare, and of better futures had a strong reverberation in this place for this reason. Usually announced as serving the wider public good, the staged promises, as the chapters have shown, made use of the faulty, derelict, or scarce post-socialist stages, like the outworn smelter or dilapidated façades and infrastructures. Such (material) "ruins of futures past" (Bryant 2021a), whose renewal was promised, allowed the reproduction of not only the different "faces of power" and authority. Through them, capitalist futures and unequal social relationships were also reproduced.

The book has shown that particular socialist legacies are today still very important for imagining the possibility of having the future in the present. The normative of the "good life" experienced during socialism, remembered as material prosperity, social security, opportunities for employment, equal access to employment benefits, free travel, and high social standards, was also a constitutive part of everyday life. Due to such lived experiences of the interplay of different past futures, ambivalence, which consisted of hope and its conflicting orientation to the future, was born out of the encounters with the staged promises. The simultaneous navigation of different scales of futures was facilitated by such encounters in the conditions where a simple "either/or" choice was very rare and where, in a context of interdependence, the actors felt "locked in" by personal, relational, or institutional commitments and constraints. While the citizens were living in the conditions shaped by global capitalism, which works on predicated futures and which opens some scales of futures possible while foreclosing others, this book has shown how such conditions, as well as the specific post-socialist conditions, facilitated a simultaneous "work" of conflicting orientations toward the futures. The navigation of different scales of futures and attachments of hope to the nearer futures allowed Borani to feel and exercise at least some agency in the midst of its lack. Such mechanics in which the individuals made the near futures more of a possibility throws light on how agency in Serbia has been explored so far, which has mainly documented the lack of it (cf. Greenberg 2010, 2011, 2014).

Paradoxically, the performances bursting with the promises of better futures evoked not hope for change but rather hope of maintaining the status quo (cf. Bryant 2019; Ringel 2018). This book has illustrated that, in fact, the staging also maintained the political and social landscape, rather than facilitating the possibility of envisioning distant futures or producing a different kind of world. In fact, the staging foreclosed possibilities of existence of any kind of prefigurative politics. This is exactly because of the performative capturing effect and how the performances engaged the audience to maintain hope that life would get better (which it rarely did). This almost paralyzing effect was ubiquitous. The literature that looked at alternatives to the political status quo (cf. Graeber 2009; Dzenovska and Arenas 2012), especially in the post-Yugoslav region (e.g., Razsa 2015; Kurtović and Hromadžić 2017; Kurtović and Sargsyan 2019), provided insightful details about different alternative practices of political organizations that are certainly indispensable for opening up routes for political enactments and futural envisioning of different realities. However, in places like Bor it was very difficult to find them. Bor shared a symptom of contemporary late-capitalism, where the performances of the promises for better futures frequently foreclosed such possibilities of hope for "something else," including the possibilities of imagining different and distant futures. In the dilapidated, deindustrialized, post-socialist mining site, which used to be the carrier of the Yugoslav socialist system and where individuals were even more dependent on the increasingly withdrawing welfare state, industry, politics, and clientelistic relationships, hope was felt differently. Such hope is today a constitutive part of the experience of being a citizen in an environment in which the conditions that create the possibility of *having the futures* strongly depend on the hegemonic political, social, and industrial relations that still maintain the everyday life. Thus, this book has shown the predicaments of future-making practices in such an environment and how they unfold at the peripheries of global capitalism.

Reproducing Hegemonic Power

The chapters in this book have described how the engagements with the staged promises reproduced hegemonic power and how authorities of power were configured through them to govern everyday life. The protagonists of this book invested themselves through their engagements with clusters of promises, to paraphrase Laurent Berlant (2011, 93). The various practices of fabrication, pretending, or mimicking, which required navigation of different scales of futures to which hope attached, with different tempos of actions, had significant consequences for the multiple (temporal) appearances of different "faces of power," which also included "the state" and "the company." The individuals I have described in this book hoped for the state as an ordering device (Jansen 2015) and discussed and elaborated on the idea of the "functioning state" but also the "functioning company," entities of power which were based on welfare rather than domination (Obeid 2015; Jansen 2015). This was why, inter alia, the interlocutors of this book were sometimes willing to get involved in performances of better futures offered by such authorities of power, since my interlocutors hoped that "the state" and "the company" had the power to contribute to making desired individual and collective futures a reality. I showed how hope was invested within the frameworks of the state and not outside of it (Navaro-Yashin 2002; Nuijten 2003; Harvey 2005; Jansen 2009a, 2009b, 2015; Greenberg 2014; Simić 2014; Obeid 2015; Rajković 2018a). Moreover, it was not that the state *only* mattered through its general presence or absence or only mattered as the "state effect," a set of effects of practices that make ideological, processual, imaginary, illusory, partial, and provisional structures appear to exist (Mitchell 1999). "The state" mattered greatly when "the state" ought to have done things, was supposed to do things, and could produce "things."[1]

The chapters have shown that, as the result of the global dynamics and the specific local configurations, as well as due to the legacy of socialism which structured the relationships between the residents, the town, and the company, the "state" was often seen as an increasingly present mechanism for regulating everyday lives. As a documented legacy of how social transformations were experienced by the people who desired the regulatory frameworks of the state and the company, Bor highlights the global involvement of the frameworks of the state power and political elite to increasingly regulate the market. This trend has become especially visible during the COVID-19 pandemic, which fueled technologies of control and increased the authority of the state in all domains, as well as in various other contemporary examples.[2]

In Bor, it was not that the company "jumped in" in the absence of the state, a characteristic often delineated in studies of mining and other resource-based contexts (Krupa and Nugent 2015; Banks 2017; Rajak 2011). Rather, the state and the company "worked" in tandem through their interpenetration (cf. Rogers 2015), arbitrarily and interchangeably. Such thorough interpenetration of the state and the company described in this book should be mainly understood through how the company was embedded in the political post-socialist terrain. Interestingly, in spite of the global dismantling of job security and the political and economic insecurities, Bor offers an intricate case of the specific production of authority and power through the state-managed, rundown, resource-based company, which appeared to the citizens as a "social welfare" institution that offered some opportunities and certain protection, which was a material experience of living in late socialism. As the state power was materialized and configured through, perhaps, a seemingly divergent site—the industrial company—the book in fact illustrates Douglas Rogers's contention that there is an "increasing involvement of corporations in direct governance of human and cultural lives" (Rogers 2015, 147). The book adds to his argument that the contemporary global processes of the state and corporate entanglement also occur through people's yearnings *for* the frameworks of the regulatory state (cf. Jansen 2015) and "capable management" of the extractive companies and other kinds of power to regulate everyday lives. The distinctiveness of the example brought by the ethnographic chapters in this book is that they have shown how the interpenetration of such powers was not conducted through some rich, profitable company, which is usually the focus of anthropological studies of resource-based capitalist relations.[3] Rather, the entanglements were conducted though a derelict, corrupt, and highly indebted post-socialist company, used as a stage to make capitalist futures seem more certain and possible. While I have offered an insight into the configuration of "politicized capitalism," in chapter 1, I have also shown how, through performing the promises of the company's successful futures, the very industrial futures were secured, which allowed the company, despite being disadvantaged on the global market, to be included in the circulation of capital. Hence, the former RTB cannot (and should not) be seen as some anachronistic leftover from the socialist past. As the book has shown, it was a major locus of power where capitalist relations were remade through performative enactments.

Bor was not only a site of extraction of copper resources that were sold on the global market but also a site of the reproduction of power both in socialist times and today. By looking into the details of which material conditions and social relations were necessary to make certain hopes and scales of futures possible in the town embedded within late capitalism, the book has shown how the proliferation of theatrical performances of promises of (better) futures and of welfare became not only a vehicle for remaking capitalist relations but also a resource for attracting particular kinds of capital and for further extraction of capital. The global post-socialist peripheries, just like Bor, are increasingly becoming frontiers for the exploitation of capital where promissory performances play an important role in their attraction and maintenance. This book warns that such processes do not and cannot take place without hijacking distant and long-term futures from people's horizons.

Notes

INTRODUCTION

1. This alluded to the material from which the statue was made—wire with red lights. The wire was compared to the cheap, poor quality string lights for Christmas trees that one could buy in so-called Chinese shops, usually owned by Chinese citizens selling goods imported from China.

2. A reference to a male sexual organ.

3. The recent literature in this field is multifarious: Erdei 2007; Vodopivec 2010; Perić 2012; Bonfiglioli 2013, 2014, 2019; Kirin and Blagaić 2013; Potkonjak and Škokić 2013; Rajković 2018a; Hodges 2019; Petrović 2020.

4. The literal translation of this Serbian saying is "dandy outside, wishbone inside."

5. See further: Navaro-Yashin 2007; Brandtstädter 2009; Lin 2011; Crăciun 2012, 2014; Reeves 2013; McConnell 2016; and Bryant 2021b. The contestations over the fakes and over what constitutes authenticity, "truth," and blurring of the distinction between reality and its direct and true representation have been analyzed in the past, see Benjamin 2007 and Baudrillard 1994.

6. For reasons of anonymity, I am unable to disclose the particulars of what I call the "cultural" centers.

7. Such a notion could be found, for example, in Miyazaki's (2004) work, as argued by Jansen (2014a).

8. I thank Stef Jansen for his suggestion on this.

9. See, for instance, Ledeneva (2006, 2013) for understanding the use of personal networks, Petrović (2018) for political parodies, and Schielke (2015) for contradictory stances regarding confrontation with great promises and grand schemes. Kierans and Bell (2017) discuss ambivalence as a methodological heuristic in regard to ambivalence toward anthropologists' political advocacy. See also Razinsky (2016) for the philosophical debates on ambivalence.

10. For ambiguity, see Knudsen and Frederiksen 2015; Pinker and Harvey 2015; and Brković 2017.

1. FABRICATING

1. This line of argumentation follows the preoccupation with "actually existing success" of certain future-oriented projects that materially resulted even in urban planning forms, which carried promises of the futures. Hence, it follows Michał Murawski's (2018) argumentation of "actually existing success" of socialist urbanism, while inviting the contemporary scholarship to avoid the "dominance of failure-centrism" of socialist architectural and urban planning forms.

2. This number is according to RTB representation in the media in 2012 and 2013. According to the head director's speech given on Miner's Day on August 6, 2013, which I attended, the company had taken on a further 1,063 workers since the new management came into power in 2009 and, according to him, the average RTB salary was 71,000 Serbian dinars per month (approximately 823 US dollars/600 euros). Conversions from Serbian dinars (RSD) to US dollars in this book were conducted according to the historical exchange rates for the particular period/date by using the online converter

Oanda.com. The amounts stated in this book always refer to their value in the particular period. In this book, I sometimes provide amounts in euros only, because that was how my interlocutors expressed the values.

3. The Kilometers (colloquial name for parts of the town) do not always correspond to actual kilometer measures.

4. For analysis of experiences of labor migration and export of "know-how" of RTB Bor to the Iranian copper-processing company between 1981 and 1990, which was a collaboration facilitated through the Non-Aligned Movement, see Jovanović and Stojmenović 2022.

5. I am careful to take into account the critique of the concept (Burawoy and Verdery 1999; Hann 2002; Mandel and Humphrey 2002) of the implied (neoliberal) teleology, and I sometimes use the term *transformation*, "which has fewer teleological resonances than 'transition'" (Burawoy and Verdery 1999, 14–15).

6. After the decomposition of the holding company RTB Bor and privatization of its subsidiaries, the company operated as a single system with four main production subsidiaries: Mining and Smelting Combine Bor—Parent Company, Copper Mines Bor, Copper Mine Majdanpek, and Bor Copper Smelter Refinery.

7. The literal translation of *kolektiv* is "a collective," which refers to a workers' commune.

8. Signing potential nondisclosure agreement (NDA) contracts with the company might also close the door to academic freedom, which Rosenblat (2018) discusses.

9. The name of the general manager was Blagoje Spaskovski. His name is the only name that is not anonymized in this book as he was a public figure.

10. I thank Dejan Nikolić for this translation. This song is performed by a popular folk singer, Mitar Mirić.

11. The zoo was RTB's project, founded as a municipal institution, ran by the municipality, and directed by a party-political friend of the general manager.

12. Characteristics of boomtowns were delineated by Thomas Hylland Eriksen in his ethnography of the industrial town of Gladstone in Australia (Eriksen 2018, 74–98).

13. Only to maintain the old infrastructure with even fewer people in the town, which I describe in chapter 4.

14. The company claimed on their website that the mining and processing project of the "Upper Zone of the Čukaru Peki Copper and Gold Mine in Serbia is designed to process 3.3 million tonnes of ore per annum." It was expected, according to them, that 91,000 tons of copper and 2.5 tons of gold would be produced per annum after production commenced (*Zijin Mining* 2021).

2. MIMICKING

1. Some ethnographic descriptions and arguments that appear in the following three subsections were published in Jovanović 2018a.

2. The examples are vast, coming from, for instance, the former salt mine of Wieliczkain in Poland to the famous Icehotel in Kiruna in Sweden, where iron mines are located.

3. I thank an anonymous reviewer of this book manuscript for this valuable suggestion.

4. Part of the Nova Tržnica building was renovated in September 2015 and became a supermarket, owned by a chain of supermarkets from Eastern Serbia.

5. See also Krisztina Fehérváry's (2013) analysis of politicized aesthetics of daily life within domestic space in Hungary from the 1950s through the 1990s, where she also detects and analyzes grayness as an emic metaphor.

3. BARGAINING

1. The ambassador refers here to RTB company, not the town.

2. The metallurgical facilities of the copper smelter, where copper ore was processed, emitted large amounts of sulfur dioxide (170,000–2,500,000 tons per year), around 1,000–1,300 tons of soot and heavy metals, 250–1,000 tons of arsenic, 100–500 tons of lead, 300 tons of zinc, and 850–3,600 kilos of mercury (Šerbula 2013, 19).

3. I thank the anonymous reviewer of this manuscript for their insightful suggestions on this.

4. *Šmeker* refers to a person, usually male, who is charming, well-mannered, and sometimes flirtatious, handsome, and stylish.

5. The "Psycho-Social Study of Bor" (Beograd projekt—centar za planiranje urbanog razvoja 1978a, 1978b), based on 150 interviews conducted with the residents for the purpose of making a new General Urban Plan in the late 1970s, also revealed how the residents complained about severe pollution in the 1970s, emphasizing it as one of the biggest concerns in their daily lives. Many saw relocation of the whole town as a solution to the severe pollution, since the pollution seemed irresolvable. Such a plan was discussed by officials in the past but has never been realized.

6. The ethnographic descriptions in this subsection are published in Jovanović 2018b.

7. Approximately 1,156 US dollars (approximately 893 euros), which was almost three times the national average salary at that time

8. The arguments from this subsection were adapted from Jovanović 2018b.

9. For aspects of waiting as a result of interaction between the citizens and the state bureaucracy in a heavily polluted environment, see Auyero and Swistun 2009.

4. (DIS)CONNECTING

1. The only exception in Serbia, besides Bor, was the town of Obrenovac, close to Belgrade, which had constant delivery of heating. This exception was possible because the heating network actually obtained heat from the national electric plant and therefore it was not possible to disconnect the heating from it.

2. Out of a total of 14,200 households in the whole town, the district heating covers 11,000 flats and around 1,400 houses and heats hospitals, kindergartens, schools, and all public and private institutions. Practically, the plant heats around 680,000 square meters of household units in total and around 125,000 square meters of business units.

3. The studies on socialist architectural and urban planning forms showed how such forms did not meet their proclaimed ideas and aims as intended in terms of both their physical qualities and the molding of new ways of living and reaching intended social values (Kotkin 1995; Buchli 1999; Fehérváry 2013; Lebow 2013; Le Normand 2014; Schwenkel 2015). For an argument on how ideology appears in and is produced by material structures not straightforwardly but fractally, see Humphrey 2005.

4. Regarding unequal access to housing, see Archer 2016 for Belgrade in the 1980s; see also Simmie and Dekleva 1991; for an overview of the studies on housing in the region from a comparative perspective, see Archer 2016. For a wider discussion of unequal housing in socialism, see Szelényi 1983.

5. Free travel and consumerism in everyday life reflected the "Western" nature of Yugoslav socialism (cf. Duda 2010; Patterson 2011).

6. *Komuna* was the basic foundation of a socioeconomic self-managed "cell" of the political system.

7. Nowadays, the heating power plant delivers heat from a single source (two boilers) and uses 45,000 to 50,000 metric tons of coal per year on average as fuel (coal was used

during socialism as well) (from a private correspondence with the PR officer of the Heating Plant).

8. The mentioned person was at that time the CEO of Elixir Group, a Serbian agribusiness company. The company was privatized and was part of RTB Bor. The IHP Prahovo factory, part of Elixir Group, located close to the town of Negotin in East Serbia, produced superphosphate and mineral fertilizers and phosphorus-based mineral nutrients.

9. The ethnographic descriptions that relate to Katarina and her family, which appear in this subsection were published in Jovanović 2019. Some arguments from the same publication were adapted in the following subsection.

10. Such conditions are shared across different locations across former Yugoslavia (Jovanović 2019).

11. For post-socialist housing policy transformation in Yugoslavia and Belgrade, see further Petrović 2001; for the transformation of housing, see Mandič 2010; on the aspect of privatization of housing and changing property rights in in Bosnia and Herzegovina, Croatia, Serbia, and Montenegro, see the UN-Habitat report from 2005 (Mikelić, Schoen, and Benschop 2005).

5. PRETENDING

1. The name of the organization is invented by the author.

2. For example, air-conditioning, cash-register servicing, English language, accountancy, and so on.

3. By following Dorinne Kondo's (1990) Foucauldian approach to self-crafting in relation to power, gender, and identity in a Japanese working-class area, I see these women not as pre-given entities but as constituted through relationships and immersed within power relationships. As Kondo argues, selves are crafted in their multiplicity and are ambiguous, open-ended, in constant flux, and negotiations between Self and Others occur within discursive fields of power (Kondo 1990, 24).

4. This figure was provided by RTB's Public Relations Officer in the media and was a success according to the company (*Al Jazeera* 2013).

5. The price was 100 Serbian dinars (approximately 1 US dollar/0.9 euros) for a smaller mat or 200 Serbian dinars (2 US dollars/1.8 euros) for a bigger and much more suitable one.

6. Vlach language is an Eastern Romance language, spoken among the Vlach minority in Southeastern Europe.

7. Hotel Jezero (Lake) was owned and renewed by RTB until the company was privatized.

8. A hat was estimated to be worth around 2,000 Serbian dinars, equivalent to 23 US dollars/18 euros.

9. At the time of my presence in Bor, in 2012 and 2013, there were two conditions for acquiring a pension in Serbia. One option was to get a pension based on age: for women, when they became sixty years old and had acquired a minimum of fifteen years of service; for men, when they turned sixty-five and had acquired at least fifteen years of service. The other option was when one collected enough years of service: for women, when they turned fifty-three years and had thirty-five of years of service; for men, when they turned fifty-three years and had forty years of service. The age bar has been increased ever since. The average pension in Serbia in February 2012 was 40,003 Serbian dinars (493 US dollars/375 euros) (Makroekonomija 2012).

10. EthnoCraft was granted two public work projects in 2011. One was created only for women with disabilities. Since the state decided to fund only projects that involved people with disabilities due to its increasingly limited budget, in September 2013, only women with disabilities eventually started the *javni rad* that EthnoCraft was granted.

11. For anthropological insights into waiting, see Crapanzano 1985, Hage 2009, Reed 2011, Čelebičić 2014, Janeja and Bandak 2018, and Minnegal 2009.

12. *Socijalni slučaj* (a welfare case) is a colloquial term (and frequently a derogatory one with a connotation of pity) for people who have insufficient means and whose living standard is a result of some external cause (the cases emerging from disability, sickness, unemployment, tragic events, family circumstances, migration, and so on).

13. Being a "coffee lady" in a socially owned enterprise was a common thing. A "coffee lady" was often a woman who made Turkish coffee for the management and directors of the company and their guests.

14. The statistics show that there was actually serious unemployment in the 1970s and 1980s in Socialist Federal Republic of Yugoslavia compared to other European countries. See also Woodward 1995.

15. The products attained a certain connotation of "backwardness" when situated in urban environments, especially in the context of modernization. This is how "*šustikla*" (a doily) placed on the TV or other electrical appliances became a "rural" signifier, often distinguished by younger "urban" generations. It relates to the rural–urban division as a striking axis of differentiation in Yugoslav and post-Yugoslav context.

6. ACCELERATING

1. Eight kilometers from Bor is Brestovačka banja, a health resort (spa) that offers a couple of natural mineral and thermal springs.

2. Private universities in Serbia may be affordable in Serbia, but their quality is regarded as lower compared to the state universities.

3. The Heating Power Plant, a public enterprise in Niš, a city in southern Serbia, attracted media attention because of this and was just one of many examples in the country (Miladinović 2014).

4. Bor had a couple of (mainly technical) faculties that were affiliated with Belgrade University.

CONCLUSION

1. I thank the anonymous reviewer for their valuable suggestion on this.

2. For example, in 2018, the German government brought in tighter regulatory conditions under which China could buy a share of the Daimler Company, and in 2019 Donald Trump, then president of the United States, banned the operation of the Chinese telecommunication company Huawei in the United States.

3. See Shever 2012 for discussion on Shell in Argentina; Rogers 2015 for Lukoil in Russia; and Welker 2014 for Newmont Mining Corporation in Indonesia and the United States.

References

Abram, Simone. 2014. "The Time It Takes: Temporalities of Planning." *Journal of the Royal Anthropological Institute* 20 (S1): 129–47.

Abram, Simone, and Gisa Weszkalnys, eds. 2013. *Elusive Promises.* Oxford: Berghahn.

Abrams, Philip. 1988. "Notes on the Difficulty of Studying the State (1977)." *Journal of Historical Sociology* 1 (1): 58–89.

Adams, Laura L. 2010. *The Spectacular State: Culture and National Identity in Uzbekistan.* Durham, NC: Duke University Press.

Al Jazeera. 2013. "Osmi mart za volanom dampera od 220 tona [The Eight of March behind the Wheel of a 220-Tons Dumper]." August 3. http://balkans.aljazeera.net/vijesti/osmi-mart-za-volanom-dampera-od-220-tona.

Alexander, Catherine. 2007a. "Almaty: Rethinking the Public Sector." In *Urban Life in Post-Soviet Central Asia,* edited by Catherine Alexander, Victor Buchli, and Caroline Humphrey, 70–101. London: University College London Press.

Alexander, Catherine. 2007b. "Soviet and Post-Soviet Planning in Almaty, Kazakhstan." *Critique of Anthropology* 27 (2): 165–81.

Alexander, Catherine. 2008. "Privatization: Jokes, Scandal and Absurdity in a Time of Rapid Change." In *Ethnographies of Moral Reasoning: Living Paradoxes of a Global Age,* edited by Karen Sykes, 43–67. New York: Palgrave Macmillan.

Alexander, Catherine, and Andrew Sanchez, eds. 2018. *Indeterminacy: Waste, Value, and the Imagination.* Wyse Series in Social Anthropology, Volume 7. New York: Berghahn.

Allen, Barbara L. 2003. *Uneasy Alchemy: Citizens and Experts in Louisiana's Chemical Corridor Disputes.* Urban and Industrial Environments. Cambridge, MA: MIT Press.

Anand, Nikhil. 2017. *Hydraulic City: Water and the Infrastructures of Citizenship in Mumbai.* Durham, NC: Duke University Press.

Anand, Nikhil, Akhil Gupta, and Hannah Appel. 2018. *The Promise of Infrastructure.* Durham, NC: Duke University Press.

Anderson, Benedict. 1991. *Imagined Communities: Reflections on the Origin and Spread of Nationalism.* London: Verso.

Appadurai, Arjun. 2013. *The Future as Cultural Fact Essays on the Global Condition.* London: Verso.

Appadurai, Arjun. 2016. "Moodswings in the Anthropology of the Emerging Future." *HAU: Journal of Ethnographic Theory* 6 (2): 1–4.

Appel, Hannah C. 2012. "Walls and White Elephants: Oil Extraction, Responsibility, and Infrastructural Violence in Equatorial Guinea." *Ethnography* 13 (4): 439–65.

Archer, Rory. 2016. " 'Paid for by the Workers, Occupied by the Bureaucrats': Housing Inequalities in 1980s Belgrade." In *Social Inequalities and Discontent in Yugoslav Socialism,* edited by Rory Archer, Igor Duda, and Paul Stubbs, 58–76. New York: Routledge.

Archer, Rory, and Goran Musić. 2017. "Approaching the Socialist Factory and Its Workforce: Considerations from Fieldwork in (Former) Yugoslavia." *Labor History* 58 (1): 44–66.

Arditi, Benjamín. 2015. "Insurgencies Don't Have a Plan—They Are the Plan. Political Performatives and Vanishing Mediators." In *The Promise and Perils of Populism: Global Perspectives*, edited by Carlos De la Torre, 113–39. Lexington: University Press of Kentucky.

Aretxaga, Begoña. 2003. "Maddening States." *Annual Review of Anthropology* 32: 393–410.

Armbrust, Walter. 2017. "Trickster Defeats the Revolution: Egypt as the Vanguard of the New Authoritarianism." *Middle East Critique* 26 (3): 221–39.

Armbrust, Walter. 2019. *Martyrs and Tricksters: An Ethnography of the Egyptian Revolution*. Princeton, NJ: Princeton University Press.

Ashwin, Sarah. 1999. *Russian Workers: The Anatomy of Patience*. Manchester: Manchester University Press.

Austin, John L. 1958. "Pretending." *Proceedings of the Aristotelian Society* 32: 261–78.

Austin, John L. 1962. *How to Do Things with Words*. Oxford: Oxford University Press.

Auyero, Javier. 2012. *Patients of the State: The Politics of Waiting in Argentina*. Durham, NC: Duke University Press.

Auyero, Javier, and Debora Swistun. 2008. "The Social Production of Toxic Uncertainty." *American Sociological Review* 73 (3): 357–79.

Auyero, Javier, and Débora Alejandra Swistun. 2009. *Flammable: Environmental Suffering in an Argentine Shantytown*. Oxford: Oxford University Press.

B92. 2010a. "Dačić: RTB Bor Je Strateški Bitan [Dačić: RTB Bor is Strategically Important]." April 20. http://www.b92.net/biz/vesti/srbija.php?yyyy=2010&mm=04&dd=20&nav_id=425601.

B92. 2010b. "Dinkić: RTB Bor Će Biti Lider u JiE [Dinkić: RTB Bor Will Become a Leader in Southeastern Serbia]." November 12. http://www.b92.net/biz/vesti/srbija.php?yyyy=2010&mm=12&dd=11&nav_id=478391.

B92. 2012. "RTB Bor: Plata 600 Evra. Doprinosi? [RTB Bor: Salary 600 Euros. Contributions?]." March 4. http://www.b92.net/biz/vesti/srbija.php?yyyy=2012&mm=03&dd=04&nav_id=587761.

B92. 2013. "Koordinator UN: Renesansa u RTB Boru [UN Coordinator: Renaissance in RTB Bor]." May 8. http://www.b92.net/biz/vesti/srbija.php?yyyy=2013&mm=08&dd=05&nav_id=739650.

Bach, Jonathan P. G. 2002. "'The Taste Remains': Consumption, (N)ostalgia, and the Production of East Germany." *Public Culture* 14 (3): 545–56.

Barnes, Jessica. 2017. "States of Maintenance: Power, Politics, and Egypt's Irrigation Infrastructure." *Environment and Planning D: Society and Space* 35 (1): 146–64.

Bateson, Gregory. 1972. *Steps to an Ecology of Mind: Collected Essays in Anthropology, Psychiatry, Evolution, and Epistemology*. Chicago: University of Chicago Press.

Baudrillard, Jean. 1994. *Simulacra and Simulation*. Translated by Sheila Faria Glaser. Ann Arbor: University of Michigan Press.

Bauman, Zygmunt. 1991. *Modernity and Ambivalence*. Ithaca, NY: Cornell University Press.

Beck, Ulrich. 1992. *Risk Society: Towards a New Modernity*. Newbury Park, CA: Sage.

Beckert, Jens. 2016. *Imagined Futures*. Cambridge, MA: Harvard University Press.

Beek, Jan, Cassis Kilian, and Matthias Krings. 2019. "Mapping out an Anthropology of Defrauding and Faking." *Social Anthropology* 27 (3): 425–37.

Benjamin, Walter. 2007. "The Work of Art in the Age of Mechanical Reproduction." In *Illuminations: Essays and Reflections*, edited by Hannah Arendt and translated by Harry Zohn, 217–51. New York: Schocken.

Banks, Emma. 2017. "We Are Bruno: Citizens Caught between an Absentee State and a State-Like Corporation during Water Conflicts in La Guajira, Colombia." *Urban Anthropology* 46: 1–2.

Bennett, Jane. 2010. *Vibrant Matter: A Political Ecology of Things*. Durham, NC: Duke University Press.

Beograd projekt—centar za planiranje urbanog razvoja. 1978a. *Socio-psihološka studija Bora* [Socio-Psychological Study of Bor]. Beograd: Beograd projekt.

Beograd projekt—centar za planiranje urbanog razvoja. 1978b. *Socio-psihološka studija Bora* [Socio-Psychological Study of Bor]. Beograd: Beograd projekt.

Berdahl, Daphne, Matti Bunzl, and Marta Lampland, eds. 2000. *Altering States: Ethnographies of Transition in Eastern Europe and the Former Soviet Union*. Ann Arbor: University of Michigan Press.

Berlant, Lauren. 2007. "Nearly Utopian, Nearly Normal: Post-Fordist Affect in La Promesse and Rosetta." *Public Culture* 19 (2): 273–301.

Berlant, Lauren. 2011. *Cruel Optimism*. Durham, NC: Duke University Press.

Beyer, Judith. 2015. "Constitutional Faith Law and Hope in Revolutionary Kyrgyzstan." *Ethnos* 80 (3): 320–45.

Bhabba, Homi K. 1994. *The Location of Culture*. London: Routledge.

Bjelotomić, Snežana. 2018. "China's Zijin Mining Chosen as Strategic Partner for RTB Bor." *Serbian Monitor*, September 3. https://www.serbianmonitor.com/en/chinas-zijin-mining-chosen-as-strategic-partner-for-rtb-bor/.

Blagojević, Marina. 2009. *Knowledge Production at the Semiperiphery: A Gender Perspective*. Beograd: Institut za kriminološka i sociološka istraživanja.

Bloch, Ernst. 1986. *The Principle of Hope*. London: Blackwell.

Boholm, Åsa, and Hervé Corvellec. 2011. "A Relational Theory of Risk." *Journal of Risk Research* 14 (2): 175–90.

Bonfiglioli, Chiara. 2013. "Gendering Social Citizenship: Textile Workers in Post-Yugoslav States." CITSEE Working Paper Series, School of Law, University of Edinburgh. https://papers.ssrn.com/sol3/papers.cfm?abstract_id=2388858.

Bonfiglioli, Chiara. 2014. "Gender, Labour and Precarity in the South East European Periphery: The Case of Textile Workers in Štip." *Contemporary Southeastern Europe* 1 (2): 7–23.

Bonfiglioli, Chiara. 2019. *Women and Industry in the Balkans: The Rise and Fall of the Yugoslav Textile Sector*. London: Tauris.

Bourdieu, Pierre. 1990. *The Logic of Practice*. Stanford, CA: Stanford University Press.

Bouzarovski, Stefan. 2007. *Energy Poverty in Eastern Europe: Hidden Geographies of Deprivation*. London: Routledge.

Bouzarovski, Stefan. 2018. *Energy Poverty: (Dis)Assembling Europe's Infrastructural Divide*. Cham, Switzerland: Palgrave Macmillan.

Boyer, Dominic. 2006. "Ostalgie and the Politics of the Future in Eastern Germany." *Public Culture* 18 (2): 361–81.

Boyer, Dominic, and Alexei Yurchak. 2010. "American Stiob: Or, What Late-Socialist Aesthetics of Parody Reveal about Contemporary Political Culture in the West." *Cultural Anthropology* 25 (2): 179–221.

Boym, Svetlana. 2002. *The Future of Nostalgia*. New York: Basic Books.

Brandtstädter, Susanne. 2009. "Fakes: Fraud, Value-Anxiety, and the Politics of Sincerity." In *Ethnographies of Moral Reasoning*, edited by Karen Skyles, 139–60. New York: Palgrave Macmillan.

Brkić, Miša. 2019. "Koliko Nas Koštaju Trovači u Boru [How Much Do the Poisoners Cost Us in Bor]." *Danas*, October 29. https://www.danas.rs/dijalog/licni-stavovi/koliko-nas-kostaju-trovaci-u-boru/.

Brković, Čarna. 2017. *Managing Ambiguity: How Clientelism, Citizenship and Power Shapes Personhood in Bosnia and Herzegovina*. Easa Series, 31. New York: Berghahn.

Bryant, Rebecca. 2019. "The Stubborn Stasis of the Status Quo." In "Orientations to the Future," edited by Rebecca Bryant and Daniel M. Knight. *American Ethnologist*, March 8. http://americanethnologist.org/features/collections/orientations-to-the-future/the-stubborn-stasis-of-the-status-quo.

Bryant, Rebecca. 2021a. "In the Ruins of Futures Past: Potentiality, Planning and the Contested Revival of Cyprus's Ghost City." Online Lecture, October 28, Max Planck Institute for the Study of Religious and Ethnic Diversity, Göttingen, Germany.

Bryant, Rebecca. 2021b. "Sovereignty in Drag: On Fakes, Foreclosure, and Unbecoming States." *Cultural Anthropology* 26 (1): 52–82.

Bryant, Rebecca, and Daniel M. Knight. 2019. *The Anthropology of the Future*. New Departures in Anthropology. Cambridge: Cambridge University Press.

Bryson, Lois, Kathleen McPhillips, and Kathryn Robinson. 2001. "Turning Public Issues into Private Troubles: Lead Contamination, Domestic Labor, and the Exploitation of Women's Unpaid Labor in Australia." *Gender and Society* 15 (5): 754–72.

Bubandt, Nils. 2009. "From the Enemy's Point of View: Violence, Empathy, and the Ethnography of Fakes." *Cultural Anthropology* 24 (3): 553–88.

Buchli, Victor. 1999. *An Archaeology of Socialism*. Oxford: Berg.

Buchli, Victor. 2007. "Astana: Materiality and the City." In *Urban Life in Post-Soviet Central Asia*, edited by Catherine Alexander, Victor Buchli, and Caroline Humphrey, 40–70. London: University College London Press.

Buchli, Victor. 2013. *An Anthropology of Architecture*. New York: Bloomsbury Academic.

Burawoy, Michael, and Katherine Verdery, eds. 1999. *Uncertain Transition: Ethnographies of Change in the Postsocialist World*. Lanham, MD: Rowman and Littlefield.

Burtynsky, Edward. 2007. *Quarries*. Göttingen: Steidl.

Butler, Judith. 1990. *Gender Trouble: Feminism and the Subversion of Identity*. Thinking Gender. New York: Routledge.

Čelebičić, Vanja. 2014. "'Waiting Is Hoping': Future and Youth in a Bosnian Border Town." Master's thesis, University of Manchester.

Chesnokov, Ivan. 2018. "No Future in Karabash, One of Russia's Most Polluted Towns." *openDemocracy*, January 18. https://www.opendemocracy.net/en/odr/no-future-in-karabash/.

Chu, Julie Y. 2014. "When Infrastructures Attack: The Workings of Disrepair in China." *American Ethnologist* 41 (2): 351–67.

Cocović-Krstić, Mirjana. 1990. "Privredni razvoj opštine Bor bez Rudarsko-topioničarskog Basena Bor u periodu 1965–1988." *Razvitak*, 14–25.

Collier, Stephen J. 2011. *Post-Soviet Social: Neoliberalism, Social Modernity, Biopolitics*. Princeton, NJ: Princeton University Press.

Crăciun, Magdalena. 2012. "Rethinking Fakes, Authenticating Selves." *Journal of the Royal Anthropological Institute* 18 (4): 846–63.

Crăciun, Magdalena. 2014. *Material Culture and Authenticity: Fake Branded Fashion in Europe*. Materializing Culture. London: Bloomsbury.

Crapanzano, Vincent. 1985. *Waiting: The Whites of South Africa*. New York: Random House.

Crapanzano, Vincent. 2004. *Imaginative Horizons: An Essay in Literary-Philosophical Anthropology*. Chicago: University of Chicago Press.

Cross, Jamie. 2014. *Dream Zones: Anticipating Capitalism and Development in India*. London: Pluto.

CRTA. 2021. "Bor i zvanično industrijski kontaminirano područje [Bor Officially Industrially Contaminated Area]." June 28. https://crta.rs/gradjani_imaju_moc/bor-i-zvanicno-industrijski-kontaminirano-podrucje/.

Cushman, Thomas. 2004. "Anthropology and Genocide in the Balkans: An Analysis of Conceptual Practices of Power." *Anthropological Theory* 4 (1): 5–28.

Cvetanović, Ninoslav. 2005. *Bakar u svetu* [Copper in the World]. Beograd: Nauka.

Đaković, Petrica. 2020. "Na političkom tržištu sva roba je falš [On the Political Market All Products Are Fake]." *NIN*, May 28.

Dalakoglou, Dimitris, and Penny Harvey. 2012. "Roads and Anthropology: Ethnographic Perspectives on Space, Time and (Im)Mobility." *Mobilities* 7 (4): 459–65.

Daly, Tom. 2017. "Gold Companies Take a Shine to China's Silk Road." *Reuters*, September 24. https://www.reuters.com/article/china-metals-gold-idUSL4N1M5089.

Das, Veena, and Deborah Poole, eds. 2004. *Anthropology in the Margins of the State.* Santa Fe, NM: School of American Research Press.

Denich, Bette. 1977. "Women, Work and Power in Modern Yugoslavia." In *Sexual Stratification*, edited by Alice Schlegel, 215–44. New York: Columbia University Press.

Denich, Bette. 1994. "Dismembering Yugoslavia: Nationalist Ideologies and the Symbolic Revival of Genocide." *American Ethnologist* 21 (2): 367–90.

Đorđević, Dina. 2021. "Za zagađenje vazduha u Boru kompanija Zidin kažnjena sa milion Dinara [For Air Pollution in Bor Zijin Company Punished with Million Dinars]." *CINS*, November 16. https://www.cins.rs/za-zagadjenje-vazduha-u-boru-kompanija-zidjin-kaznjena-sa-milion-dinara/.

Dostaler, Ned. 2017. "On Hope and Indeterminacy." Member Voices. *Fieldsights*, June 8. https://culanth.org/fieldsights/on-hope-and-indeterminacy.

Douglas, Mary, and Aaron Wildavsky. 1983. *Risk and Culture: An Essay on the Selection of Technological and Environmental Dangers.* Berkeley: University of California Press.

Dragojlo, Saša. 2021. "'Like Prisoners': Chinese Workers in Serbia Complain of Exploitation." *BIRN*, January 26. https://balkaninsight.com/2021/01/26/like-prisoners-chinese-workers-in-serbia-complain-of-exploitation/.

Duda, Igor. 2010. *Pronađeno blagostanje: svakodnevni život i potrošačka kultura u Hrvatskoj 1970-Ih i 1980-Ih* [Wellbeing Found: Everyday Life and Consumer Culture in Croatia in the 1970s and 1980s]. Zagreb: Srednja Europa.

Dunk, Thomas, Stephen McBride, and Randle W. Nelson, eds. 1996. *The Training Trap: Ideology, Training and the Labour Market.* Vol. 11. Halifax, NS: Fernwood.

Dunn, Elizabeth C. 2004. *Privatizing Poland: Baby Food, Big Business, and the Remaking of Labor.* Ithaca, NY: Cornell University Press.

Đurašović, Aleksandra. 2016. *Ideology, Political Transitions and the City: The Case of Mostar, Bosnia and Herzegovina.* New York: Routledge.

Dzenovska, Dace. 2018. "Emptiness and Its Futures: Staying and Leaving as Tactics of Life in Latvia." *Focaal* 2018 (80): 16–29.

Dzenovska, Dace. 2020. "Emptiness: Capitalism without People in the Latvian Countryside." *American Ethnologist* 47 (1): 10–26.

Dzenovska, Dace, and Iván Arenas. 2012. "Don't Fence Me in: Barricade Sociality and Political Struggles in Mexico and Latvia." *Comparative Studies in Society and History* 54 (3): 644–78.

Edelstein, Michael R. 1988. *Contaminated Communities: The Social and Psychological Impacts of Residential Toxic Exposure.* Boulder, CO: Westview.

Edwards, Paul N. 2003. "Infrastructure and Modernity: Force, Time, and Social Organization in the History of Sociotechnical Systems." *Modernity and Technology* 1: 185–226.

Einhorn, Barbara. 1993. *Cinderella Goes to Market: Citizenship, Gender, and Women's Movements in East Central Europe.* London: Verso.

Elson, Diane, and Ruth Pearson. 1981. "'Nimble Fingers Make Cheap Workers': An Analysis of Women's Employment in Third World Export Manufacturing." *Feminist Review* 7 (1): 87–107.

Empson, Rebecca. 2018. "Claiming Resources, Honouring Debts: The Cosmoeconomics of Mongolia's Mineral Economy." *Ethnos* 84 (2): 263–82.

Enslev, Lea, Lykke Mirsal, and Brit Ross Winthereik. 2018. "Anticipatory Infrastructural Practices: The Coming of Electricity in Rural Kenya." *Energy Research and Social Science* 44: 130–37.

Erdei, Ildiko. 2007. "Dimenzije ekonomije—prilog promišljanju privatizacije kao sociokulturne transformacije [Dimensions of Economy—Contribution towards Thinking about Privatization as Socio-Cultural Transformation]." In *Antropologija postsocijalizma—Zbornik Radova*, edited by V. Ribić, 76–127. Beograd: Srpski genealoški centar.

Eriksen, Thomas Hylland. 2018. *Boomtown: Runaway Globalisation on the Queensland Coast*. London: Pluto.

Eriksen, Thomas Hylland, and Elisabeth Schober. 2018. "Economics of Growth or Ecologies of Survival?" *Ethnos* 83 (3): 416–606.

European Commission. 2016. "EU Je poduzeo pravne korake protiv ograničenja izvoza kineskih sirovina [EU Takes Legal Action against Limitation of Export of Chinese Minerals]." July 19. https://ec.europa.eu/commission/presscorner/detail/hr/IP_16_2581.

Evans, Gillian. 2020. "Introduction." In *Post-Industrial Precarity: New Ethnographies of Urban Lives in Uncertain Times*, edited by Gillian Evans. Wilmington, DE: Vernon.

Ezrahi, Yaron. 2012. *Imagined Democracies: Necessary Political Fictions*. Cambridge: Cambridge University Press.

Fehérváry, Krisztina. 2002. "American Kitchens, Luxury Bathrooms, and the Search for a 'Normal' Life in Postsocialist Hungary." *Ethnos* 67 (3): 369–400.

Fehérváry, Krisztina. 2013. *Politics in Color and Concrete: Socialist Materialities and the Middle Class in Hungary*. Bloomington: Indiana University Press.

Fennell, Catherine. 2011. "'Project Heat' and Sensory Politics in Redeveloping Chicago Public Housing." *Ethnography* 12 (1): 40–64.

Fennell, Catherine. 2015. *Last Project Standing: Civics and Sympathy in Post-Welfare Chicago*. A Quadrant Book. Minneapolis: University of Minnesota Press.

Ferguson, James. 1999. *Expectations of Modernity: Myths and Meanings of Urban Life on the Zambian Copperbelt*. Berkley: University of California Press.

Ferguson, James. 2002. "Of Mimicry and Membership: Africans and the 'New World Society.'" *Cultural Anthropology* 17 (4): 551–69.

Ferguson, James. 2005. "Seeing Like an Oil Company: Space, Security, and Global Capital in Neoliberal Africa." *American Anthropologist* 107 (3): 377–82.

Ferguson, James, and Akhil Gupta. 2002. "Spatializing States: Toward an Ethnography of Neoliberal Governmentality." *American Ethnologist* 29 (4): 981–1002.

Fernandes, Leela. 1997. *Producing Workers: The Politics of Gender, Class, and Culture in the Calcutta Jute Mills*. Critical Histories. Philadelphia: University of Pennsylvania Press.

Ferry, Elizabeth Emma, and Mandana E. Limbert. 2008. *Timely Assets: The Politics of Resources and Their Temporalities*. School for Advanced Research Advanced Seminar Series. Santa Fe, NM: School for Advanced Research Press.

Fortun, Kim. 2009. *Advocacy after Bhopal: Environmentalism, Disaster, New Global Orders*. Chicago: University of Chicago Press.

Fortun, Kim. 2012. "Ethnography in Late Industrialism." *Cultural Anthropology* 27 (3): 446–64.

Fox, Samantha Maurer. 2022. "I Feel Brandenburg: Temporality, Vacancy, and Migration in Germany's Model Socialist City." *Anthropological Quarterly* 95 (2): 437–64.

Furlong, Kathryn. 2011. "Small Technologies, Big Change: Rethinking Infrastructure through STS and Geography." *Progress in Human Geography* 35 (4): 460–82.

Gal, Susan, and Gail Kligman. 2000a. "Introduction." In *Reproducing Gender: Politics, Publics, and Everyday Life after Socialism*, edited by Susan Gal and Gail Kligman. Princeton, NJ: Princeton University Press.

Gal, Susan, and Gail Kligman. 2000b. *Reproducing Gender: Politics, Publics, and Everyday Life after Socialism*. Princeton, NJ: Princeton University Press.

Galbraith, Marysia. 2008. "Choosing and Planning in a Climate of Insecurity: Balancing Professional Work and Family Life in Poland." *Journal of the Society for the Anthropology of Europe* 8 (2): 16–30.

Gardner, Katy. 2012. *Discordant Development: Global Capitalism and the Struggle for Connection in Bangladesh*. London: Pluto.

Gibson, William. 2012. *Distrust That Particular Flavor*. New York: Putnam.

Giddens, Anthony. 1991. *Modernity and Self-Identity: Self and Society in the Late Modern Age*. Cambridge: Polity.

Gilbert, Andrew, Jessica Greenberg, Elissa Helms, and Stef Jansen. 2008. "Reconsidering Postsocialism from the Margins of Europe: Hope, Time and Normalcy in Post-Yugoslav Societies." *Anthropology News* 49 (8): 10–11.

Gilberthorpe, Emma, and Dinah Rajak. 2017. "The Anthropology of Extraction: Critical Perspectives on the Resource Curse." *Journal of Development Studies* 53 (2): 186–204.

Goffman, Erving. 1969 [1956]. *The Presentation of Self in Everyday Life*. London: Allen Lane.

Golub, Alex. 2014. *Leviathans at the Gold Mine: Creating Indigenous and Corporate Actors in Papua New Guinea*. Durham, NC: Duke University Press.

Golubović, C. M. 1978. "Razvoj komunalnog Sistema u Opštini Bor (1955–1974) [Development of Communal System in Bor Municipality]." *Razvitak*, 10–22.

Golubović, C. M. 1979. "Razvoj komunalnog sistema u Opštini Bor (1955–1974) [Development of Communal System in Bor Municipality]." *Razvitak*, 9–21.

Graeber, David. 2009. *Direct Action: An Ethnography*. Edinburgh: AK Press.

Graeber, David. 2013a. "It Is Value That Brings Universes into Being." *HAU: Journal of Ethnographic Theory* 3 (2): 219–43.

Graeber, David. 2013b. "On the Phenomenon of Bullshit Jobs: A Work Rant." *Strike Magazine* 3: 1–5.

Graham, Stephen, and Simon Marvin. 2001. *Splintering Urbanism: Networked Infrastructures, Technological Mobilities and the Urban Condition*. London: Routledge.

Graham, Stephen, and Nigel Thrift. 2007. "Out of Order: Understanding Repair and Maintenance." *Theory, Culture and Society* 24 (3): 1–25.

Green, Hardy. 2012. *The Company Town: The Industrial Edens and Satanic Mills That Shaped the American Economy*. New York: Basic Books.

Greenberg, Jessica. 2010. "'There's Nothing Anyone Can Do about It': Participation, Apathy, and 'Successful' Democratic Transition in Postsocialist Serbia." *Slavic Review* 69 (1): 41–64.

Greenberg, Jessica. 2011. "On the Road to Normal: Negotiating Agency and State Sovereignty in Postsocialist Serbia." *American Anthropologist* 113 (1): 88–100.

Greenberg, Jessica. 2014. *After the Revolution: Youth, Democracy, and the Politics of Disappointment in Serbia*. Stanford, CA: Stanford University Press.

Guyer, Jane I. 2007. "Prophecy and the Near Future: Thoughts on Macroeconomic, Evangelical, and Punctuated Time." *American Ethnologist* 34 (3): 409–21.

Hage, Ghassan. 2009. "Waiting out the Crisis: On Stuckedness and Governmentality." In *Waiting*, edited by Hage Ghassan, 97–106. Melbourne: Melbourne University Press.

Halpern, Joel Martin, and David A. Kideckel., eds. 2000. *Neighbors at War: Anthropological Perspectives on Yugoslav Ethnicity, Culture, and History*. University Park: Pennsylvania State University Press.

Halvaksz, Jamon Alex. 2008. "Whose Closure? Appearances, Temporality, and Mineral Extraction in Papua New Guinea." *Journal of the Royal Anthropological Institute* 14 (1): 21–37.

Hann, Chris M. 2019. "Anthropology and Populism." *Anthropology Today* 35 (1): 1–2.

Hann, Chris M., ed. 2002. *Postsocialism: Ideals, Ideologies, and Practices in Eurasia.* London: Routledge.

Hansen, Thomas Blom, and Finn Stepputat, eds. 2001. "Introduction: States of Imagination." In *States of Imagination: Ethnographic Explorations of the Postcolonial State.* Durham, NC: Duke University Press.

Harvey, David. 2007. *A Brief History of Neoliberalism.* Oxford: Oxford University Press.

Harvey, Penny. 2005. "The Materiality of State-Effects: An Ethnography of a Road in the Peruvian Andes." In *State Formation: Anthropological Perspectives*, edited by Christian Krohn-Hansen and Knut Nustad, 123–41. Cambridge: Pluto.

Harvey, Penny, and Hannah Knox. 2012. "The Enchantments of Infrastructure." *Mobilities* 7 (4): 521–36.

Hayden, Robert M. 1996. "Constitutional Nationalism and the Logic of the Wars in Yugoslavia." *Problems of Post-Communism Problems of Post-Communism* 43 (5): 25–35.

Herzfeld, Michael. 1997. *Cultural Intimacy: Social Poetics in the Nation-State.* New York: Routledge.

High, Steven C. 2003. *Industrial Sunset: The Making of North America's Rust Belt, 1969–1984.* Toronto, ON: University of Toronto Press.

Hodges, Andrew. 2019. "Psychic Landscapes, Worker Organizing and Blame. Uljanik and the 2018 Croatian Shipbuilding Crisis." *Südosteuropa* 67 (1): 50–74.

Hönke, Jana. 2014. "Business for Peace? The Ambiguous Role of 'Ethical' Mining Companies." *Peacebuilding* 2 (2): 172–87.

Humphrey, Caroline. 2003. "Rethinking Infrastructure: Cities and the Great Freeze of January 2001." In *Wounded Cities: Destruction and Reconstruction in a Globalized World*, edited by Jane Schneider and Ida Susser, 91–107. Oxford: Berg.

Humphrey, Caroline. 2005. "Ideology in Infrastructure: Architecture and Soviet Imagination." *Journal of the Royal Anthropological Institute* 11 (1): 39–58.

Humphrey, Caroline. 2007. "New Subjects and Situated Interdependence: After Privatisation in the City of Ulan-Ude." In *Urban Life in Post-Soviet Asia*, edited by Catherine Alexander, Victor Buchli, and Caroline Humphrey, 175–207. London: University College London Press.

Institut za javno zdravlje Srbije. 2020. *Unapređenje upravljanja kontaminiranim lokalitetima u Srbiji* [The Advancement of the Management of Contaminated Sites]. Beograd: Institut za javno zdravlje Srbije "Dr Milan Jovanović Batut."

Jackson, Anthony, ed. 1987. *Anthropology at Home: Selection of Papers Presented at the Asa Conference, Held at the University of Keele, England, in March 1985.* Asa Monographs, 25. London: Tavistock.

Janeja, Manpreet K., and Andreas Bandak, eds. 2018. *Ethnographies of Waiting: Doubt, Hope and Uncertainty.* London: Bloomsbury Academic.

Janković, Marija. 2018. "RTB Bor: Ko su Kinezi koji dolaze [RTB Bor: Who Are the Chinese That Are Coming to Bor]." *BBC News Serbia*, August 31. https://www.bbc.com/serbian/lat/svet-45369112.

Jansen, Stef. 2005. *Antinacionalizam: Etnografija otpora u Beogradu i Zagrebu [Anti-Nationalism: Ethnography of Resistance in Belgrade and Zagreb].* Beograd: Biblioteka XX vek.

Jansen, Stef. 2009a. "After the Red Passport: Towards an Anthropology of the Everyday Geopolitics of Entrapment in the EU's 'Immediate Outside.'" *Journal of the Royal Anthropological Institute* 15 (4): 815–32.

Jansen, Stef. 2009b. "Hope and the State in the Anthropology of Home: Preliminary Notes." *Ethnologia Europaea* 39 (1): 54–60.

Jansen, Stef. 2014a. "Hope for/against the State: Gridding in a Besieged Sarajevo Suburb." *Ethnos* 79 (2): 238–60.

Jansen, Stef. 2014b. "On Not Moving Well Enough: Temporal Reasoning in Sarajevo Yearnings for 'Normal Lives.'" *Current Anthropology* 55 (S9): S74–84.

Jansen, Stef. 2015. *Yearnings in the Meantime: 'Normal Lives' and the State in a Sarajevo Apartment Complex.* Dislocations, 15. New York: Berghahn.

Jansen, Stef. 2016. "For a Relational, Historical Ethnography of Hope: Indeterminacy and Determination in the Bosnian and Herzegovinian Meantime." *History and Anthropology* 27 (4): 447–64.

Jeffrey, Craig. 2010. *Timepass: Youth, Class, and the Politics of Waiting in India.* Stanford, CA: Stanford University Press.

Jensen, Casper Bruun. 2017. "Pipe Dreams: Sewage Infrastructure and Activity Trails in Phnom Penh." *Ethnos* 82 (4): 627–47.

Johnson, Charlotte. 2013. *"Infrastructures of Continuity and Change. A Material Culture Approach to Finance, Heating and Maintenance in Belgrade Homes."* Master's thesis, Newcastle University.

Johnson, Charlotte. 2016. "District Heating as Heterotopia: Tracing the Social Contract through Domestic Energy Infrastructure in Pimlico, London." *Economic Anthropology* 3 (1): 94–105.

Johnson, Charlotte. 2018. "The Moral Economy of Comfortable Living: Negotiating Individualism and Collectivism through Housing in Belgrade." *Critique of Anthropology* 38 (2): 156–71. https://doi.org/10.1177/0308275X18758874.

Jovanović, Božin, and Đurđević Miodrag. 2005. *Sto godina Borskog rudarstva: 1903–2003 [One Hundred Years of Bor's Mining].* Bor: Rudarsko-topioničarski basen Bor.

Jovanović, Deana. 2016. "Ambivalence and the Study of Contradictions." *HAU: Journal of Ethnographic Theory* 6 (3): 1–6. https://doi.org/10.14318/hau6.3.002.

Jovanović, Deana. 2018a. "The Politics of Simulation. Fake Repairs in a Serbian Industrial Town." *Comparative Southeast European Studies* 66 (1): 27–44. https://doi.org/10.1515/soeu-2018-0003.

Jovanović, Deana. 2018b. "Prosperous Pollutants: Bargaining with Risks and Forging Hopes in an Industrial Town in Serbia." *Ethnos: Journal of Anthropology* 83 (3): 489–504. https://doi.org/10.1080/00141844.2016.1169205.

Jovanović, Deana. 2019. "The Thermodynamics of the Social Contract: Making Infrastructures Visible in the Case of District Heating in Two Towns in Serbia and Croatia." In *Post-Socialist Urban Infrastructures*, edited by Tauri Tuvikene, Wladimir Sgibnev, and Carola S. Neugebauer, 38–53. London: Routledge. https://doi.org/10.4324/9781351190350.

Jovanović, Deana. 2021. "Infrastructural Stripping and 'Recycling' of Copper: Producing the State in an Industrial Town in Serbia." *Social Anthropology* 29 (3): 586–601.

Jovanović, Deana, and Dragan Stojmenović. 2022. "The Export of Know-How at the (Semi-)peripheries: The Case of Yugoslav–Iranian Industrial Collaboration and LABOR Mobility (1980–1991)." *Labor History* 64 (4): 443–59. https://doi.org/10.1080/0023656X.2023.2173728.

Jovanović, Matija. 2015. "Poglavlje 27: Zaštita životne sredine na kredit [Chapter 27: Protecting the Environment on Credit]." *Mašina*, January 30. http://www.masina.rs/?p=848.

Jovanović, Slobodan. 1987. "Društveni i kulturni procesi u Boru u istorijskom kontekstu između dva rata [Social and Cultural Processes in Bor in Historical Context between Two Wars]." *Zbornik radova Muzeja rudarstva i metalurgije Bor* V–VI: 189–211.

Jovanović, Slobodan. 2001. *Bor—Istorijski putokazi [Bor—Historical signposts]*. Bor: Skupština opštine Bor.

Kalb, Don. 2011. "Introduction. Headlines of Nation, Subtexts of Class: Working-Class Populism and the Return of the Repressed in Neoliberal Europe." In *Headlines of Nation, Subtexts of Class: Working-Class Populism and the Return of the Repressed in Neoliberal Europe*, edited by Gábor Halmai and Don Kalb, 1–36. EASA Series, 15. New York: Berghahn.

Kallianos, Yannis. 2018. "Infrastructural Disorder: The Politics of Disruption, Contingency, and Normalcy in Waste Infrastructures in Athens." *Environment and Planning D: Society and Space* 36 (4): 758–75.

Kandiyoti, Deniz. 2002. "How Far Do Analyses of Postsocialism Travel." In *Postsocialism: Ideals, Ideologies, and Practices in Eurasia*, edited by Chris M. Hann, 238–57. London: Routledge.

Kideckel, David. 2004. "Miners and Wives in Romania's Jiu Valley: Perspectives on Postsocialist Class, Gender, and Social Change." *Identities* 11 (1): 39–63.

Kideckel, David A. 2008. *Getting by in Postsocialist Romania: Labor, the Body and Working-Class Culture*. Bloomington: Indiana University Press.

Kierans, Ciara, and Kirsten Bell. 2017. "Cultivating Ambivalence: Some Methodological Considerations for Anthropology." *HAU: Journal of Ethnographic Theory* 7 (2): 23–44.

Kirin, Renata Jambrešić, and Croatia Marina Blagaić. 2013. "The Ambivalence of Socialist Working Women's Heritage: A Case Study of the Jugoplastika Factory." *Croatian Journal of Ethnology and Folklore Research/Narodna Umjetnost* 50 (1): 40–72.

Kirsch, Stuart. 2014. *Mining Capitalism: The Relationship between Corporations and Their Critics*. Oakland: University of California Press.

Kleist, Nauja, and Stef Jansen. 2016. "Introduction: Hope over Time—Crisis, Immobility and Future-Making." *History and Anthropology* 27 (4): 373–92.

Knight, Daniel M. 2020. "Sun Grab: Failing Futures in Greece." Theorizing the Contemporary. *Fieldsights*, March 24. https://culanth.org/fieldsights/sun-grab-failing-futures -in-greece.

Knudsen, Ida Harboe, and Martin Demant Frederiksen. 2015. *Ethnographies of Grey Zones in Eastern Europe: Relations, Borders and Invisibilities*. Anthem Series on Russian, East European and Eurasian Studies. London: Anthem.

Knudsen, Ståle. 2018. "Is Corporate Social Responsibility Oiling the Neoliberal Carbon Economy?" *Ethnos* 83 (3): 505–20.

Kolektiv. 1977. *Kolektiv: List Rudarsko-topioničarskog basena Bor* [Collective. Newspapers of Mining and Smelting Basin Bor] XXXI (1). January 14, 1977.

Kondo, Dorinne K. 1990. *Crafting Selves: Power, Gender, and Discourses of Identity in a Japanese Workplace*. Chicago: University of Chicago Press.

Kotkin, Stephen. 1995. *Magnetic Mountain: Stalinism as a Civilization*. Berkeley: University of California Press.

Kovačević, Aleksandar. 2004. "Stuck in the Past: Energy, Environment and Poverty in Serbia and Montenegro." *Oil, Gas and Energy Law* 2 (4).

Krstić, Branko. 1982. *Čovjek i prostor. Pristup prostornom uređenju [Man and Space. Approach to Spatial Planning]*. Sarajevo: Svijetlost.

Krupa, Christopher, and David Nugent. 2015. "Off-Centered States: Rethinking State Theory through an Andean Lens." In *State Theory and Andean Politics: New Approaches to the Study of Rule*, 1–31. Philadelphia: University of Pennsylvania Press.

Kurtović, Larisa. 2019. "Interpellating the State: Activists Seek Political Authority in Postwar Bosnia and Herzegovina." *American Ethnologist* 46 (4): 444–56.

Kurtović, Larisa, and Azra Hromadžić. 2017. "Cannibal States, Empty Bellies: Protest, History and Political Imagination in Post-Dayton Bosnia." *Critique of Anthropology* 37 (3): 262–96.

Kurtović, Larisa, and Azra Hromadžić. 2020. "Socialist Greens: On Vernacular Environmentalisms." Theorizing the Contemporary. *Fieldsights*, March 24. https://culanth.org/fieldsights/socialist-greens-on-vernacular-environmentalisms.

Kurtović, Larisa, and Nelli Sargsyan. 2019. "After Utopia: Leftist Imaginaries and Activist Politics in the Postsocialist World." *History and Anthropology* 30 (1): 1–19.

Lakićević, Mijat. 2018. "RTB i PKB: Prodaja ili poslednji dani. [RTB and PKB: Selling or the Last Days]." August 23. http://mijatlakicevic.com/zasto-prodati-rtb-a-kako-pkb/.

Lambek, Michael. 2010. *Ordinary Ethics: Anthropology, Language, and Action.* New York: Fordham University Press.

Larkin, Brian. 2013. "The Politics and Poetics of Infrastructure." *Annual Review of Anthropology* 42 (1): 327–43.

Laszczkowski, Mateusz. 2011. "Building the Future: Construction, Temporality, and Politics in Astana." *Focaal* 60 (1): 77–92.

Laszczkowski, Mateusz. 2015. "Scraps, Neighbors, and Committees: Material Things, Place-Making, and the State in an Astana Apartment Block." *City and Society* 27 (2): 136–59.

Laszczkowski, Mateusz. 2016. *"City of the Future": Built Space, Modernity and Urban Change in Astana.* Integration and Conflict Studies, Vol. 14. New York: Berghahn.

Laszczkowski, Mateusz, and Medeleine Reeves. 2015. "Introduction: Affective States—Entanglements, Suspensions, Suspicions." *Social Analysis* 59 (4): 1–14.

Latour, Bruno. 1993. *We Have Never Been Modern.* Cambridge, MA: Harvard University Press.

Lazić, Mladen, and Jelena Pešić. 2012. *Making and Unmaking State-Centered Capitalism in Serbia.* Belgrade: Čigoja Štampa.

Le Normand, Brigitte. 2014. *Designing Tito's Capital: Urban Planning, Modernism, and Socialism.* Pittsburgh, PA: University of Pittsburgh Press.

Lebow, Katherine. 2013. *Unfinished Utopia: Nowa Huta, Stalinism, and Polish Society, 1949–56.* Ithaca, NY: Cornell University Press.

Ledeneva, Alena V. 2006. *How Russia Really Works: The Informal Practices That Shaped Post-Soviet Politics and Business.* Ithaca, NY: Cornell University Press.

Ledeneva, Alena V. 2013. *Can Russia Modernise? Sistema, Power Networks and Informal Governance.* Cambridge: Cambridge University Press.

Lee, Ching Kwan. 2017. *The Specter of Global China: Politics, Labor, and Foreign Investment in Africa.* Chicago: University of Chicago Press.

Li, Fabiana. 2011. "Engineering Responsibility: Environmental Mitigation and the Limits of Commensuration in a Chilean Mining Project." *Focaal* 2011 (60): 61–73.

Li, Fabiana. 2015. *Unearthing Conflict: Corporate Mining, Activism, and Expertise in Peru.* Durham, NC: Duke University Press.

Limbert, Mandana. 2010. *In the Time of Oil: Piety, Memory, and Social Life in an Omani Town.* Stanford, CA: Stanford University Press.

Lin, Yi-Chieh Jessica. 2011. *Fake Stuff: China and the Rise of Counterfeit Goods.* New York: Routledge.

Little, Peter C. 2014. *Toxic Town: IBM, Pollution, and Industrial Risks.* New York: New York University Press.

Mah, Alice. 2012. *Industrial Ruination, Community, and Place: Landscapes and Legacies of Urban Decline.* Toronto, ON: University of Toronto Press.

Mah, Alice, and Xinhong Wang. 2019. "Accumulated Injuries of Environmental Injustice: Living and Working with Petrochemical Pollution in Nanjing, China." *Annals of the American Association of Geographers* 109 (6): 1961–77.

Makroekonomija. 2012. "Penzije u Srbiji, II 2012 [Pensions in Serbia, II 2012]." *Makroekonomija*, April 18. http://www.makroekonomija.org/penzije/penzije-u-srbiji-ii-2012/.

Mandel, Ruth Ellen, and Caroline Humphrey. 2002. *Markets and Moralities: Ethnographies of Postsocialism*. Oxford: Berg.

Mandič, Srna. 2010. "The Changing Role of Housing Assets in Post-Socialist Countries." *Journal of Housing and the Built Environment* 25 (2): 213–26.

Mann, Michael. 1984. "The Autonomous Power of the State: Its Origins, Mechanisms and Results." *European Journal of Sociology/Archives Européennes de Sociologie* 25 (2): 185–213.

Marković, Radmilo. 2016. "Intervju—Zoran Drakulić, *Point Group*: O Boru i srpskim privrednicima. [Interview—Zoran Drakulić, *Point Group*: About Bor and Serbian Enterpreneurs]." *Vreme*, August 12. https://www.vreme.com/vreme/o-boru-i-srpskim-privrednicima/.

Markowitz, Gerald E., and David Rosner. 2013. *Deceit and Denial: The Deadly Politics of Industrial Pollution*. Berkeley: University of California Press.

Matošević, Andrea. 2010. "Industry Forging Masculinity: 'Tough Men', Hard Labour and Identity." *Narodna Umjetnost* 47 (1): 29–47.

Matošević, Andrea. 2015. *Socijalizam s udarničkim licem: entografija radnog pregalaštva [Socialism with a Shock-Work Face. Ethnography of Working Zeal]*. Zagreb: Biblioteka Nova Etnografija.

McConnell, Fiona. 2016. *Rehearsing the State: The Political Practices of the Tibetan Government-In-Exile*. Rgs-Ibg Book Series. Chichester: Wiley.

Medija Centar Bor. 2013. "Spaskovski: ja sam Vučićev Ronaldo! [Spaskovski: I Am Vučić's Ronaldo]." June 19. https://www.mc.kcbor.net/spaskovski-ja-sam-vucicev-ronaldo/.

Merton, Robert K. 1976. *Sociological Ambivalence and Other Essays*. New York: Free Press.

Migdal, Joel S. 2001. *State in Society: Studying How States and Societies Transform and Constitute One Another*. Cambridge: Cambridge University Press.

Mikelić, Veljko, Torsten Schoen, and Marjolein Benschop. 2005. *Housing and Property Rights in Bosnia and Herzegovina, Croatia and Serbia, and Montenegro*. Nairobi: UN-Habitat.

Mikuš, Marek. 2016. "The Justice of Neoliberalism: Moral Ideology and Redistributive Politics of Public Sector Retrenchment in Serbia." *Social Anthropology* 24 (2): 211–27.

Miladinović, Zorica. 2014. "Deca nasleđuju radna mesta u javnom preduzeću [Children Inheriting Job Positions in Public Companies]." *Danas*, May 14. http://www.danas.rs/danasrs/ekonomija/deca_nasledjuju_radna_mesta_u_javnom_preduzecu.4.html?news_id=281451.

Mills, Mary Beth. 2003. "Gender and Inequality in the Global Labor Force." *Annual Review of Anthropology* 32: 41–62.

Mining.com. 2021. "Copper Price Tops $10,000 a Tonne for First Time in Ten Years." April 29. https://www.mining.com/copper-extends-rally-to-10000-for-the-first-time-since-2011/.

Mining Technology. 2021. "Zijin Commissions Cukaru Peki Copper and Gold Mine in Serbia." October 25. https://www.mining-technology.com/news/zijin-cukaru-peki-mine-serbia/.

Minnegal, Monica. 2009. "The Time Is Right: Waiting, Reciprocity and Sociality." In *Waiting*, edited by H. Ghassan, 89–97. Melbourne: Melbourne University Press.

Mirić, Mitar. 1989. "Ne može nam niko ništa." On *Ne može nam niko ništa*. Diskos.

Mitchell, Timothy. 1999. "Society, Economy, and the State Effect." In *State/Culture: State-Formation after the Cultural Turn*, edited by George Steinmetz, 76–90. Ithaca, NY: Cornell University Press.

Mitrović, Igor. 2012. "Spaskovski: topionica i nova sumporna će biti završena na vreme [Spaskovski: The Smelting Plant and New Acid Plant Will Be Finished in Time]." *Bor030*, March 10. http://www.bor030.net/spaskovski-topionica-i-nova-sumporna -bice-zavrsene-na-vreme.

Mitrović, Igor. 2013. "Plate RTB-a podižu cene u Boru [RTB Salaries Raise Prices in Bor]." *Bor030*, April 16. http://www.bor030.net/plate-u-rtb-u-podizu-cene-u -boru.

Miyazaki, Hirokazu. 2004. *The Method of Hope: Anthropology, Philosophy, and Fijian Knowledge.* Stanford, CA: Stanford University Press.

Morris, Jeremy. 2016. *Everyday Post-Socialism—Working-Class Communities in the Russian Margins.* London: Palgrave Macmillan.

Murawski, Michał. 2018. "Actually-Existing Success: Economics, Aesthetics, and the Specificity of (Still-)Socialist Urbanism." *Comparative Studies in Society and History* 60 (4): 907–37.

N1. 2018a. "Brkić: Tender za RTB Bor 'fingiran' [Brkić: Public Procurement for RTB Bor 'Faked']." February 9. http://rs.n1info.com/Biznis/a416780/comments/Misa-Brkic -gost-Novog-dana.html#.

N1. 2018b. "Vučić i 'brat' Li—Kinezi stižu i do Bora? [Vučić and 'Brother' Li—Chinese Are Coming All the Way to Bor?]." May 7. http://rs.n1info.com/Biznis/a401658 /Vucic-i-brat-Li-Kinezi-stizu-i-do-Bora.html.

Nash, June. 1979. *We Eat the Mines and the Mines Eat Us: Dependency and Exploitation in Bolivian Tin Mines.* New York: Columbia University Press.

Navaro-Yashin, Yael. 2002. *Faces of the State: Secularism and Public Life in Turkey.* Princeton, NJ: Princeton University Press.

Navaro-Yashin, Yael. 2007. "Make-Believe Papers, Legal Forms and the Counterfeit: Affective Interactions between Documents and People in Britain and Cyprus." *Anthropological Theory* 7 (1): 79–98.

Nee, Victor, and Sonja Opper. 2012. *Capitalism from below: Markets and Institutional Change in China.* Cambridge, MA: Harvard University Press.

Newell, Sasha. 2012. *The Modernity Bluff.* Chicago: University of Chicago Press.

Newell, Sasha. 2013. "Brands as Masks: Public Secrecy and the Counterfeit in Côte d'Ivoire." *Journal of the Royal Anthropological Institute* 19 (1): 138–54.

Nuijten, Monique. 2003. *Power, Community and the State: The Political Anthropology of Organisation in Mexico.* Anthropology, Culture, and Society. London: Pluto.

Obeid, Michelle. 2015. "'States of Aspiration': Anthropology and New Questions for the Middle East." In *A Companion to the Anthropology of the Middle East*, edited by Soraya Altorki, 434–52. Hoboken, NJ: Wiley-Blackwell.

Ong, Aihwa. 1988. "The Production of Possession: Spirits and the Multinational Corporation in Malaysia." *American Ethnologist* 15 (1): 28–42.

Ortner, Sherry B. 1997. "Thick Resistance: Death and the Cultural Construction of Agency in Himalayan Mountaineering." *Representations* 59 (59): 135–62.

Oštrić, Zoran. 1992. "Ekološki pokreti u Jugoslaviji. Građa za proučavanje razdoblja 1971–1991 [Ecological Movements in Yugoslavia. Material for Studying 1971–1991 Period]." *Socijalna ekologija: časopis za ekološku misao i sociologijska istraživanja okoline* 1 (1): 83–104.

Palmberger, Monika. 2019. "Relational Ambivalence: Exploring the Social and Discursive Dimensions of Ambivalence—The Case of Turkish Aging Labor Migrants." *International Journal of Comparative Sociology* 60 (1–2): 74–90.

Parry, Jonathan P. 2003. "Nehru's Dream and the Village 'Waiting Room': Long-Distance Labour Migrants to a Central Indian Steel Town." *Contributions to Indian Sociology* 37 (1–2): 217–49.

Patterson, Patrick Hyder. 2011. *Bought and Sold: Living and Losing the Good Life in Socialist Yugoslavia*. Ithaca, NY: Cornell University Press.

Pelkmans, Mathijs. 2013. "Ruins of Hope in a Kyrgyz Post-industrial Wasteland." *Anthropology Today* 29 (5): 17–21.

Perić, Sabrina. 2012. *"Silver Bosnia: Precious Metals and Society in the Western Balkans."* Master's thesis, Harvard University.

Petrović, Ivica. 2012. "Srbija je na ivici bankrota [Serbia Is on the Verge of Bankruptcy]." *Deutsche Welle*, July 25. http://www.dw.com/sr/srbija-je-na-ivici-bankrota/a -16122674.

Petrović, Mina. 2001. "Post-Socialist Housing Policy Transformation in Yugoslavia and Belgrade." *European Journal of Housing Policy* 1 (2): 211–31.

Petrović, Tanja. 2010. "'When We Were Europe': Socialist Workers in Serbia and Their Nostalgic Narratives. The Case of the Cables Factory Workers in Jagodina (Serbia)." In *Remembering Communism: Genres of Representation*, edited by Maria N. Todorova, 127–53. New York: Social Science Research Council.

Petrović, Tanja. 2016. "Divided Modernities: Citizenship, Agency and Public Spaces in a Central Serbian Town." *Etnološka Tribina* 49 (39): 111–25.

Petrović, Tanja. 2018. "Political Parody and the Politics of Ambivalence." *Annual Review of Anthropology* 47: 201–16.

Petrović, Tanja. 2020. "Fish Canning Industry and the Rhythm of Social Life in the Northeastern Adriatic." *Narodna Umjetnost* 57 (1): 33–49.

Petryna, Adriana. 2013. *Life Exposed: Biological Citizens after Chernobyl*. Princeton, NJ: Princeton University Press.

Phillimore, Peter, and Patricia Bell. 2005. "Trust and Risk in a German Chemical Town." *Ethnos* 70 (3): 311–34.

Pine, Frances. 1998. "Dealing with Fragmentation: The Consequences of Privatisation for Rural Women in Central and Southern Poland." In *Surviving Post-Socialism: Local Strategies and Regional Responses in Eastern Europe and the Former Soviet Union*, edited by Frances Pine and Susan Bridger, 106–23. London: Routledge.

Pine, Frances. 2002. "Retreat to the Household? Gendered Domains in Postsocialist Poland." In *Postsocialism: Ideals, Ideologies and Practices in Eurasia*, edited by Chris M. Hann, 95–113. London: Routledge.

Pinker, Annabel, and Penny Harvey. 2015. "Negotiating Uncertainty: Neo-Liberal Statecraft in Contemporary Peru." *Social Analysis* 59 (4): 15–31.

Popović, Ivan. 2015. "KAO FENIKS. Ovaj srpski grad je bio sinonim za propast, a sada je jedan od najlepših [LIKE A PHOENIX. This Serbian Town Was a Synonym for Ruination, and Now It Is One of the Most Beautiful]." *Blic*, January 9. https:// www.blic.rs/vesti/srbija/kao-feniks-ovaj-srpski-grad-je-bio-sinonim-za-propast -a-sada-je-jedan-od-najlepsih/2gctwwf.

Potkonjak, Sanja, and Tea Škokić. 2013. "'In the World of Iron and Steel': On the Ethnography of Work, Unemployment and Hope." *Narodna Umjetnost* 1 (50): 74–95.

Privatization Agency—Republic of Serbia, The. 2006. "Environmental Assessment of RTB Bor Operations—Final Report." Unpublished Report.

Pupavac, Vanessa. 2010. "Weaving Postwar Reconstruction in Bosnia? The Attractions and Limitations of NGO Gender Development Approaches." *Journal of Intervention and Statebuilding* 4 (4): 475–93.

Radenković, Ivan. 2015. "Borski kombinat Bakra: nova topionica—stara priča [Bor's Basin: New Smelting Factory—Old Story]." *Bilten*, January 26. http://www.bilten .org/?p=4247.

Radulović, Miroslav. 1987. *Priča o mom gradu [The Story about My Town]*. Bor: Radna organizacija Štampa, radio i film.

Rajak, Dinah. 2011. "Theatres of Virtue: Collaboration, Consensus, and the Social Life of Corporate Social Responsibility." *Focaal* 2011 (60): 9–20.

Rajković, Ivan. 2017. "Concern for the State: 'Normality', State Effect and Distributional Claims in Serbia." Гласник Етнографског Института САНУ 65 (1): 31–45.

Rajković, Ivan. 2018a. "For an Anthropology of the Demoralized: State Pay, Mock-Labour, and Unfreedom in a Serbian Firm." *Journal of the Royal Anthropological Institute* 24 (1): 47–70.

Rajković, Ivan. 2018b. "Stvarnost prezaduženih gradova. Mere štednje i lokalna politika u Srbiji [Reality of over-indebted Towns. Austerity Measures and the Local Politics in Serbia]." *Le Monde Diplomatique*, August 4.

Razsa, Maple. 2015. *Bastards of Utopia: Living Radical Politics after Socialism.* Global Research Studies. Bloomington: Indiana University Press.

Razinsky, Hili. 2016. *Ambivalence: A Philosophical Exploration.* London: Rowman and Littlefield.

Reed, Adam. 2011. "Hope on Remand." *Journal of the Royal Anthropological Institute* 17 (3): 527–44.

Reeves, Madeleine. 2013. "Clean Fake: Authenticating Documents and Persons in Migrant Moscow." *American Ethnologist* 40 (3): 508–24.

Reeves, Madeleine. 2017. "Infrastructural Hope: Anticipating 'Independent Roads' and Territorial Integrity in Southern Kyrgyzstan." *Ethnos* 82 (4): 711–37.

Reeves, Madeleine, Judith Beyer, and Johan Rasanayagam. 2014. "Introduction. Performances, Possibilities, and Practices of the Political in Central Asia." In *Ethnographies of the State in Central Asia: Performing Politics*, edited by Madeleine Reeves, Judith Beyer, and Johan Rasanayagam, 1–26. Bloomington: Indiana University Press.

Reuters. 2019. "China's Zijin Buys Freeport's Copper-Gold Assets in Serbia for up to $390 Million." November 4. https://www.mining.com/web/chinas-zijin-buys-freeports-copper-gold-assets-in-serbia-for-up-to-390-million/.

Ringel, Felix. 2016. "Can Time Be Tricked? A Theoretical Introduction." *Cambridge Journal of Anthropology* 34 (1): 22–31.

Ringel, Felix. 2018. *Back to the Postindustrial Future: An Ethnography of Germany's Fastest Shrinking City.* Easa Series, 33. New York: Berghahn.

Rogers, Douglas. 2015. *The Depths of Russia: Oil, Power, and Culture after Socialism.* Ithaca, NY: Cornell University Press.

Rose, Nikolas. 1999. *Powers of Freedom: Reframing Political Thought.* Cambridge: Cambridge University Press.

Rosenblat, Alex. 2018. *Uberland: How Algorithms Are Rewriting the Rules of Work.* Oakland: University of California Press.

RTS. 2009. "Novi socijalni program za radnike RTB Bor [New Severance Payment Programs for RTB Workers]." January 26. http://www.rts.rs/page/stories/sr/story/125/Dru%C5%A1tvo/40851/Novi+socijalni+program+za+radnike+RTB+Bor.html.

RTS. 2013. "Najveći ekološki projekat na Balkanu [The Biggest Ecological Project on the Balkans]." May 24. https://www.rts.rs/page/stories/sr/story/13/ekonomija/1330364/najveci-ekoloski-projekat-na-balkanu.html.

Rutar, Sabine. 2005. "Arbeit und Überleben in Serbien. Das Kupfererzbergwerk Bor im Zweiten Weltkrieg." *Geschichte Und Gesellschaft* 31 (1): 101–34.

Ružica, Miroslav. 2010. "Država i/ili tržište—neoliberalizam i/ili socijaldemokratija [State and/or Market—Neoliberalism and/or Social-Democracy]." In *Kako građani srbije vide tranziciju: istraživanje javnog mnjenja tranzicije*, edited by Srećko Mihajlović, Miroslav Ružica, Tanja Jakobi, Zoran Đ. Slavujević, Mirjana Vasović, Bora Kuzmanović, Dragan Popadić, et al., 29–46. Belgrade: Friedrich Ebert Stiftung.

Ružica, Miroslav. 2013. "Od Kratkoročnog Razmišljanja Se Ne Živi, Ali Se (Na Žalost) Zahvaljujući Njemu Vlada [From Short-Term Thinking One Cannot Live, but Thanks to It, It Is (Unfortunately) Being Governed]." *Biznis i Finansije*, June 8. https://old.bif.rs/2013/08/miroslav-ruzica-sociolog-od-kratkorocnog-razmisljanja-se-ne-zivi-ali-se-na-zalost-zahvaljujuci-njemu-vlada/.

Şalaru, Maria. 2018. *BLOCUL—an Ethnography of a Romanian Block of Flats*. PhD diss., University of Oxford.

Samimian-Darash, Limor, and Paul Rabinow, eds. 2015. *Modes of Uncertainty: Anthropological Cases*. Chicago: University of Chicago Press.

Savić, Ljubodrag. 2014. "Industrialization—Myth or Reality?" In *Moguće strategije razvoja Srbije* [Possible Development Strategies of Serbia], edited by Časlav Ocić, 297–309. Belgrade: Serbian Academy of Arts and Sciences, Social Sciences Department.

Schielke, Samuli. 2015. *Egypt in the Future Tense: Hope, Frustration, and Ambivalence before and after 2011*. Public Cultures of the Middle East and North Africa. Bloomington: Indiana University Press.

Schwartz, Barry. 1974. "Waiting, Exchange, and Power: The Distribution of Time in Social Systems." *American Journal of Sociology* 79 (4): 841–70.

Schwenkel, Christina. 2015. "Spectacular Infrastructure and Its Breakdown in Socialist Vietnam." *American Ethnologist* 42 (3): 520–34.

Serbia Energy Mining News. 2019. "Expansion of Chinese Zidjin in Serbia." December 29. https://serbia-energy.eu/expansion-of-chinese-zidjin-in-serbia/.

Šerbula, Snežana. 2013. "Environmental Pollution in the Bor Region." In *Environmental Protection in Pančevo and Bor: Challenges of Participation to Environmental Governance*, edited by Mina Petrović and Jelisaveta Vukelić, 15–28. Belgrade: Institute for Sociological Research, Faculty of Philosophy, University of Belgrade.

Shever, Elana. 2012. *Resources for Reform: Oil and Neoliberalism in Argentina*. Stanford, CA: Stanford University Press.

Shove, Elizabeth. 2003. "Users, Technologies and Expectations of Comfort, Cleanliness and Convenience." *Innovation: The European Journal of Social Science Research* 16 (2): 193–206.

Simić, Andrei. 1973. *The Peasant Urbanites: A Study in Rural-Urban Mobility in Serbia*. New York: Seminar Press.

Simić, Marina. 2010. "Fieldwork Dillemas: Problems of Location, Insiderhood and Implicit Discourses." *Glasnik Etnografskog Instituta Sanu* 58 (2): 29–42.

Simić, Marina. 2014. *Kosmopolitska čežnja: etnografija srpskog postsocijalizma [Cosmopolitan Yearning: Ethnography of Serbian Post-socialism]*. Edicija Postkultura 1. Beograd: Centar za Studije kulture, Fakulteta političkih nauka.

Simić, Marina. 2017. "Anthropological Research of the State: A View on Postsocialism." Гласник Етнографског Института САНУ 65 (1): 15–29.

Simmie, James. 1991. "Housing and Inequality under State Socialism: An Analysis of Yugoslavia." *Housing Studies* 6 (3): 172–81.

Simmie, James, and Jože Dekleva, eds. 1991. *Yugoslavia in Turmoil after Self-Management?* London: Pinter.

Smelser, Neil J. 1998. "The Rational and the Ambivalent in the Social Sciences: 1997 Presidential Address." *American Sociological Review* 63 (1): 1–16.

Sneath, David. 2009. "Reading the Signs by Lenin's Light: Development, Divination and Metonymic Fields in Mongolia." *Ethnos* 74 (1): 72–90.

Solecki, William D. 1996. "Paternalism, Pollution and Protest in a Company Town." *Political Geography* 15 (1): 5–20.

Spasić, Ivana, and Ana Birešev. 2012. "Social Classifications in Serbia Today: Between Morality and Politics." In *Social and Cultural Capital in Serbia*, edited by Predrag Cvetičanin et al., 139–58. Niš, Serbia: Centre for Empirical Cultural Studies of South-East Europe.

Špirić, Jovanka. 2018. "Ecological Distribution Conflicts and Sustainability: Lessons from the Post-Socialist European Semi-Periphery." *Sustainability Science* 13 (3): 661-76.

Ssorin-Chaikov, Nikolai V. 2003. *The Social Life of the State in Subarctic Siberia*. Stanford, CA: Stanford University Press.

Stanojević, J. 2011. "Nova Životna Energija Grada [New Life Energy of the City]." *Kolektiv* 2217, September 30, 22–21.

Star, Susan Leigh. 1999. "The Ethnography of Infrastructure." *American Behavioral Scientist* 43 (3): 377–91.

Statista. 2019. "Distribution of Refined Copper Consumption Worldwide in 2019, by Region." *Statista.com*, May 19. https://www.statista.com/statistics/693466/distribution -of-global-refined-copper-consumption-by-region/.

Statistical Office of the Republic of Serbia. 2014a. *"2011 Census of Population, Households and Dwellings in the Republic of Serbia."* Belgrade: Statistical Office of the Republic of Serbia.

Statistical Office of the Republic of Serbia. 2014b. *"Comparative Overview of the Number of Population in 1948, 1953, 1961, 1971, 1981, 1991, 2002 and 2011."* Republika Srbija: Republički zavod za statistiku. https://view.officeapps.live.com/op/view .aspx?src=https%3A%2F%2Fwww.stat.gov.rs%2Fmedia%2F3760%2F1_uporedni -pregled-broja-stanovnika.xls&wdOrigin=BROWSELINK.

Steinmüller, Hans. 2013. *Communities of Complicity: Everyday Ethics in Rural China*. Dislocations, Vol. 10. New York: Berghahn.

Stevanović, Mirjana N. 2020. "Država u Boru prevarila i građane i Kineze [The State Deceived Both the Citizens and the Chinese]." *Danas*, January 22. https://www .danas.rs/ekonomija/drzava-u-boru-prevarila-i-gradjane-i-kineze/.

Stevanović, Mirjana. 2021. "Za 'već Urađen' posao, Ziđin sad Mora da uloži još 220 miliona evra [For 'Already Done' Job, Zijn Now Has to Invest 220 Million Euros]." *Danas*, August 23. https://www.danas.rs/vesti/ekonomija/za-vec-uradjen-posao -zidjin-sad-mora-da-ulozi-jos-220-miliona-evra/.

Strangleman, Tim. 2013. "'Smokestack Nostalgia,' 'Ruin Porn' or Working-Class Obituary: The Role and Meaning of Deindustrial Representation." *International Labor and Working-Class History* 84: 23–37.

Street, Alice. 2012. "Affective Infrastructure: Hospital Landscapes of Hope and Failure." *Space and Culture* 15 (1): 44–56.

Stubbs, Paul. 2018. "Slow, Slow, Quick, Quick, Slow: Power, Expertise and the Hegemonic Temporalities of Austerity." *Innovation: The European Journal of Social Science Research* 31 (1): 25–39.

Szelényi, Iván. 1983. *Urban Inequalities under State Socialism*. Oxford: Oxford University Press.

Taş, Hakkı. 2022. "The Chronopolitics of National Populism." *Identities* 29 (2): 127–45.

Taussig, Michael. 1993. *Mimesis and Alterity: An Alternative History of the Senses*. London: Routledge.

Telegraf. 2014. "Vučić: Topionica je ponos Srbije, građanima osigurana budućnost! [Vučić: Smelter Is the Pride of Serbia, Citizens Are Assured of the Future!]." December 23. https://www.telegraf.rs/vesti/politika/1363746-vucic-topionica-u -boru-je-nase-malo-cudo.

Telegraf. 2017. "Stanovnici Bora bez grejanja drugi dan, među njima i bolnica: pacijenti se smrzavaju, RTB Bor priskočio u pomoć (FOTO) [The Inhabitants of Bor without

Heating Second Day, among Them Hospital as Well: The Patients Are Freezing, RTB Bor Jumped in to Help Out (PHOTO)]." December 7. https://www.telegraf.rs/vesti/srbija/2917717-stanovnici-bora-bez-grejanja-drugi-dan-medju-njima-i-bolnica-pacijenti-se-smrzavaju-rtb-bor-priskocio-u-pomoc-foto.

Tilt, Bryan. 2013. "Industrial Pollution and Environmental Health in Rural China: Risk, Uncertainty and Individualization." *China Quarterly* 214: 283–301.

Todorova, Maria, and Zsuzsa Gille. 2012. *Post-Communist Nostalgia*. New York: Berghahn.

Tončev-Vasilić, G. 2012. "'Bolje prvi u selu, nego poslednji u gradu' [Better to Be First in the Village Than Last in the Town]." *Kolektiv* 2226, September 17.

Turner, Víctor. 1974. *Dramas, Fields, and Metaphors: Symbolic Action in Human Society*. Ithaca, NY: Cornell University Press.

Turner, Víctor. 1986. *The Anthropology of Performance*. New York: PAJP.

Tuvikene, Tauri, Wladimir Sgibnev, Daniela Zupan, Deana Jovanović, and Carola S. Neugebauer. 2020. "Post-Socialist Infrastructuring." *Area* 52 (3): 575–82.

van Marrewijk, Alfons H. 2014. "Exceptional Luck? Conducting Ethnographies in Business Organizations." *Anthropologist* 18 (1): 33–42.

Venkatesan, Soumhya. 2010. "Learning to Weave; Weaving to Learn . . . What?" *Journal of the Royal Anthropological Institute* 16 (S1): S158–75.

Vesković, Milica. 2013. "Public Health Ethics and Ecology." In *Environmental Protection in Pančevo and Bor: Challenges of Participation to Environmental Governance*, edited by Mina Petrović and Jelisaveta Vukelić, 193–212. Belgrade: Institute for Sociological Research, Faculty of Philosophy, University of Belgrade.

Večernje novosti. 2012. "Prosečna plata u Srbiji 40.562 dinara [An Average Salary in Serbia 40.562 Serbian Dinars]." April 27. http://www.novosti.rs/vesti/naslovna/aktuelno.239.html:377424-Prosecna-plata-u-Srbiji-40562-dinara.

Vlaović, Gojko. 2019. "Šta je uzrok velikih oblaka dima koji su već mesecima redovna pojava u Boru? [What Is the Cause of Huge Clouds That Could Be Seen in Bor for Months?]." *Danas*, December 14. https://www.danas.rs/ekonomija/manja-prerada-sumporne-kiseline-u-zidjinu-povecala-zagadjenje/.

Vodopivec, Nina. 2010. "Textile Workers in Slovenia: From Nimble Fingers to Tired Bodies." *Anthropology of East Europe Review* 28 (1): 165–83.

Vodopivec, Nina. 2012. "On the Road to Modernity: Textile Workers and Post-Socialist Transformations in Slovenia." *History* 97 (328): 609–29.

Walley, Christine J. 2013. *Exit Zero: Family and Class in Postindustrial Chicago*. Chicago: University of Chicago Press.

Wallman, Sandra. 2003. *Contemporary Futures: Perspectives from Social Anthropology*. London: Routledge.

Watson, Peggy. 1993. "Eastern Europe's Silent Revolution: Gender." *Sociology* 27 (3): 471–87.

Weber, Cynthia. 1998. "Performative States." *Millennium* 27 (1): 77–95.

Wedeen, Lisa. 1999. *Ambiguities of Domination: Politics, Rhetoric, and Symbols in Contemporary Syria*. Chicago: University of Chicago Press.

Welker, Marina. 2014. *Enacting the Corporation: An American Mining Firm in Post-Authoritarian Indonesia*. Berkeley: University of California Press.

Weszkalnys, Gisa. 2016. "A Doubtful Hope: Resource Affect in a Future Oil Economy." *Journal of the Royal Anthropological Institute* 22 (S1): 127–46.

Woodward, Susan L. 1995. *Socialist Unemployment: The Political Economy of Yugoslavia, 1945-1990*. Princeton, NJ: Princeton University Press.

Woodward, Susan L. 2003. "The Political Economy of Ethno-Nationalism in Yugoslavia." *Socialist Register* 39: 73–92.

Yurchak, Alexei. 2006. *Everything Was Forever, Until It Was No More: The Last Soviet Generation*. Princeton, NJ: Princeton University Press.

Yurchak, Alexei. 2018. "Fake, Unreal, and Absurd." In *Fake. Anthropological Keywords*, edited by Jacob Copeman and Giovanni da Col, 91–108. Chicago: University of Chicago Press.

Zaloom, Caitlin. 2004. "The Productive Life of Risk." *Cultural Anthropology* 19 (3): 365–91.

Zijin Mining. 2021. "Cukaru Peki Copper-Gold Mine in Serbia Begins Trial Production." June 16. https://www.zijinmining.com/news/news-detail-119136.htm.

Zonabend, Françoise. 1993. *The Nuclear Peninsula*. Cambridge: Cambridge University Press.

Index

Figures and maps are indicated by "f" and "m" following page numbers.

www.ingramcontent.com/pod-product-compliance
Lightning Source LLC
Chambersburg PA
CBHW030406270326
41926CB00009B/1294